D1542223

08/21
STRAND PRICE
$5.00

Managing the Risks of International Agreement

Managing the Risks of International Agreement

RICHARD B. BILDER

THE UNIVERSITY OF WISCONSIN PRESS

Published 1981

The University of Wisconsin Press
114 North Murray Street
Madison, Wisconsin 53715

The University of Wisconsin Press, Ltd.
1 Gower Street
London WC1E 6HA, England

Copyright © 1981
The Board of Regents of the University of Wisconsin System
All rights reserved

First printing

Printed in the United States of America

For LC CIP information see the colophon

ISBN 0–299–08360–8

For Sally,
Mary Sarah, Anne,
David, and Debbie,
with love,

and in memory of my father,
Walter J. Bilder

Contents

Preface

This book discusses a variety of techniques by which nations can manage the risks of their international agreements and other cooperative arrangements. It attempts to call attention to the importance of risk management in facilitating cooperation among nations, to suggest a possible framework of analysis of risk-management problems and techniques, and to pull together some experiences relating to the use of risk-management techniques. But risk management is a broad and complex subject, and further work—particularly empirical research—will be needed if we are to more fully understand and effectively deal with these problems.

Most of this book consists of a survey or catalogue of risk-management techniques. Yet an understanding of how best to use them requires some awareness of both the broader context in which the need for these techniques has developed and the general limitations and alternative approaches which bear on their appropriate use. Consequently, my discussion is organized as follows: Chapter 1 is a general discussion of the nature and importance of international agreements, the problems of risk, the options open to nations in attempting to deal with these problems, and some *caveats* to this study. Chapter 2 is a survey of very general risk-management techniques, designed to give a nation broad protection against the risk that it may later decide, for any reason, that it no longer wishes to participate in the agreement, and to give it flexibility to limit or escape from its obligations if it subsequently changes its mind. Chapter 3 is a survey of techniques designed specifically to protect a nation against the risk that the intrinsic value of the agreement to it may decline. Chapter 4 is a survey of techniques designed specifically to protect a nation against the risk that its potential treaty partner or partners may not perform the obligations promised, or may do so inadequately. Chapter 5 discusses some general limitations on the use of the specific risk-management techniques dealt with in the study; the relevance of alternative risk-management approaches, particularly attitudes of trust; and some things that might be done to make risk management more effective. A checklist of the various techniques discussed in this book is set out in the Appendix.

Certain frequently mentioned treaties and other international agreements are referred to in the text and notes by short titles; the full titles and citations of these agreements are set out in the list of Short Titles and Abbreviations preceding the notes at the back of the book.

This study assumes that the international system will be based for some time to come on the existence of a number of separate nation-states, cooperating principally through international agreements. I share with many the hope that we will someday find a better way to organize our world. But until that time, we have no choice but to try to use our present system as effectively as we can. While the book is primarily addressed to foreign office officials, international lawyers, and others interested in foreign relations and international affairs, I hope it may also be useful to lawyers and others concerned with facilitating co-operative arrangements in domestic as well as international contexts. Cooperation is an important and pervasive aspect of all social behavior, and experience and lessons drawn from one type or level of human interaction often have applications or analogies in others.

I would like to express my appreciation to the University of Wisconsin Sea Grant Program and the University of Wisconsin-Madison Graduate School Research Committee for their support of parts of this project, and to a number of colleagues—including Professors Richard Baxter, Thomas Franck, Wesley Gould, Richard Lillich, Stewart Macaulay, Gerald Marwell, Peter Rohn, and Oscar Schachter—for their encouragement. I would also like to thank Violette Moore for her competence, patience, and unfailing good humor in typing the manuscript through several revisions; and Thomas Klancnik, William Mansell, and Sherry Steffel for help in checking the citations and quotations. My debt and gratitude to my family for their support over the course of this work is beyond measure.

Madison, Wisconsin
July 1, 1980

Managing
the Risks
of International
Agreement

CHAPTER 1

Risk as an Obstacle to International Agreement

International agreements are the principal means of cooperation among nations. But agreements frequently involve risks, and since nations are reluctant to enter into agreements involving substantial risks, it is important to improve their ability to deal with these risks if wider international agreement and cooperation is to be achieved. The premise of this study is that nations can often overcome the obstacles that risks pose for cooperation through the appropriate use of risk-management techniques.

Over thousands of years of living together, human beings have developed a variety of devices for controlling the risks involved in cooperation. Many of these techniques are familiar from common experience with personal and business arrangements, such as marriage, employment, and commercial contracts, and they are often used by individuals and lawyers in arranging private transactions. But these techniques play an important role in international cooperative arrangements as well, and the way in which nations use or misuse them can greatly influence the success or failure of cooperative efforts.

There has been a good deal of study of some of these risk-management techniques, particularly those using third parties to resolve disputes.[1] But there has as yet been little attempt to organize our knowledge about risk management more broadly in a systematic and comprehensive way.[2] For example, diplomats and international lawyers have acquired considerable practical experience in the uses of various techniques, but few efforts have been made to collect, analyze, and transmit this experience.[3] The purpose of this study is to at least begin this work, in the hope that a greater awareness and understanding of these techniques will help nations to overcome problems of risk in the negotiation of their agreements and lead to greater international cooperation.

1. The Importance of International Agreements

Cooperation is an important aspect of all social life.[4] Indeed, there is much to suggest that the ability to cooperate may be among the most basic distinguishing features of the human species. Leakey and Lewin, in their book on human origins, suggest "a deep-seated biological urge toward cooperation" and comment: "The cooperative behavior born of our hunting-gathering heritage combines with the long-established social nature of primates to galvanize social units with an extraordinary ability to tackle environmental challenges. This is, of course, why we were so successful as an evolving species."[5]

Thus, it is not surprising that cooperation, including closely associated types of social behavior such as exchange, plays a significant role in international relations as well as in other types of relations between and among human individuals and groups. As in other situations of social interdependence, nations must often cooperate if they are to achieve their individual goals. In recent years, a growing awareness of the dimensions, complexity, and significance of global problems has brought broad acceptance of the need for greater international cooperation. U.N. Secretary General Waldheim, for example, has noted that the necessity for international cooperation "has never been so great or so urgent.''[6] It has become clear that nations can hope to meet the profound challenges that currently confront humanity only by working together.

The most important way in which nations reach cooperative arrangements is by negotiating and concluding written international agreements or treaties.[7] Indeed, they have done so for at least 5,000 years: archaeologists have discovered a treaty between the city states of Umma and Lagash written in the Sumerian language on a stone monument and concluded about 3100 B.C.[8] An international agreement is simply the analogue in international relations of the familiar private contract, the parties, however, being nation-states or governments rather than private individuals, businesses, or associations. An international agreement can be broadly defined as an exchange of conditional promises by which each nation declares that it will act in a certain way on condition that the other nation acts in accordance with its promises.[9] More technically, the Vienna Convention on the Law of Treaties, which is widely accepted as reflecting the customary international law of treaties,[10] defines a treaty, for the purposes of the convention, as ''an international agreement concluded between States in written form and governed by international law, whether embodied in a single instrument or in two or more related instruments and whatever its particular designation.''[11] Thus, nations may give their international agreements different titles—''treaty,'' ''convention,'' ''charter,'' ''statute,'' ''articles of agreement,'' ''agreement,'' ''protocol,'' or ''exchange of notes''—but if these otherwise establish legally binding international obligations between or among the nations' parties, they are all what are generally considered international agreements.[12]

International agreements are typically used to establish exchange or cooperative relationships between or among nations, based on reciprocity. They will occasionally, however, be used to serve other purposes as well, such as to communicate foreign policy positions, convey threats, encourage the growth of international institutions, achieve propaganda objectives, lay a basis for future bargaining, or accomplish primarily internal purposes.[13] As of 1980, there were probably over 15,000 international agreements in force between or among nations,[14] which, among other things, established some 280 international organizations;[15] about 1,000 new agreements were being concluded each year.[16] By 1980 the United States alone was party to over 7,000 international agreements and participated in some 80 international organizations.[17] Collectively, these agreements establish an extensive and intricate network of cooperation on a wide variety of subjects, ranging from the broad concerns embraced in the United Nations Charter, Charter of the Organization of American States, or International Covenants on Human Rights, to the narrower and more specialized problems dealt with in agreements on radio frequencies, oil pollution, control of narcotics, fisheries, or uniform weights and measures.

International agreements are a particularly useful way of arranging international cooperation and exchange for several reasons:

(1) A written agreement increases the reliability and stability of a cooperative arrangement by providing a means through which nations can rationally plan the arrangement and communicate to each other and publicly record the precise terms of their cooperation. A written agreement can make clear what each is to do or not do, when, and how; what conduct constitutes breach; the means of restoring complementarity if breach occurs; and so forth. In effect, the agreement serves to lay down for the actors who are to be involved in the cooperative undertaking—diplomats, lawyers, and other government officials—what the rules governing the cooperation are to be and how the game is to be played.

(2) By embodying their cooperative arrangement in the form of a legally binding written agreement, the nations participating in the arrangement can increase the chances it will be kept. More specifically, the written agreement furnishes nations with a

formal or ritual device through which they can clearly character-
ize their cooperative relationship as one based upon mutual
reliance and trust, and invoke the normative and sanctioning
system of the broader international legal order in its support. The
customary international law principle of *pacta sunt servanda*, as
now codified in the Vienna Convention on the Law of Treaties,
provides that "[e]very treaty in force is binding upon the parties
to it and must be performed by them in good faith."[18] By
entering into an international agreement, nations can commit
themselves to the cooperative arrangement in the sense of
exposing themselves to criticism or condemnation and possibly
sanctions if they fail to live up to their obligations.[19]

(3) A written agreement facilitates the negotiation of a cooperative arrangement by permitting nations to place their offers
and counteroffers in a common frame of reference, to assess
more easily the comparative benefits and costs of alternative
cooperative arrangements, and to fix a single point of commitment at which negotiations cease and the cooperative bargain is
struck.

(4) As will be discussed in some detail in this study, a written
agreement provides a standardized framework in which nations,
through a choice of risk-management provisions and techniques, can adjust and manage the risks of their cooperative
arrangement.[20]

In the last analysis, of course, international agreements are
only pieces of paper and nations can and on occasion do violate
their agreements. But agreements are very special pieces of
paper, which serve to reinforce the expectations of their parties
by drawing upon deeply and widely held human norms, developed over millennia of social experience, supporting the sanctity
of solemnly made promises. There is ample evidence that
nations generally take their agreements very seriously, treat
them as real commitments, and do not enter into them lightly.[21]
Indeed, if nations did not believe international agreements were
useful and effective, they would not bother to enter into so many

of them and would enter into them with less care and deliberation than they usually do. The time, effort, and concern given by the United States and the Soviet Union to negotiation and questions of ratification of the SALT II treaty is an example. Moreover, in almost all cases nations carry out their agreements in good faith. While there are occasional instances of clear and deliberate breach, and nations sometimes get away with it, these are by far the exception rather than the rule. In the rare cases where a flagrant breach does occur, it will often be in a context where there has been a dramatic change in the circumstances underlying the agreement or the relations between the parties, such as where the government of one party undergoes a revolutionary change. This was the case, for example, with respect to Iran's seizure of the American embassy in Tehran and taking as hostages American diplomatic and consular personnel, found by the International Court of Justice to have been in violation of Iran's obligations to the United States under several different international agreements.[22]

The various factors which influence nations to observe their treaty obligations have often been noted.[23] First, since cooperative agreements are consensual, a nation will not usually enter into such an agreement unless it believes that the agreement is in its interest and intends to comply with it; thus, if for no other reason, a nation will normally perform its part of the bargain because it wants reciprocal performance by its treaty partner. Second, nations share a common interest in maintaining the usefulness of the treaty device as a way of ensuring stable expectations and will not lightly impair the integrity of this device. Third, most nations and government officials feel a normative sense of obligation to prove trustworthy and keep their word and will not want to be thought of as untrustworthy or "cheaters." Henkin points out that "[e]very nation's foreign policy depends substantially on its 'credit'—on maintaining the expectation that it will live up to international mores and obligations. Considerations of 'honor,' 'prestige,' 'leadership,' 'influence,' 'reputation,' which figure prominently in government decisions, often weigh in favor of observing law. Nations generally desire a reputation for principled behavior, for propriety and respectability.''[24] Fourth, nations and their officials have a very practical stake in maintaining a reputation for credibility and living up to their commitments; if they break their treaties, other nations will be less willing to enter into further agreements with them. As Schelling comments, ''[W]hat makes many agreements enforceable is only the recognition of future opportunities for agreement that will be eliminated if mutual trust is not created and maintained and whose value outweighs the monetary gain from cheating in the present instance.''[25] Fifth, nations will, as we shall see, be concerned with possible retaliation or the imposition of sanctions by its treaty partner or other nations or international organizations in the event it fails to comply with its obligations. Finally, there is much to suggest that once a nation concludes an agreement, political and bureaucratic inertia alone tend to induce compliance. Bureaucrats are creatures of law and will generally find it more comfortable simply to keep a treaty than to go to the effort of breaking it. Moreover, as Chayes points out in a thoughtful article on arms control agreements, ''verification and enforcement mechanisms do not provide the only forces operating to insure compliance, and probably not the most important ones. An agreement that is adopted by a modern bureaucratic government will be backed by a broad official consensus generated by the negotiating process, and will carry personal and political endorsement across the spectrum of bureaucratic and political leadership. These are exceedingly hard to undo and reverse, the more so since, once the treaty goes into effect, they are reinforced by the ponderous inertia of the bureaucracy.''[26] Iklé similarly notes that ''[w]here breach of an agreement necessitates a clear-cut action requiring complicated decisions, democratic governments may encounter institutional obstacles to a violation.''[27] In short, a fear that nations enter into international agreements with the idea of cheating or tricking the other party assumes a Machiavellian rationality and flexibility of which most governments are not capable in the real world.

Nonetheless, to say that international agreements usually work does not mean that nations regard them as establishing completely rigid commitments or deal with treaty problems solely in legalistic terms. As I have suggested more fully elsewhere, government officials probably look at questions of treaty obligation and breach more flexibly and in a broader context than traditional legal analysis assumes.[28] For them, an agreement will often be not simply an instrument for creating legal rights and obligations but a multipurpose foreign policy tool, constituting only one element in the more complex pattern of their nation's overall foreign policy. In this broader context, other foreign policy objectives will sometimes be more important than ensuring performance of the agreement. Indeed, decisions respecting international agreements will sometimes turn on solely domestic rather than foreign policy considerations; internal political pressures may dictate participation in agreements which otherwise make little sense, or prevent participation in agreements of great potential benefit. Moreover, government officials will recognize that agreements are made with varying degrees of commitment—that some are meant to be taken less seriously than others; that changing expectations and external or domestic circumstances can create pressures for one or more parties which must be pragmatically dealt with if the agreement is not to break; and that treaty disputes are more likely to signal real problems in the balance and fairness of the agreement than to result from attempts to "cheat." Consequently, they will tend to see the obligation to perform agreements in good faith in terms of these realities, to be interpreted and judged not only by the past balance of forces in which the treaty was formed but also by the present and future balance of forces in which it must be implemented. Finally, while legal rights and obligations will affect the perceived legitimacy of the different parties' positions in the event of a dispute, and thus their respective strategies in trying to resolve the dispute, law alone will not necessarily determine either the parties' responses or the eventual outcome. Government officials will be aware that a particular treaty dispute is only one incident in what must inevitably be a continuing relationship with the other nation; in an interdependent world, most countries will have little choice but, sooner or later, to do business with each other. As is often the case in business contract disputes,[29] pressing one's treaty partner unduly, "taking him to court," or winning the dispute may be poor long-run policy, and accommodation and compromise through negotiation and express or tacit amendment will often appear much more sensible. The net result of these perceptions and tendencies towards accommodation is that in the real world, international agreements, far from creating once-and-for-all expectations and commitments, constantly change and evolve as the circumstances and the parties' expectations change.

2. The Problem of Risk

While the process of cooperation is complex and may involve many different kinds of problems,[30] one of the most important and pervasive obstacles to achieving international agreement is risk. *Risk* is usually defined as "the possibility of suffering harm or loss";[31] the term can connote both the existence of some hazard or exposure to loss or injury, and the amount or extent of such an exposure to loss or injury.

Risk is an inevitable aspect of life and social interaction. Human beings often have to make decisions or take actions under conditions of uncertainty, in which they cannot be sure what the consequences will be, and whether a particular decision or action will ultimately prove helpful rather than harmful.[32] Government officials making foreign policy decisions find themselves in this position as well. Thus, a nation will normally enter into an international agreement only if it believes that the outcome of such participation is likely to be favorable— that its prospective benefits will exceed, or at least not be less than, its prospective costs. But every nation knows that the future is uncertain and unpredictable, that even its best judgments and assessments may prove wrong, and that, under certain circumstances, a proposed agreement which now seems to be a good deal may turn out to be a bad one which leaves it worse off than before. Where a nation believes that there is a possibility that a prospective agreement may turn out badly, it will have to take this possibility into account in deciding whether or not it is worth its while to enter into the agreement. In general, a nation's decision to enter into an international agreement or other cooperative arrangement will involve considerations of risk when that nation believes that its commitment to the agreement may, depending on the occurrence or nonoccurrence of particular future events or outcomes, expose it to an eventual outcome which has a net negative utility or is harmful in that its costs exceed its benefits.

Experience suggests that risk is a major reason why nations fail to reach otherwise mutually useful agreements. Where a nation sees a prospective agreement as involving substantial risks, and it cannot find some way of compensating for or controlling them, it will often choose not to enter into the agreement. Research in cooperation between individuals tends to support this hypothesis. Experiments by the sociologists Marwell and Schmitt indicate that risk disrupts interpersonal cooperation; that this disruption of cooperation is substantial even when the risk is small and is almost total when the risk is large; that increasing the magnitude of potential rewards from cooperating does not appear substantially to reduce the disruptive effect of large risk; and that, in order for cooperation to occur or resume, it is necessary to reduce or somehow deal with what the participants see as the risks involved.[33]

While risk presupposes uncertainty, uncertainty does not in itself necessarily involve risk. Thus, a nation will often be uncertain as to whether another nation will perform its obligations under an agreement or as to other events relating to the agreement. But these uncertainties will not in themselves involve risk unless, under the most pessimistic assumptions, a nation's participation in that agreement could result in that nation's experiencing a net loss, leaving it in a worse position than if it had not entered into the agreement. For example, human rights agreements, obligating the participating nations to protect certain rights of their citizens, may involve uncertainty but little risk to a nation such as the United States, which is already committed by its Constitution and other internal laws to respecting the rights covered in the agreement; it undertakes little additional burden or risk in agreeing internationally to do what its laws and traditions already require it to do. The United States may be uncertain whether other nations will similarly respect their obligations to respect the rights of their own citizens, but should they fail to do so, it will not be worse off than before—though it may be disappointed.

Risks will, of course, differ both in nature and extent: some agreements will be very risky; others will involve little or no risk. Typically, risk will be thought of in terms of general probabilities, or chances, although these probabilities will often reflect only the roughest kinds of judgments or visceral hunches. Moreover, a nation's decisions concerning international agreements will be influenced, if at all, by its *perceptions* and *beliefs* concerning the presence of uncertainty and risk rather than by the facts as they actually exist.[34] Perceptions of risk will be affected by a variety of factors—the scope and nature of the prospective agreement; whether a prospective treaty partner is a friendly, adversary, or neutral nation; whether its leadership is of proven or doubtful competence; whether it is potentially stable or volatile internally; and so forth. The extent to which a nation's subjective perceptions or beliefs in this respect do or do not correspond to objective reality will depend upon factors such as its psychological predispositions or preconceptions; its access to relevant information; its skill and judgment in accurately interpreting and assessing that information; and its ability to ensure receipt of the information by relevant decisionmakers in a usable form. Thus, different nations (or particular officials involved) may have different propensities to perceive risk or different "security levels" or propensities to accept risk.[35] Some may be very trusting and may readily discount risks; others may be pathologically distrustful and see perils at every turn. Some may be more risk-prone and willing to accept a given risk in order to achieve agreement; others may be more risk-averse, less inclined to stick their necks out, and more likely to forego agreement rather than face such a risk. Where a nation or its officials are particularly eager to reach an agreement—perhaps because the officials involved have spent a great deal of time and effort in its negotiation and feel a need for something to show for their efforts—there may be a tendency to discount risks below what objective assessment might suggest. For all of these reasons, a given type or level of risk may affect some nations more than others.

In general, a nation is likely to be concerned with one or more of several broad types of risk in considering an international agreement. These are

1. The risk that the nation may later change its mind or decide, for extraneous reasons, that it no longer wishes to participate in the agreement (for example, it may wish to get out of the agreement because some other nation has offered it a better deal);

2. The risk that the intrinsic utility of the agreement to the nation may decline to the extent that the prospective benefits from the agreement no longer equal or exceed its costs (for example, the cost or burden of performing as promised may increase, or the benefit or value to it of the other nation's performance may decline); or

3. The risk that the other nation may not perform as promised (for example, a nation's treaty partner may completely withhold performance or perform only partially or inadequately).

Each of these situations can expose a nation participating in an agreement to possible loss.

Where a nation is interested in cooperating with another, but is uncertain whether to do so because it fears the risks of the agreement may outweigh its benefits, it can attempt to deal with the problem in one or more of several ways. It can, first, simply refuse to enter into the agreement. But nonagreement can also have risks and opportunity costs. A nation choosing this course—and the other nation or nations involved—loses the benefits that it would otherwise have achieved through the proposed cooperation. Indeed, since international cooperative arrangements frequently produce indirect benefits and external economies even for nations not directly involved and for the international system more generally, a failure to reach agreement can have substantial opportunity costs for the broader international community as well. For example, U.S. refusal to ratify the SALT II treaty might protect the United States against any immediate risks that agreement might pose—but it could also result in an increase in the arms race, heightened U.S.–Soviet tensions, and a greater danger of nuclear war. The threat of nonagreement will, of course, play a key part in each nation's bargaining strategy and be a major factor in producing mutual concessions in their negotiations.

Second, a nation may decide to ignore the problem of risk for the time being, in the hope that such problems will not arise or that, if they do, they can be dealt with by further negotiations at that time or through norms and procedures established by the broader international legal order—in particular, the rules of customary international law relevant to the interpretation and application of international agreements. This approach is, in effect, "We'll cross that bridge when we come to it." In actuality, however, a nation is unlikely to ignore problems of risk unless it believes that they are unlikely to be substantial or that, if they should arise, it will be in a good position to protect itself. Where a nation believes that risks are significant and difficulties may well occur, it is unlikely to leave these problems to so chancy a solution.

Third, a nation can change its perceptions of the risks involved in the agreement, deciding that they are not as great as it had initially thought. Its reassessment may be the result of learning more facts, more careful evaluation of the facts, or persuasion by the other nation. An agreement that at first seems very risky may turn out, on more careful analysis, to be one in which the risks really are not so great after all. But perceptions of risk may have deep psychological roots, closely related to distrust, and be resistant to change. Even the most solid facts and careful reasoning may be unable to eliminate a nagging doubt that something, somewhere, may go wrong.

Fourth, a nation can attempt to obtain an adjustment of the substantive terms of the agreement to compensate it for encountering the risks it perceives. Presumably, there will in most situations be some point at which the potential benefits or return a nation hopes to receive from an agreement will be so high as to make it worth that nation's while to take even a very substantial risk; the other nation may be able to ''make it an offer it can't refuse.''[36] For example, some commentators suggest that Israel should logically be willing to gamble on an agreement establishing a West Bank Palestinian state, despite Israel's belief that this involves serious risks and Israel's distrust for the other parties, since in their view this offers the only chance of achieving a lasting and peaceful solution of Middle East problems.[37] Yet, the possibilities of substantive adjustment in the terms of an agreement will often be limited. In many cases, particularly where the risks involved relate to vital national interests or to national survival, nations may be unwilling to accept these risks at any price. For example, since Israel appears, at least at present, to see the establishment of a completely independent

West Bank Palestinian state as an extremely grave threat to its existence, there may be no offer, no matter how generous, which would induce it to agree to the establishment of such a state. It will simply not be prepared to gamble on this matter. Moreover, perceptions of the same risks may often differ; while one nation views its risks as substantial, the other may see these perceptions as unrealistic and exaggerated and be unwilling to offer an inducement of the size demanded, since in its view this would unbalance the agreement. For example, even if there were some high price at which Israel might be prepared to accept the risks of an agreement establishing a wholly independent West Bank Palestinian state, it is unlikely that the Arab nations would be willing to meet such a price—or, indeed, if it were offered, that Israel would believe the Arab nations meant their offer.

Fifth, a nation may overcome its concern for risk in an agreement simply by trusting its prospective treaty partner to behave in a way that will avoid subjecting it to harm. That is, a nation may choose to believe that the other nation involved is highly likely—because of factors such as the other nation's benevolent attitude; an innate sense of honesty, integrity, and responsibility; a practical stake in maintaining a reputation for trustworthiness and keeping its commitments; and so forth—to fully perform the agreement and not otherwise take advantage of it, even if breach or exploitative behavior might be in the other nation's immediate self-interest and there is no way of subjecting it to sanctions if it decides not to comply with its promises. Trust is a generalized, simple, low-cost way of dealing with risk in social relations, and most societies support it through strong moral and legal norms. But trust may not exist between the nations considering agreement, and where important national interests are at stake, one or both nations may in any event be reluctant to rely on trust alone.[38] We will return to the role of trust in international agreements in Chapter 5.

Finally, a nation can deal with the risks of agreement by

seeking to include in the agreement specific risk-management provisions which change or reduce its perceptions of risk to an extent where it is willing to enter into the agreement. It is with this approach to risk management that this book is principally concerned.

Of course, nations typically use a combination of these approaches to deal with risk. By using skill, judgment, and imagination, diplomats and lawyers can often successfully meld these different approaches in ways which give nations sufficient assurance to make agreement possible.

3. Some Caveats

Risk management is a very broad topic, and any broad study necessarily involves some generalization and simplification. In reading this discussion, certain points should be kept in mind:

(a) *This study is not an exhaustive inventory of risk-management techniques.* The primary purpose of the survey is to offer a framework of analysis rather than a complete catalog. There are a large number of these techniques, and much could be said about each of them. Many societies have developed their own unique ways of handling the risks of cooperation—often ways especially suited to their own culture—and the process of social innovation in this respect is continuing. Moreover, there are clearly ways other than that used in this study in which these techniques might be classified and analyzed. Indeed, any single classification tends to obscure the fact that many of these techniques (such as those relating to withdrawal, timing of performance, and verification) have multiple risk-management functions.

(b) *This study does not deal with the complexity or diversity of different national foreign policy processes.* To simplify the analysis, the discussion treats nations abstractly as if they were unitary actors with respect to their foreign policy attitudes, decisions, and interactions.[39] We will speak, for example, of the United States "deciding" to enter into an agreement with the Soviet Union, or of nation A "distrusting" nation B or "fearing" that it may cheat. But nations do not act or reach decisions in the same way as rational individuals. Instead, foreign policy decisions typically emerge only out of a complex interaction of interest-group and bureaucratic politics and pressures, and the nature of this process differs among countries and circumstances.[40] Moreover, some of the most important players in the game of international cooperation are the diplomats, lawyers, and other officials who do the actual work of negotiating, implementing, and adjusting disputes concerning agreements. It is likely that factors such as their shared professional values, desire to maintain good continuing working relationships, personal contacts and "old boy" networks, career aspirations, and so forth, have some influence on the way the game is played.[41]

(c) *Risk-management techniques differ considerably in both their nature and application.* As has been indicated, some techniques are very general, designed to deal with all of the kinds of risks involved in an agreement; others are more specific, designed to deal in a more individual way either with risks relating to the inherent value of the agreement, or with risks relating to the other state's nonperformance, or with risks relating to one's own obligation to perform. Some techniques are directed at reducing a party's uncertainty; others are intended to reduce its vulnerability; still others may affect both a party's uncertainty and vulnerability. Some techniques relate primarily to managing risks arising from external conditions; others are directed more particularly at managing the ways in which the nations involved perceive or respond to these conditions. Some techniques are integrally related to the basic terms of the substantive exchange involved in the agreement; others are essentially auxiliary techniques, which may be either contained in the agreement itself or embodied in collateral agreements. Some techniques are applicable or relevant only to agreements involving tangible exchanges of persons, goods, or property; others can apply to agreements involving intangible kinds of behavior. Some techniques are most useful in the case of agreements involving a single or short-term exchange or cooperative transaction; others are more applicable to agreements involving multiple exchanges or long-term cooperative relations. Finally, some techniques can be implemented by a nation itself, through self-help; others are dependent upon the collateral behavior of third parties, whether another nation, a group of nations, a public international organization such as the United Nations, or an international institution such as the International Court of Justice.

(*d*) *Risk-management techniques can be combined in a variety of ways.* Designing an effective risk management system requires a careful choice of those techniques best suited to meet the parties' concerns. The particular combination of techniques selected should be functional, imaginative, and internally consistent. Innovation in risk management can be achieved not only by developing new techniques, but by using and combining old ones in new ways. The possibilities of combination are not unlimited, however. While some techniques are interrelated and fit together, others will be inconsistent or redundant. For example, provisions for a buffer zone are frequently combined with provisions for some form of inspection or surveillance. On the other hand, where an agreement includes strong general risk-management provisions limiting the subject matter or duration of the agreement or providing for easy withdrawal, there will be less need for other more specific risk-management provisions.

(*e*) *Nations may include risk-management techniques in their agreements for reasons unrelated to any concern with risk or even any belief in the efficacy of such techniques.* Certain types of provisions, such as "final clauses" dealing with dispute settlement and amendment, have now become standardized clauses or "boiler-plate" in international agreements, and may be included from routine or habit, because of a desire for completeness and conformity with other agreements, or simply because (as is often the case) one agreement is copied closely from another. Where other agreements of a similar type typically include particular risk-management provisions, they will usually be written into an agreement as a matter of course, and a lawyer responsible for the drafting of such an agreement may feel uncomfortable and open to criticism if they are omitted. Again, where one nation wishes to include a particular risk-management technique in an agreement, the technique will usually be demanded by and made available to the other nation or nations involved in order to give the agreement the appearance of equity, reciprocity, and symmetry, even if the other party has little real interest in such protection. In some cases, risk-management techniques may be included primarily for face-saving purposes or to satisfy internal political objectives or public opinion. For example, negotiators may include dispute settlement, verification, or other risk-control provisions as a protection against the possibility of domestic criticism on grounds that they have been overtrusting, unconcerned for risks, or careless. Negotiators may wish to include such provisions for these reasons even if they believe there is very little chance that the other party will violate the agreement, or doubt that such provisions will have any practical value in deterring or sanctioning violations.

(*f*) *Every prospective cooperative arrangement raises its own unique problems and requires its own special solutions.* Effective risk management must be tailored to the special needs of the particular agreement involved. The art of successful negotiation—a process in which the international lawyer can play a significant role—includes skill in designing that particular mix of risk-management techniques which can, under the specific circumstances, bring otherwise hesitant nations together into agreement. A truce or arms limitation agreement will require a mix of techniques different from those involved in a human rights agreement. An agreement between traditional enemies, involving strong distrust, will require different techniques from those in one between traditional friends, with a long history of mutual cooperation and trust. There are no certain rules as to what particular techniques or mix of techniques will or will not, in any given case, serve to meet the particular concerns of the particular nations involved. Experiment may be called for.

(*g*) *Risk-management techniques have inherent limitations and costs which constrain their usefulness.* As will be apparent throughout the discussion and further developed in Chapter 5, specific risk-management techniques cannot solve all problems of risk. It is usually impossible to avoid all uncertainty and risk in an agreement; specific risk-management techniques can serve to reduce risks or change their character but cannot remove them completely. Moreover, in some cases, the limitations or costs or particular techniques will make their use not worthwhile. Thus, there will be situations in which specific techniques of the kind described in this study will not alone be able to meet the problems of risk involved in an agreement, and where the parties, if they are to reach agreement, will have to rely also on more general approaches to risk management, such as trust and good faith. And there will also be situations in which problems of risk prove insuperable and agreement and cooperation cannot be achieved.

CHAPTER 2

General Risk-Management Techniques

Many of the techniques nations use to protect themselves against the risk of international agreements are very general and designed to deal with a broad range of risks. Some are intended to limit the extent to which a nation can be held to performing its obligations under the agreement, permitting it to escape from these obligations if it believes the agreement no longer serves its interests. Others are intended to limit the significance of the interests a nation has at risk in the agreement so that, if the agreement turns out badly, a nation's costs will be within the range of what it is prepared to accept.

General techniques of this type are widely employed even when officials can identify the particular risks which worry them—concern about their own ability to perform the agreement, the probability that the other nation or nations involved will perform, the intrinsic value of the agreement, or some combination of these. While narrower risk-management devices might be able to handle these specific problems, officials may consider a broad escape clause safer and less likely to run into snags if invoked. But broad risk-management techniques can be particularly useful when officials are apprehensive about entering into a proposed agreement but have difficulty in pointing to specific risks as the cause of their uneasiness; they simply have a hunch that the agreement is one that can somehow turn out badly. This may be the case, for example, where nations have had little experience in cooperating with each other or have a history of mutual distrust. In these situations, techniques which broadly control and limit the risks of the nations involved may serve to meet their apprehensions sufficiently to permit cooperation to proceed.

1. Nonbinding Arrangements

One obvious way in which a nation can minimize the risk of being held to compliance with an international agreement or other cooperative arrangement is by making it clear that the arrangement is not intended to be legally binding. A "nonbinding" international agreement has been defined as an agreement among nations which "does not engage their legal responsibility" and in which "noncompliance by a party would not be a ground for a claim for reparation or for judicial remedies."[1]

Generally speaking, an international agreement is not legally binding unless the parties intend it to be.[2] Nations can enter into consensual arrangements on whatever terms and with whatever understandings they wish, and the parties' intentions are controlling. International law, now largely codified in the Vienna Convention on the Law of Treaties, provides a detailed set of rules and formalities governing the ways in which nations enter into agreements intended to create legal rights and obligations and to have international legal effect.[3] Thus, nations can manifest their intention that their arrangement *not* be legally binding by reaching the arrangement through a procedure and expressing it in a form other than that usually used and recognized in international law as establishing legally binding agreements, or by otherwise clearly indicating, in the arrangement itself or in the negotiations for the agreement, that it is to be regarded as nonbinding.

By deliberately choosing to embody their cooperative arrangement in a nonbinding rather than binding form, nations indicate that they regard their mutual undertakings as only tentative and that they contemplate and accept the possibility that each may, without incurring legal sanctions, decide not to comply. Thus, a nonbinding agreement falls short of full commitment and is understood to provide the parties broad flexibility. But the fact that the agreement is not legally binding does not mean that it cannot be an effective means of achieving cooperation. Even if the agreement is nonbinding, it still enables the parties to spell out clearly what each expects that it and the other will do and provides some normative underpinning to support these expectations. And where the arrangement serves both nations' interests, there can still be relatively firm expectations that they will each continue to abide by it despite the fact it is nonbinding. To illustrate the fact that nations take nonbinding agreements seriously, Schachter cites testimony of then Secretary of State Kissinger before the U.S. Senate Foreign Relations Committee in connection with the Sinai Disengagement Agreements of 1975. Kissinger "noted that certain of the undertakings were 'not binding commitments of the United States,' but he went on to say that that 'does not mean, of course, that the United States is morally or politically free to act as if they did not exist. On the contrary, they are important statements of diplomatic policy and engage the good faith of the United States as long as the circumstances that gave rise to them continue.' "[4] Indeed, where nations are too apprehensive to enter into a firm legal commitment, where a binding agreement is legally impossible or politically impractical, or where circumstances otherwise suggest that a binding agreement is not at the time sensible or attainable, a nonbinding agreement may in many cases effectively meet the parties' needs. In any event, it may be better than no agreement at all. As Schacter notes, "As long as they do last, even nonbinding agreements can be authoritative and controlling for the parties. There is no *a priori* reason to assume that the undertakings arc illusory because they are not legal.''[5]

Nonbinding agreements provide broad flexibility to the parties; they are not, however, completely free of risk. First, the price a nation pays for preserving its own option not to perform is that it cannot be sure of the other nation's performing. Second, unless the nations involved very clearly indicate their intention not to establish a binding agreement, conflicting interpretations as to their intentions may be possible, and an arrangement which one nation intended and understood to be nonbinding may subsequently be argued by another—in good faith or otherwise—to be legally binding.[6] Thus, any type of arrangement raises the possibility of disputes. Third, while a nonbinding agreement avoids formal legal obligations, it may still be regarded by other nations and by the public as establishing at least political and moral expectations and commitments, and noncompliance may still give rise to allegations of bad faith and involve political risks.[7] In practice, the distinction between ''legal'' and ''nonlegal'' obligations is not a sharp line but a gradual continuum. Often, this distinction will be lost on the public, and a failure to comply with even nonbinding agreements or other arrangements may be generally perceived as illegitimate.

Finally, even participation in an agreement which is clearly intended not to be legally binding may nevertheless, under certain circumstances, indirectly give rise to legal obligations. For example, where one nation over a long period behaves in a particular way, inducing reliance by another nation that it will continue to behave in that way, the other nation may claim that such conduct has become legally obligatory under principles of estoppel.[8] In the International Court of Justice's 1951 decision in the *Fisheries* case between the United Kingdom and Norway, the Court held that the United Kingdom's long-standing abstention from fishing in certain waters off Norway which Norway regarded as its ''internal waters'' supported Norway's claim that it was legally entitled to exclude British trawlers from fishing in these waters.[9] Arguably, long-standing mutual compliance with and reliance on a nonbinding arrangement could, over time, independently of the nonbinding intent of the agreement, create legitimate expectations and legal obligations among the nations involved. Moreover, a long-continued and consistent practice among particular nations, even if initially generated by a clearly nonbinding agreement, may over time take on an increasingly normative character and at some point be argued to have become binding as customary international law. For example, in the International Court's 1960 decision in the case concerning *Right of Passage over Indian Territory*, between Portugal and India, the Court held that India's long-standing practice of noninterference with the passage of private persons, officials, and general goods over Indian territory between India's coasts and certain Portuguese enclaves within Indian territory gave rise to a legal duty on the part of India not to interfere with such passage.[10]

Now let us look at several of the most important ways in which nations can reach nonbinding agreements.

a. Tacit Agreements

As indicated, any express agreement always carries the risk that another party may argue that it involves legal or at least political or moral commitments. Thus, a nation can seek to protect itself against any implication of commitment by avoiding entering into any express written or oral agreement, attempting instead to reach cooperative arrangements through solely tacit understandings. One way in which nations can reach such tacit agreements is by engaging in deliberately reciprocal behavior. For example, Brazil might unilaterally indicate that it will not acquire nuclear weapons so long as Argentina also refrains from doing so. Argentina might announce or adopt a similar stance. Taken together, the continued conduct or restraint of each nation, while ostensibly unilateral, may in effect constitute a tacit understanding recognized by both nations as contingent upon continuing reciprocity.

Tacit agreements of this kind play a pervasive and important role in international affairs. Henkin gives several examples in arms control:

> [T]here was in effect a tacit agreement between the United States and Great Britain (later with Canada) not to fortify the frontiers between the United States and Canada. There was perhaps a tacit agreement during the Second World War that neither side would use chemical warfare. It is not unrealistic to say that there was a tacit agreement during the Korean War that the United Nations Command would not bomb across the Yalu River, and the Communist Chinese would not bomb United States bases outside Korea. For some years there was a tacit agreement between the United States and the Soviet Union not to aggravate tensions in Berlin and not to accelerate the arms race by major increases in military budgets. Many believe there is a tacit agreement between the United States and the Soviet Union not to give nuclear weapons to other nations, including their respective allies.[11]

A more recent example is the "parallel unilateral policy declarations" by the United States and Soviet Union announcing that they would each continue to adhere to the SALT I interim agreement limits even after that agreement expired on October 3, 1977, while nevertheless indicating that no formal agreement would be in effect.[12] Tacit agreements are, of course, also pervasive in interpersonal and business relations. For example, private companies in certain industries may use the device of tacit agreement or "conscious parallelism" to avoid price or market competition in situations where express agreements might incur public disapproval or run afoul of national antitrust laws.[13]

Tacit agreement can be particularly useful not only where the nations concerned are distrustful of each other or uncertain as to the benefits of cooperation and consequently wish to avoid any express commitment, but also where internal or external political constraints make express agreement impossible. Henkin suggests a number of advantages of this technique: "A tacit agreement does not entail difficult negotiation or drafting, needs no ratification or proclamation. Its very existence can be denied if that proves desirable for political reasons, foreign or domestic. It can be terminated by either side at will, without legal liability, political onus or sanction, or stigma in world opinion."[14] Moreover, while tacit agreements are clearly not legally binding in themselves, nations can normally be expected to continue to observe them and carry out their cooperation within this framework as long as the arrangement continues to serve each of their interests. As Henkin points out, "Even more than with formal agreements . . . the principal inducement to compliance is the desire to have the agreement continue."[15]

But tacit agreements also have many obvious drawbacks. They are particularly uncertain and unreliable. They can establish cooperation respecting only relatively simple and salient types of behavior—for example, a mutual restraint on acquisition or use of particular weapons—and they cannot effectively deal with problems where cooperation requires more complex behavior by the parties. Moreover, even tacit agreements are not entirely free of risk. Under certain conditions, even unilateral statements may be argued to give rise to international obligations.[16] In the 1974 *Nuclear Tests* cases, the International Court of Justice indicated that unilateral statements by French officials that France intended to cease conducting nuclear tests in the atmosphere in the South Pacific could have binding legal effect.[17] Indeed, the legal adviser of the U.S. Department of State has taken the position that "parallel" unilateral undertakings by two or more states may constitute an international agreement.[18] More broadly, Baxter has commented: "The *Nuclear Tests* cases have provided a basis for thinking that there are many forms of international commitments that are not treaties in the technical sense of the Vienna Convention, and it may very well be that a customary international law of treaties, embracing a much wider range of international agreements than under the Convention, continues to exist and to give binding force to international undertakings of one sort or another."[19]

Again, participation in a tacit agreement may, over time, give rise to expectations of continued compliance which can be violated only at a political cost.[20] If, for example, Brazil and Argentina each refrain for a long time from acquiring nuclear weapons, pursuant to an apparent tacit agreement not to do so, Brazil's sudden acquisition of such weapons might well be viewed by Argentina and by the international community as a breach of at least a moral commitment to Argentina and occasion widespread criticism and even political reprisal against Brazil. Finally, as previously indicated, even tacit agreements, if long continued, may be argued by a party to have established legal obligations, either through the operation of principles of estoppel or through the gradual development of expectations of continued compliance with the practice to the point where nations have come to consider the practice as one which has become obligatory under customary international law.

b. Arrangements in a Form Indicating Nonbinding Intent

In many cases, nations may wish to express a particular co-operative arrangement in writing, while at the same time avoiding legal obligation. They may wish a written instrument, for example, in order to spell out the arrangement more clearly or in detail, to provide public notice of the arrangement, or to indicate that it is meant to have a normative, though not legal, effect. In this case, one way the parties can indicate their intent that the arrangement not be legally binding is by deliberately utilizing some form and procedure which is generally understood not to create legally binding obligations. While the title or specific form of an instrument is not necessarily controlling as to the intentions of the parties to establish or not to establish a legally binding agreement, their use of forms and procedures different from those which nations normally use in concluding legally binding agreements will usually indicate that the establishment of legal obligations is not intended. Nations, in their international relations, have in fact developed many types of instruments which are generally understood not to be legally binding. These include declarations and resolutions of international organizations and conferences (for example, the 1974 United Nations General Assembly Declaration and Action Program on the Establishment of a New International Economic Order);[21] recommendations of international organizations or conferences (for example, the Organization for Economic Cooperation and Development's Recommendation on Principles Governing Transfrontier Pollution);[22] international codes of conduct (for example, the Guidelines for Multinational Enterprises adopted in 1976 by the Council of the Organization for Economic Cooperation and Development);[23] and other internationally recommended standards or action plans. When nations wish to make such arrangements legally obligatory, they usually subsequently negotiate and conclude a separate formal international agreement on the subject.[24] For example, the U.N. General Assembly's 1963 Resolution on Principles Governing the Exploration and Use of Outer Space[25] ultimately evolved into the U.N.'s 1967 Treaty on Outer Space.[26]

Once again, however, an arrangement may involve risks even when embodied in presumably nonbinding forms. That the agreement is in writing tends to legitimate it and impose at least some political and moral, if not legal, obligation on the nations involved to comply. Moreover, other nations may argue that, despite its form, the arrangement was in fact intended to be legally binding. Finally, the arrangement, if broadly accepted and referred to as if it were normative by nations, may gradually become obligatory and eventually be argued to have become legally binding as customary international law. For example, while the Universal Declaration of Human Rights,[27] adopted as a resolution by the United Nations General Assembly in 1948, was clearly intended to be nonbinding, it has over time taken on an increasingly normative character. In a number of recent instances, nations and private groups have accused other nations of "violation" of the standards established by the declaration, and some scholars contend that the declaration, or at least some of its provisions, has now, through wide recognition and acceptance, become legally binding as customary international law.[28] Indeed, it is sometimes argued that a very widely approved United Nations resolution or declaration may in some circumstances have immediate legal effect as "instant" customary international law.[29]

c. Agreements Expressing Nonbinding Intent

Even where nations negotiate what looks like a formal and binding agreement, they can make it clear that it is not intended to be legally binding, either by including express provisions to this effect in the text of the agreement or by statements to this effect in the related negotiations. But even where nations apparently do not intend an agreement to be binding, they do not always manifest their intention clearly and unambiguously. Schachter, in a thoughtful article on nonbinding agreements, notes that "governments tend to be reluctant . . . to state explicitly in an agreement that it is nonbinding or lacks legal force."[30] Consequently, even an agreement which the parties initially understood to be nonbinding, can, in the absence of an express statement to this effect, subsequently be argued to have been intended to be binding.

Some frequently cited examples of nonbinding agreements are so-called gentlemen's agreements, such as the 1908 U.S.–Japanese agreement relating to Japanese immigration and the 1946 orally concluded London Agreement concerning the distribution of seats among the nonpermanent members of the U.N. Security Council, and the recently concluded Final Act of the 1975 Helsinki Conference.[31] A more recent example is the 1978 "Joint Statement on International Terrorism" by representatives of Canada, the Federal Republic of Germany, France, Italy, the United Kingdom, and the United States, "committing" these nations to halt flights to or from countries which have refused extradition or prosecution of persons who have hijacked an aircraft, or which do not return a hijacked aircraft.[32]

The 1975 Helsinki Final Act[33] suggests the ambiguity of such agreements when nonbinding intent is less than completely clear. The Final Act, which was signed by the heads of state and other "high representatives" of thirty-five nations and is intended to establish a broad framework of East-West cooperation in a great number of fields, is a sixty-page instrument which on its face looks and reads much like a treaty. There is no express provision in the Final Act stating that it is not intended to have legal effect; in fact, in the final paragraph of the text the parties express their determination "to act in accordance with the provisions contained in the above texts."[34] In another paragraph of the Final Act, however, the parties state that they do not regard the instrument as a treaty or international agreement eligible for registration under Article 102 of the U.N. Charter.[35] Moreover, during the conference a number of delegations, including the U.S. and other Western delegations, clearly expressed their understanding that the Final Act was not intended to involve a "legal" commitment or to be binding upon the signatory powers.[36] Thus, there is considerable evidence that the act was not intended to establish legal obligations. Nevertheless, nations have treated the Final Act as embodying important political and moral commitments, and there have been a number of instances in which various Western nations have accused the Soviet Union and other Communist signatory nations of "violating" its human rights provisions.[37] In support of such efforts, Henkin notes that while the Helsinki Accord is nonbinding and without "legal remedies," it is an "international undertaking" and violations are a "proper basis for international (nonlegal) recourse and remedy by other participants."[38]

Agreements of this type permit nations to come close to firm obligations without taking the final step of binding legal commitment. Often, nations will be willing to carry their cooperative experiments further under this kind of nonbinding arrangement than would be the case if the agreement were legally binding. Thus, it can be argued that the nonbinding nature of the Helsinki Final Act has permitted experiments in East-West cooperation in sensitive areas where more binding and riskier commitments could not possibly have been achieved. This seems particularly true of the human rights provisions embodied in ''Basket Three'' of the Final Act.

2. Agreements to Agree

A nation can avoid incurring any immediate risk in a proposed cooperative arrangement by entering only into some preliminary type of general understanding which, while legally binding, is in practical effect devoid of specific substantive commitments. Agreements ''to agree'' and agreements limited to an obligation ''to cooperate'' are of this character.[39] In essence, such agreements involve only a commitment to future negotiation. For example, the U.S.–Soviet Agreement on Environmental Cooperation provides that ''the parties will develop cooperation in the field of environmental protection on the basis of equality, reciprocity, and mutual benefit.''[40] Again, a number of agreements on delimitation of the continental shelves between two countries contain clauses providing generally for cooperation between them in the event a mineral deposit common to both shelves is discovered in the future.[41] Under such an agreement, the parties have at least an obligation to engage in good faith attempts to work out some type of substantive cooperation in the future. Frequently, such agreements establish joint committees or other procedures to attempt to implement their cooperative objective.

The principle that nations may commit themselves to good

faith negotiation of a common problem, without necessarily committing themselves to reaching a final agreement on it, is suggested in the 1957 Lake Lanoux Arbitration between France and Spain, involving French diversion of waters of a river system shared by the two countries. In that case, the arbitral tribunal indicated that relevant treaties between the two countries establishing procedures for cooperation in use of these waters at least required France to consult, though not necessarily reach agreement, with Spain with respect to the river diversion, although it also held that France had in fact met these obligations. The tribunal noted that ''the reality of the obligations thus undertaken is incontestable and sanctions can be applied in the event, for example, of an unjustified breaking off of the discussions, abnormal delays, disregard of agreed procedures, systematic refusals to take into consideration adverse proposals or interests, and, more generally, in cases of violations of the rules of good faith.''[42]

Despite the absence of specific substantive obligation, an agreement to agree can often serve a very useful function. For example, in situations where nations are not yet prepared to commit themselves fully to an agreement, an agreement to agree can at least commit the nations concerned to the principle of cooperation in the area in question. More specifically, it can provide an institutional framework for and facilitate such future cooperation, while permitting the parties to work out the specific terms and details of their cooperation over time or in the light of developing conditions. An agreement to agree can also be useful in establishing a broad framework for potential cooperation among nations in cases where a problem is still relatively unimportant and does not appear presently to warrant the negotiation of detailed cooperative arrangements, or where the exact nature of the problem is as yet undefined and it is not presently feasible to decide on specific arrangements. Finally, an agreement to agree can be useful in providing an ''umbrella'' understanding in situations where the practical implementation of cooperation is likely to require a variety of different and often short-lived subsidiary arrangements, none of which is worth embodying in a formal international agreement.

3. Option Agreements

A nation may preserve its choice to enter into a particular cooperative arrangement with another nation, while deferring the risks which might be involved in a present binding decision, by entering into some kind of option agreement with the other nation. Under an option agreement, one nation promises another the privilege of deciding either to go ahead with a future agreement or to not do so, as the nation securing the option may subsequently unilaterally determine.[43] While the nation giving the option is contingently committed to the agreement, the nation having the option is not. Of course, in most cases a nation will have to pay something for, or "purchase," such an option. But its immediate risk in such cases is limited to this price it has paid to secure the option. For example, one nation might wish to obtain an assured right to purchase certain quantities of grain from another nation at a given price at a particular date if it subsequently decides it needs such grain; it may be willing to pay certain claims or make other concessions to the supplier state in order to obtain an agreement giving such assurances. Again, an atomic energy cooperation agreement may give a recipient nation the right to purchase from the supplier nation such amounts of special nuclear material, up to a certain limit, as the recipient subsequently decides to buy from the supplier, without any obligation by the recipient to make such purchases.[44]

An option agreement permits the nation securing the option to preserve its privilege of entering into a particular cooperative arrangement while retaining a further opportunity to assess the potential usefulness of the arrangement, explore possibly more desirable alternatives, and see what develops. In effect, it serves as a hedge against opportunity costs. It can also be useful where costs are involved in deciding whether one wishes to or will be able to enter into a particular agreement—costs of attempting to secure relevant information, legislative authority, necessary financing, or so forth—and it is not worthwhile even to begin these processes unless the opportunity to eventually conclude the deal, if desired, is assured. If the option is free or given at low cost, a nation will have little to lose in obtaining such an option, except perhaps a political identification with the other nation granting the option, through public knowledge that it is considering "doing business" with the other nation. On the other hand, a nation will not need such an option if it believes the opportunity to cooperate will be there even if it does not obtain a formal option. Thus, it will be interested in an option agreement only if it believes that the other nation may change its mind as to its willingness to enter into a particular future agreement, or will decide instead to cooperate exclusively with some alternative partner.

Of course, there are not many situations in which one nation is interested in giving another such an option, since the nation giving the option commits itself without receiving any commitment in return. It may take the position, "Come and see us when you are really ready to talk business." A nation is likely to give an option only in exchange for some *quid pro quo*, or if it believes the option agreement is necessary to maintain the other nation's interest in eventual agreement and increase the chances that it will ultimately choose to enter into it.

4. Equivocal Agreements

Nations often seek to preserve broad flexibility in their agreements through the deliberate use of very general, equivocal, or ambiguous language which is capable of being interpreted by each of them, if necessary, as protecting their own interests and positions.[45] (We have already seen that very general or imprecise language may also indicate the parties' lack of intent that the agreement be legally binding.)[46] Of course, ambiguity may occur other than deliberately. Thus, ambiguity will frequently occur in an agreement despite the parties' efforts to achieve clarity, reflecting unintentional misunderstandings or inherent difficulties in anticipating future situations to which the agreement may be applicable. But ambiguity can also be used as a conscious technique, clearly understood and recognized by the parties, for dealing with risks they perceive. For example, several nations may reach agreement that, when any of them expropriates or nationalizes alien property within their territories, the owners shall be entitled to ''appropriate'' compensation—but each nation may hold different views, clearly reflected in their negotiations, as to what compensation is ''appropriate'' under this standard.[47] Or nations may agree that the resources of the deep-sea bed should be regarded as the ''common heritage of mankind,'' but differ markedly as to what this principle means or what it implies as to how the exploitation of these resources is actually to be controlled or the revenues produced from such activities are to be shared.[48] Equivocal language may relate to issues central to agreement or to less important or peripheral issues.

Views differ as to the usefulness of this technique. Some commentators believe that equivocal or ambiguous international agreements are wholly illusory and not useful, giving the appearance of genuine agreement and shared understandings when in fact there is none. Thus, Kindleberger suggests that ''[w]hen minds do not meet, it is a mistake to agree on a form of words that papers the cracks, since the paper bargain struck will not be kept.''[49] This illusion of agreement may even be harmful. It may relax the pressure on the parties to reach an agreement capable of really dealing with the problem involved, induce false public expectations, and, when these expectations are disappointed, lead to increased conflict and more difficulty in reaching real agreement.[50] In this view, it is usually better to postpone the conclusion of any formal agreement until such time as genuine agreement can be reached.

Others argue that deliberate equivocality or ambiguity often serves a useful function. Even where the parties cannot reach common understandings as to issues central to their agreement, ambiguous or equivocal language permits them at least to commit themselves to cooperative approaches to the problem. Moreover, simply having a written agreement may promote general attitudes and establish an institutional framework and negotiating parameters in which a more genuine agreement can, over time, be more easily achieved. The agreement will probably embody real consensus on at least some issues, and these at least can be disposed of once and for all. The argument is that it may be worthwhile, for example, to reach even an equivocal agreement on principles furthering resolution of the Arab-Israeli dispute, or the principle that the deep-sea beds are the "common heritage of mankind," or the principle that "aggression" is illegal, even if there is considerable uncertainty and disagreement as to the meaning and application of these principles. This is particularly so where the only alternative is to defer attempts to reach agreement to a future time when, as the context of negotiation changes, divergent interests become more apparent, and positions harden and become more fixed, even equivocal agreement may be unattainable. In such cases, an equivocal agreement performs functions similar to an agreement to agree in furnishing at least an established basis for further negotiation. In short, where genuine agreement is presently unattainable, an equivocal or ambiguous agreement may be better than no agreement at all.

This debate will doubtless long continue, since it is difficult to generalize on the virtues or drawbacks of ambiguity apart from the facts of a particular situation. Sometimes equivocal language will be helpful, sometimes not. One seasoned diplomat, Abba Eban, comments:

Equivocal language is often used in diplomacy to cover up disagreement on issues which must be included for some reason in a larger settlement, or which must be dealt with as if there was agreement. In other words, there is a degree of complicity involved in the ambiguous language. There is nothing inherently wrong in this practice, so long as the parties know what they have done and do not delude themselves with the hope that their joint signature creates a common policy.[51]

In any case, equivocal or ambiguous language can be particularly useful in helping the parties to bridge disagreements as to minor or more peripheral provisions of a proposed arrangement, permitting them to reach an overall agreement dealing with the principal issues involved. If nations can agree on the basic and most important provisions of a cooperative arrangement, it makes little sense for them to allow their negotiations to fail because of differences over less important provisions. In practice, nations often use equivocal language to bypass such peripheral issues, leaving them to later negotiation should they arise and their solution prove necessary. For example, nations often disagree as to the phrasing in an agreement of abstract legal positions which have little relation to the agreement's actual purposes or implementation but on which, as matters of principle or precedent, neither nation is prepared to yield. Agreements such as the 1959 Antarctic Treaty and the 1972 U.S.– Brazilian Shrimp Agreement[52] were successfully concluded only because the parties refused to become bogged down in abstract, complex, and controversial legal issues of title and jurisdiction and instead bypassed them and focused their attention on the practical issues requiring solution.

5. Limiting the Importance of the Subject Matter

A nation may reduce the risks of cooperation by limiting its agreement with another nation to less important and less risky subjects. For example, the United States may conclude an agreement with the Soviet Union for an exchange of information on cancer research rather than for a limitation on strategic missiles. Obviously, the risks involved in a mistaken assessment of the value of the arrangement or of the Soviet Union's trustworthiness will be less in the one case than in the other.

Many commentators have suggested that cooperation between initially unenthusiastic, apprehensive, or distrustful nations can be developed through tentative experiments with relatively limited, less important, and less risky agreements. Their assumption is that successful cooperation in such low-risk agreements will lead to growing mutual trust and confidence, which will in turn form the basis for agreements on more important subjects.[53] For example, Schelling suggests that

confidence does not always exist; and one of the purposes of piecemeal bargains is to cultivate the necessary mutual expectations. Neither [party] may be willing to trust the other's prudence . . . on a large issue. But, if a number of preparatory bargains can be struck on a small scale, each may be willing to risk a small investment to create a tradition of trust. The purpose is to let each party demonstrate that he appreciates the need for trust and that he knows the other does so too. So, if a major issue is to be negotiated, it may be necessary to seek out and negotiate some minor items for "practice," to establish the necessary confidence in each other's awareness of the long-term value of good faith.

Similarly, Marwell and Schmitt note that

[t]he absolute size of the risk involved [in a cooperative arrangement] is also often subject to manipulation and, in general, should be reduced if cooperation is to be most easily achieved. By size, we mean the injury which can be inflicted from a single act of exploitation. The less costly one exploitative response, the more it is likely that partners will try again to cooperate. A small loss can be more easily ignored or regained, and may instigate the development of protective devices rather than a severance of relations. In short, a shaping process may be required for trust as well as for other forms of learned behavior.[55]

The recent U.S. policy of entering into a wide variety of minor and low-risk cooperative agreements with the Soviet Union was based, in part, on the theory that this technique would help in building mutual trust and détente.[56] A similar approach has been suggested as a way of dealing with the problems of distrust which pervade Arab-Israeli relations. Eban, commenting on the lessons of the 1979 Camp David Agreements, suggests:

> Above all, there has been vindication of a gradualist approach to conflict resolution. The interim and disengagement accords of 1974 and 1975 were indispensable stages toward peace. They proved that negotiation could produce benefits, that agreements could be kept, that there was usually more than one possible solution for dilemmas of physical security, and that modest partial agreements were more likely to develop a positive momentum toward further agreement than to "freeze" situations or "destroy incentives." . . . When you descend to earth from an exceptionally tall ladder, it is often prudent to use the intervening rungs, rather than to seek posthumous glory by a single leap.[57]

Whether a strategy of entering into less important and less risky agreements actually leads nations to a willingness to conclude more important ones—whether trust and confidence can in fact be developed through this technique—has yet to be demonstrated.[58] The strategy assumes that nations will behave consistently in all agreements with the same parties. But, a nation's past record of trustworthy performance in unimportant agreements is no guarantee that it will prove equally trustworthy in important ones. For example, the Soviet Union may have little reason to fail to perform obligations under a cancer research agreement but more incentive to fail to do so under an arms control agreement. Moreover, the technique of gradually building trust may be deliberately used as part of a confidence game, to trick another nation into entering into subsequent and more important agreements in which they can be exploited. As Gergen points out, "[I]n daily life, a person may generate trust with a series of actions at low cost to himself, only to take advantage of the other in situations where the stakes are high; or he may actually provide the other with very positive outcomes in certain areas of exchange in order to achieve high payoffs at great cost to his partner in other areas."[59]

An agreement can be structured so that, while initially limited to unimportant and low-risk matters, it can easily be extended by the parties, or even by one of them, to more important matters as their confidence in the agreement and in each other grows. Sohn has made several proposals for furthering international cooperation on the basis of this idea. One of his proposals is designed to encourage acceptance by nations of the compulsory jurisdiction of the International Court of Justice under Article 36, paragraph 2, of the Statute of the Court (the so-called optional clause) by a step-by-step acceptance of such jurisdiction.[60] The proposal envisions the establishment of a detailed list of possible categories of international legal disputes potentially subject to the Court's compulsory jurisdiction. A nation might initially agree to accept the Court's compulsory jurisdiction only as to particular very limited and unimportant categories of disputes specified in the list, such as disputes involving consular relations, but could gradually accept the Court's jurisdiction in more significant categories, such as disputes involving territorial or environmental questions, as its confidence in the International Court increases. Another of Sohn's proposals was directed at developing Soviet-American confidence in the principle of on-site inspections as a means of ensuring compliance with arms control agreements. He suggested an agreement which would initially limit on-site inspections to a small number of designated zones, but would provide for the gradual expansion of inspections over an increasing number of such zones, eventually including those in which relevant industries or installations would most likely be located.[61]

6. Limiting the Size or Scope of the Agreement

As a closely related technique, a nation may reduce its risks by limiting the size or scope of its agreement with another nation. For example, one nation may agree to sell another only one million tons of wheat rather than the five million tons the other wishes, or it may agree to lend only $100 million rather than the $200 million the other nation has requested. Or the United States and Soviet Union may agree to the mutual establishment of only a few rather than many consulates in each other's territory or to a mutual reduction in the number of their respective strategic bombers rather than of all types of nuclear weapons delivery systems. In each case, limiting the investment serves to limit the risk. At the extreme, a nation may limit the scope of its obligations to behavior it intends to engage in even in the absence of the agreement. For example, the 1974 U.S.–Soviet Vladivostok agreement between President Ford and General Secretary Brezhnev put a ceiling of 2,400 on the total number of intercontinental ballistic missiles, submarine-launched ballistic missiles, and heavy bombers for each country, a level which probably exceeded either nation's present stocks or future intentions.[62]

This technique is useful only where the size or scope of the agreement can be varied and where the risk involved in the agreement is proportionate to its size or scope. For example, a mutual defense agreement cannot easily be limited; if there is an obligation to assist an ally against attack, nations will not usually limit this obligation by providing that assistance in repelling attack will be furnished only up to a certain level, or will be forthcoming only in the event of attacks by small rather than large and powerful countries. Again, if one nation is concerned that an agreement requiring international inspection of its nuclear facilities may result in disclosure of its technical secrets, inspection of even one facility may result in disclosure, and limiting the number of inspected facilities may not reduce the risk.

Attempts to limit the size or scope of an agreement may sometimes lead to added rather than lessened risk. Thus, in some cases, cooperation may require a substantial level of mutual commitment or investment, and agreements which do not reach a sufficient level may fail. For example, an inadequate commitment of military forces to a mutual defense agreement may fail to deter an aggressor, or an inadequate commitment of resources to an economic development agreement may mean that a developing nation cannot develop the internal infrastructure and economic momentum necessary to take off on its own in coping with its problems. Again, where cooperation of a particular type, regardless of its scope, requires a nation to incur substantial preparation or reliance costs, that nation may prefer to enter into a more extensive arrangement which would justify those costs than to enter into a less extensive arrangement which would not. For example, the Soviet Union might be prepared to enter into an agreement with the United States for the linking up of U.S. and Soviet spacecraft on a large number of space missions, but not be prepared to go to the expense of specially designing a spacecraft for only a single joint mission. Finally, in certain situations a nation may have more confidence in the probability of a particular agreement's proving useful if the agreement is likely to be applied to a large number or broad range of instances than if the agreement will be applied only to a small number or limited range of instances. An agreement for a broad exchange of industrial technology and know-how between the United States and the Soviet Union may offer both sides gains, whereas a more limited exchange of technology, such as computer technology, may turn out to be an uneven exchange for one side (in the case of computer technology, probably the United States).

7. Exceptions Clauses and Reservations

Exceptions clauses and reservations are a special way of limiting the scope of an agreement. Where a nation is concerned about the risks of possible application of an agreement to a particular limited subject matter or area, it can protect itself by provisions specifically excluding these matters from the agreement. It is sometimes easier to deal with problems of risk by specifying what the agreement does *not* cover than by specifying what it does cover.

Many agreements contain exception clauses. Most U.S. commercial treaties (usually called Treaties of Friendship, Commerce, and Navigation) with other countries specifically provide that the agreement shall not preclude the right of either party to adopt measures reserving to its own nationals rights and privileges with respect to its national fisheries, measures relating to fissionable materials, statutes permitting aliens entry subject to conditions regarding their engaging in gainful occupations, and so forth.[63] Exceptions broadly preserving a nation's right to take actions it considers necessary to protect its national security or to deal with situations of national emergency are particularly common in international agreements. For example, U.S. commercial treaties usually expressly provide that the treaty ''shall not preclude the application by either Party of measures . . . necessary to fulfill its obligations for the maintenance or restoration of international peace and security, or necessary to protect its essential security interests,''[64] and Article XXI of the General Agreement of Tariffs and Trade contains a general exception to all GATT obligations for certain measures taken by a contracting party ''necessary for the protection of its essential security interests.''[65] The London Ocean Dumping Convention permits a party to issue a special permit allowing dumping of substances otherwise prohibited from being disposed of in the ocean ''in emergencies, posing unacceptable risk relating to human health and admitting no other feasible solution.''[66]

Clearly, such broad exception clauses may be open to abuse. An interesting example of a more complex ''derogation clause,'' intended to provide some constraints on improper invocation of ''national security'' exceptions, is Article 4 of the International Covenant on Civil and Political Rights, which provides:

1. In time of public emergency which threatens the life of the nation and the existence of which is officially proclaimed, the States Parties to the present Covenant may take measures derogating from their obligations under the present Covenant to the extent strictly required by the exigencies of the situation, provided that such measures are not inconsistent with their other obligations under international law and do not involve discrimination solely on the ground of race, colour, sex, language, religion or social origin.

2. No derogation from Articles 6, 7, 8 (paragraphs 1 and 2), 11, 15, 16 and 18 may be made under this provision. [These articles prohibit torture and protect certain other basic human rights.]

3. Any State Party to the present Covenant availing itself of the right of derogation shall immediately inform the other States Parties to the present Covenant, through the intermediary of the Secretary-General of the United Nations, of the provisions from which it has derogated and of the reasons by which it was actuated. A further communication shall be made, through the same intermediary, on the date on which it terminates such derogation.[67]

Reservations made by one nation at the time of its approval of the agreement serve a similar function in limiting the reserving nation's commitment with respect to the matters covered by the reservation.[68] The Vienna Convention on Treaties defines *reservation* as "a unilateral statement, however phrased or named, made by a State, when signing, ratifying, accepting, approving or acceding to a treaty, whereby it purports to exclude or to modify the legal effect of certain provisions of the treaty in their application to that state."[69]

In the case of bilateral treaties, a reservation is, in effect, a counteroffer and has to be expressly or implicitly accepted by the other party if the agreement is to have legal effect. Reservations are unusual in bilateral agreements, since the parties normally handle such questions in their negotiations and, if necessary, provide for any exceptions or clarifications in the treaty instrument itself. Thus, reservations to a bilateral agreement usually occur when one nation's legislature, which under its law must approve an agreement, refuses to do so unless specific exceptions, clarifications, or understandings are included. Such reservations may be controversial and, when put forward after negotiations have been concluded and the agreement is in final form, can give rise to charges of bad faith. Recent examples are the various amendments, conditions, reservations, and understandings adopted by the U.S. Senate in approving ratification of the 1978 U.S.–Panama Canal Treaty and Treaty Concerning the Permanent Neutrality and Operation of the Panama Canal, and attached to the treaties.[70] These included the so-called DeConcini condition to the Neutrality Treaty, which provided that U.S. ratification of that treaty was subject to the condition that ''notwithstanding the provisions of Article V or any other provision of the treaty, if the canal is closed, or its operations are interfered with, the United States of America and the Republic of Panama shall each independently have the right to take such steps as it deems necessary, in accordance with its constitutional processes, including the use of military force in Panama, to reopen the canal or restore the operations of the canal as the case may be.''[71] While the DeConcini condition occasioned considerable controversy, Panama ultimately accepted the treaties with this condition. As this is written, the possibility of extensive U.S. Senate reservations to the U.S.–Soviet SALT II Treaty has posed a similar threat to ultimate Soviet acceptance of that agreement.[72]

Reservations to multilateral agreements raise special and more complex problems which will be discussed below in Section 15(b).

In some cases, a nation may be concerned that another party to an agreement may attempt to apply the agreement to *de minimis* situations and complain of alleged violations of a trivial nature which are not subject to proof or refutation through feasible procedures. This problem can in some cases be dealt with through ''threshold'' provisions, limiting the obligations of the parties to activities whose effects exceed some stated technical or more general threshold or minimum. For example, Article III of the 1954 International Convention for the Prevention of Pollution of the Sea by Oil, as amended, provides in part that

(b) the discharge from a tanker to which the present Convention applies of oil or oily mixture shall be prohibited except when the following conditions are all satisfied:

(i) the tanker is proceeding en route;

(ii) the instantaneous rate of discharge of oil content does not exceed 60 litres per mile;

(iii) the total quantity of oil discharged on a ballast voyage does not exceed 1/15,000 of the total cargo-carrying capacity;

(iv) the tanker is more than 50 miles from the nearest land;

(c) the provisions of subparagraph (b) of this Article shall not apply to:

(i) the discharge of ballast from a cargo tank which, since the cargo was last carried therein, has been so cleaned that any effluent therefrom, if it were discharged from a stationary tanker into clean calm water on a clear day, would produce no visible traces of oil on the surface of the water.[73]

Again, Article I of the 1977 Treaty on Environmental Modification provides that "[e]ach State Party to this Convention undertakes not to engage in military or any other hostile use of environmental modification techniques having widespread, long-lasting or severe effects as the means of destruction, damage or injury to any other State Party."[74] In this last example, the phrase "widespread, long-lasting or severe effects" is clearly intended to provide a threshold for application of the treaty. Obviously, thresholds stated in such broad terms may give rise to differing interpretations and lead to future dispute. However, nations may be reluctant to accept obligations in the absence of some threshold. Where this is the case, even a broad threshold may be preferable to none at all.

8. Limiting the Duration of the Agreement

A nation may control its risk by reducing the time period during which it is committed to the agreement.[75] Thus, a nation may decide to enter into an agreement to grant concessions or engage in certain conduct for only a shorter period rather than the longer period another nation proposes. For example, while the 1962 International Coffee Agreement provided for a duration of five years, the U.S. Congress, concerned about the risk of increased coffee prices to American consumers, initially authorized U.S. participation for only two years.[76]

Most agreements are expressly limited as to their duration, although the provisions differ considerably. The 1954 U.S.–West German Treaty of Friendship, Commerce, and Navigation provides that the treaty is to remain in force for at least ten years and continue in force thereafter until terminated by either party's giving one year's written notice to the other.[77] The International Sugar Agreement, 1958, had a five-year duration.[78] The 1959 Antarctic Treaty is binding on the parties for at least thirty years from its date of ratification.[79] Organizational treaties, such as the U.N. Charter and Universal Postal Convention, are typically of indefinite duration.[80]

Shorter-term agreements are perceived as less risky than longer-term agreements presumably because (1) as the time horizon increases, a nation's confidence in its predictions decreases and its uncertainty increases; (2) the statistical chance that something will go wrong is viewed as increasing with time; and (3) the actual and psychological costs to a nation of continued commitment to an agreement that turns out to be disadvantageous may increase in proportion to the length of time that it is held to that agreement. The total loss involved if an agreement results in a nation's losing $10 million a year is less if it is bound to the agreement for only one year than if it is bound for five years.

Some types of risks may not be directly related to the duration of the agreement, however. For example, if the United States agrees to supply nuclear material and technology to Pakistan on condition that Pakistan not use this material to develop a nuclear capability, the risk of Pakistan's diverting the material arises as soon as it is delivered by the United States and cannot be directly reduced by making the agreement a short-term rather than a long-term one. (Indeed, the potential continuing benefits of a longer-term agreement may dissuade Pakistan from cheating.)

There may even be situations where a nation regards a longer-term agreement as less risky than a shorter-term one, either because the agreement requires a substantial investment on its part in terms of preparation or reliance costs which can only be recovered over a longer period, or because it sees the agreement as likely to involve net costs in the short run which, however, will be made up by greater net gains over the long run. Moreover, certain types of agreements contemplate a permanent change in status or very complex types of cooperative behavior, and the parties may not be prepared to enter into them if they are only for a limited time. A treaty providing for a common market or for demilitarization or denuclearization, for example, will make sense only if the parties can count on it over a long period.

9. Providing for a Trial Period (Provisional Application)

A nation may control its risk by providing for a trial period before it becomes definitively committed to the agreement. For example, a nation may be willing to agree to a tariff reduction agreement only on an expressly provisional basis, with the understanding that it can withdraw from the agreement at will or on very short notice. U.S. participation in the General Agreement on Tariffs and Trade was based on its signature of such a protocol of provisional application.[81]

Provisional application of an agreement for risk-management purposes differs from the occasional use of provisional application as a means of putting an agreement immediately into effect on a tentative basis pending definitive acceptance or ratification. Where the parties wish to initiate cooperation promptly under their agreement, but some considerable delay may be involved in completing the constitutional processes required for binding ratification, they may agree to implement the agreement on a nonbinding basis while these procedures are being completed.[82]

The intent in this case is not to test the agreement, but, on the contrary, to put it into operation as quickly as possible.

A trial or experimental period permits a nation to test the utility and risks of a cooperative arrangement under close to operating conditions, and to refuse to commit itself to the agreement if this experience suggests that the agreement is likely to prove unsatisfactory. There are many examples of the use of this technique in interpersonal contexts, such as the period of engagement or trial cohabitation which frequently precedes marriage, or the probationary period frequently found in employment relationships.

One problem with this device is that the trial period may not accurately reveal or reflect the conditions, stresses, or behavior that actually emerge in the course of a more permanent and committed relationship. Since the parties are aware of the tentative and testing nature of the provisional relationship, they may, on the one hand, be on their best behavior or, on the other hand, be less trusting in their behavior and less committed to the success of the relationship.

10. Providing for Unilateral Denunciation or Withdrawal

A nation may protect itself against risk by express provisions that permit it to withdraw easily and quickly from the arrangement.[83] For example, Article IV of the Nuclear Test Ban Treaty provides that "[t]his treaty shall be of unlimited duration," but "[e]ach party shall in exercising its national sovereignty have the right to withdraw from the Treaty if it decides that extraordinary events, related to the subject matter of this Treaty, have jeopardized the supreme interests of its country. It shall give notice of such withdrawal to all other Parties to the Treaty three months in advance."[84] Similar provisions are included in a number of other arms control agreements, including the proposed U.S.–Soviet SALT II Treaty, although a number of these subsequent agreements add a proviso to the effect that the notice of withdrawal "shall include a statement of the extraordinary events the notifying Party regards as having jeopardized its supreme interests."[85] Again, economic and technical cooperation agreements between the United States and other nations typically include the following provision: "All or any part of the program of assistance provided herein may . . . be terminated by either Government if that Government determines that because of changed conditions the continuation of such assistance is unnecessary or undesirable. The termination of such assistance under this provision may include the termination of deliveries of any commodities hereunder not yet delivered."[86]

Most international organizations expressly provide for withdrawal in their constitutive instruments.[87] For example, members may withdraw from the International Monetary Fund or the World Bank with immediate effect,[88] from the North Atlantic Treaty or Food and Agriculture organizations on one year's notice,[89] or from the Organization of American States or the International Labour Organization on two years' notice.[90] While the U.N. Charter does not contain any provision for withdrawal, its negotiating history suggests that withdrawal is legally permissible.[91]

Such escape hatches or outs are analytically equivalent to a right unilaterally to establish the duration of the agreement, at least for the withdrawing state. Unilateral withdrawal or termination provisions can be drawn up in various ways so as to circumscribe the exercise of such a right. For example, the right to withdraw can be conditioned on the occurrence of particular specified circumstances, the existence of appropriate cause for withdrawal can be made subject to third-party review, or a period of prior notice can be required.[92]

Provisions for easy unilateral withdrawal from an agreement raise both theoretical and practical problems. Thus, it can be argued that an agreement which permits a party to withdraw whenever it wishes embodies no real legal commitment, is in effect illusory, and consequently neither party is likely to be willing to invest in or rely on it. However, there is ample evidence—for example, in the continued observance of the Nuclear Test Ban Treaty—that nations generally treat agreements which contain such withdrawal clauses as reflecting meaningful commitments. Certainly, by entering into such an agreement, a party incurs an obligation not to exercise such a right to withdraw except in good faith. The existence of a real commitment is, of course, even more evident if a nation can withdraw only after a period of notice, or if its right to withdraw is made subject to objective criteria or third-party review.

Despite these theoretical problems, broad withdrawal provisions are widely used and appear to play an important role in giving nations a sufficient sense of flexibility to induce them to enter into otherwise risky agreements. It should be remembered that until a nation exercises a right of withdrawal (which may never occur), cooperation between the parties under the agreement continues. Moreover, if a nation is so convinced that an agreement is harmful to its interests that it wishes to withdraw, there is a substantial likelihood that it will not comply with the agreement even if it is forced to continue as a party. Where provisions of this type permit parties to cooperate where they would not otherwise be willing to do so, they clearly perform a useful function.

Yet, once again, even the broadest provision for easy withdrawal cannot completely protect a nation from the risks of an agreement. Thus, a nation must consider the risk that it may incur unrecoverable losses or costs either before it obtains information which causes it to decide to withdraw or during a possible waiting period before its withdrawal becomes effective. It must also consider the risk that it may be subject to domestic or international criticism for exercising such a right to withdraw, or that its withdrawal may be subject to other political constraints or lead to sanctions. Finally, withdrawal necessarily involves giving up the cooperative relation the parties have achieved, which may have implications for their willingness to cooperate in the future. Where a nation believes its interests are so jeopardized by remaining party to the agreement that it must seriously consider withdrawal, it may suggest that the other party or parties should consider the possibility of express or tacit revision of the agreement in order to permit cooperation to continue.

11. Breaking the Agreement into Parts

A nation may seek to control its risks by breaking down or segmenting a proposed larger cooperative arrangement into a series of separate, more limited agreements. This technique in effect combines several of the techniques previously discussed by permitting each nation to limit the subject matter, scope, or duration of each discrete segment of the overall arrangement. The nation can then reassess the value and risks of continuing cooperation on the basis of its experience with each completed stage or segment. Staging or segmenting techniques of this type have been used in armistice and arms control agreements, which are frequently broken down into a series of separate reciprocal steps, and in long-term sales agreements, which are often broken down into shorter-term segments renewable from year to year. For example, the 1975 Egypt-Israel Agreement on the Sinai and Suez Canal sets out a detailed schedule of phased and reciprocal partial withdrawal measures by each of these nations, designed when completed to produce the intended full withdrawal of forces to agreed armistice lines.[93] Similar provisions are included in the 1979 Egypt-Israel Peace Treaty.[94]

This technique is obviously not applicable where the cooperative arrangement is by its nature not capable of being segmented, nor is it useful where the practical or administrative costs of segmentation are excessive. But, as Schelling and others have pointed out, even seemingly integral arrangements can, with sufficient ingenuity, sometimes be broken down into a series of separate reciprocal steps, thus helping to meet the risk-management concerns of the parties.[95]

12. Amendment or Revision

A nation may obtain some protection against the risks involved in a long-term cooperative arrangement by providing for possible amendment or revision of the agreement.[96] However, such provisions will not, of course, protect it from costs which occur prior to the time of amendment. Moreover, the extent to which the possibility of amendment can provide protection against risk will depend upon many factors, including the procedure by which amendments can be initiated and brought into effect, and the consequences which follow if one party proposes an amendment but another party refuses to accept it. The possibility of amendment is most pertinent to a nation's concerns regarding the risk of changes in the value of the arrangement and is discussed in more detail in Chapter 3, Section 2.

13. Dispute Settlement Provisions

Dispute settlement procedures, including those employing third parties, can play a general risk-management role as well as performing other functions in facilitating cooperation.[97] In the international legal system—in contrast with domestic legal systems—international courts and arbitral tribunals have no general compulsory jurisdiction. An international tribunal can decide a dispute between or among nations only if all of the nations concerned agree to its doing so, either by giving such consent in some agreement before the dispute arises or by entering into an agreement conferring jurisdiction to decide the dispute on the tribunal after the dispute has arisen.[98] Yet even in the absence of specific provision in their agreements, nations have a general obligation to settle their disputes by peaceful means. Article 2, paragraph 3, of the U.N. Charter provides that "members shall settle their international disputes by peaceful means in such a manner that international peace and security, and justice, are not endangered." Article 33 of the charter further requires: "The parties to any dispute, the continuance of which is likely to endanger the maintenance of international peace and security, shall, first of all, seek a solution by negotiation, enquiry, mediation, conciliation, arbitration, judicial settlement, resort to regional agencies or arrangements, or other peaceful means of their own choice." Most agreements provide for some kind of dispute settlement procedures, ranging from a simple obligation to consult, to an obligation to accept submission of the dispute to binding settlement by the International Court of Justice.[99] For example, Article XXVII of the 1954 U.S.–West German Treaty of Friendship, Commerce and Navigation provides:

1. Each Party shall accord sympathetic consideration to, and shall afford adequate opportunity for consultation regarding, such representations as the other Party may make with respect to any matter affecting the operation of the present Treaty.

2. Any dispute between the Parties as to the interpretation or the application of the present Treaty which the Parties do not satisfactorily adjust by diplomacy or some other agreed means shall be submitted to arbitration or, upon agreement of the Parties, to the International Court of Justice.[100]

Dispute settlement procedures provide a nation some protection against arbitrary breach of the agreement by the treaty partner.[101] A nation will usually be more reluctant to try to evade its obligations if its actions are likely to be publicly regarded as a violation of its commitments, subjecting it to legal or political sanctions or other costs. Moreover, dispute settlement procedures can furnish a safety valve, providing a legitimate and politically acceptable way for nations to raise and attempt to resolve genuine differences while still maintaining the integrity of their agreement. Broadly speaking, the possibility of third-party involvement in dispute settlement influences the parties towards moderate behavior, since each must anticipate that it may have to persuade an impartial third party, or indirectly, the more general international community, that its actions and reactions are reasonable and legitimate. Thus, the availability of dispute settlement procedures serves to limit risk by constraining the possible consequences of agreement within more foreseeable limits.

Nevertheless, dispute settlement procedures—particularly those employing third parties—also involve certain uncertainties and risks. First, dispute settlement procedures are intended to and can restrain each party's freedom to act unilaterally to protect its interests, even if it feels that these interests are seriously threatened if it performs or if the other party fails to perform the agreement. A feeling by government officials that they have last-ditch flexibility not to comply with an agreement, or to take unilateral action to retaliate against the other party if it does not comply, may be an important factor in their willingness to accept agreement. The availability of dispute settlement procedures inevitably constrains these options. Second, these procedures may be improperly invoked by the other party or unfairly or unreasonably applied by a third party. Third, dispute settlement procedures can be costly and time-consuming—in some cases more so than their usefulness justifies. Fourth, dispute settlement procedures may prove ineffective. The parties will be under no obligation to actually settle their dispute unless the agreement provides for binding third-party settlement. Moreover, even where an agreement permits one party to submit the dispute to binding settlement by an arbitral tribunal or international court, such tribunals usually have no authority to enforce their decisions. While nations have generally abided by such decisions, at least where the jurisdiction of the tribunal has been recognized, a nation may, in practice, ignore such a decision with relative impunity. Finally, dispute settlement procedures may sometimes prove counterproductive, exacerbating rather than resolving disputes and making compromise and accommodation more difficult. Thus, a nation may resent being brought before an international tribunal as a defendant, and as a result, its position may harden and become inflexible. For example, the resolution of the 1964 U.S.–French air traffic rights controversy—involving the right of U.S. air carriers under the then existing U.S.–French Air Transport Agreement to embark passengers in Paris for Turkey and Iran, and vice versa—was probably made more difficult by a U.S. decision to take the matter to arbitration. What may well have been simply a French negotiating ploy in denying these rights, designed to place pressure on the United States to grant certain air traffic rights to the U.S. West Coast, was hardened into a highly legalistic arbitral dispute, which after considerable time was in any event decided largely against the U.S. interest.[102]

Consequently, while nations typically include some type of nonbinding dispute settlement procedures in their agreements, they are often reluctant to agree to provisions for compulsory and binding third-party settlement.[103] This has been true with respect to a number of significant multilateral "law-making" conventions negotiated in recent years. For example, the conference preparing the 1961 Vienna Convention on Diplomatic Relations rejected proposals for the inclusion of provisions for the compulsory and binding settlement of disputes in the text of the convention itself, and was able to agree only on the preparation of an entirely separate instrument, or "optional protocol," containing such provisions, subject to separate signature and ratification.[104] Again, the conferences preparing both the 1969 Vienna Convention on the Law of Treaties and the 1978 Vienna Convention on Succession of States in Respect of Treaties (with a minor exception in the case of the 1969 treaty) rejected proposals for compulsory and binding third-party settlement, and were able to agree only on provisions permitting disputes to be submitted to nonbinding third-party conciliation procedures.[105] Indeed, even where provisions for binding third-party dispute settlements are clearly provided in an agreement, they are rarely invoked. As Judge Dillard, formerly a member of the International Court, has noted, "[W]hile perhaps regrettable, it does not seem unnatural that" those in charge of the foreign affairs of governments "should prefer to settle disputes by processes with which they are familiar, that are flexible, and that remain under their control, rather than risk a settlement through processes with which they are less familiar, that appear more rigid, and that entail a loss of control."[106]

Where an agreement contemplates continuing and complex interactions and is likely to raise continuing problems, the nations parties often provide in the agreement for the establishment of a joint commission, liaison committee, or some other joint institution to deal with such questions. Joint commissions can be extremely effective, both in avoiding disputes and in handling them at a low key should they arise. For example, the U.S.–Canadian Boundary Waters Treaty of 1909 establishes a permanent binational commission—the International Joint Commission—composed of six commissioners, three appointed by each country, which has been extensively used and remarkably effective in both implementing the objectives of the convention and resolving disputes between the parties relating to their boundary waters and other boundary questions.[107] The 1979 Egypt–Israel Peace Treaty sets up a Joint Commission and a liaison system to implement certain of its provisions.[108] The 1972 U.S.–Soviet SALT I Agreement established a Standing Consultative Committee to deal with questions of compliance, and the proposed SALT II Agreement would further utilize and institutionalize this committee.[109] Joint institutions of this type have many potential advantages. Ideally, problems can be dealt with at an early stage and in a private, informal, and relatively nonpolitical atmosphere. Moreover, such groups may over time establish special expertise, special commitments to the success of the agreement, and procedures and personal associations which facilitate their ability to resolve problems that arise in implementing the agreement.

Third-party dispute settlement procedures are, of course, also employed in a variety of more specific risk-management roles, and will be further discussed in subsequent sections.

14. Risk-Spreading Devices

A nation may seek to control the risks of cooperation by spreading these risks among a number of similar agreements with several countries, or by pooling these risks with other nations facing similar risk-management problems.

Diversification—that is, entering into a number of smaller transactions with different parties rather than a single larger transaction with one party—is a widely used method of dealing with problems of uncertainty and risk. Lenders, stock market investors, and manufacturers or merchants dependent on suppliers will frequently spread their risks in this way. In effect, a nation can separate a single proposed agreement into several parts and enter into each of these parts with different nations. For example, if a nation needs certain imports of grain to meet its domestic food requirements, it may decide that, rather than dealing with only one nation as supplier of all of its needs, it will spread its risks by making arrangements with several producing nations, each of which is to supply a portion of its needs. Or, if a nation wishes assurance of at least some help in case of aggression by another state, it may decide to spread its risks by making collective security agreements with several other nations rather than with one alone.

The principle of this technique is familiar. If a nation stakes everything on a single agreement with a single other nation—in effect, puts all of its eggs in one basket—and that agreement for some reason turns out badly, the nation loses everything and may be in serious trouble. If, in contrast, it segments the transaction and divides its risk and investment among several agreements with several other nations, and one of these agreements turns out badly, its losses will be only partial and more manageable. Moreover, where it enters into several agreements with several nations, losses on one agreement may be balanced by gains in others. Chance factors will tend to even out its risks among these several agreements.

In practice, however, risk-spreading techniques probably have only limited usefulness with respect to international agreements. In many cases, cooperative possibilities will be relatively unique, involving only two or a relatively few particular nations, and it will not be possible to spread the risks involved through agreements with other different nations. It is difficult, for instance, to see how either the United States or the Soviet Union could spread among other nations the mutual risks of their strategic arms limitation arrangements. Again, while the United States can attempt to spread the risks of an interruption in oil supply by dealing with a number of oil-supplying nations, there is no way it can fill its needs other than relying substantially on supplies from potentially uncertain Middle East sources. Moreover, risk-spreading through diversification of agreements is rational only in cases where a nation has no basis for distinguishing between the uncertainty and overall utility of agreements with one or another of several potential cooperative partners. In this case, for the reasons suggested, the probability of its achieving an overall favorable outcome may be increased by diversification. But if nation A believes, for example, that there is a higher probability that nation B alone will satisfactorily meet its grain import requirements than that either nation C, D, or E will do so, it will be more reasonable for A to deal with B alone. Moreover, diversification may involve substantial extra costs which more than cancel out any risk-management benefits. Thus, a nation may have to pay more to acquire smaller amounts of grain from several different other nations than if it acquires all of its needs from only one supplier, and the transaction costs of several different arrangements are also likely to be greater than those associated with a single arrangement.

Risk-pooling, or insurance, devices are another venerable technique for dealing with problems of risk. Where a number of nations face similar risks, they may in certain situations make these risks more individually manageable by forming consortia or by collectively pooling their resources for meeting them. The principle involved in this technique is again familiar. In effect, it may make more sense in some situations for each nation to exchange the certainty or greater probability of incurring a smaller, more manageable cost (involved in its commitment to support the resource pool) for the smaller probability of incurring a much larger cost which might be beyond its capacity to handle. International analogies to such risk-pooling techniques include the International Monetary Fund's system of Special Drawing Rights for nations encountering balance-of-payments difficulties;[110] the system for collective action to share the risks of an oil boycott or other energy emergency provided by the agreement establishing the International Energy Agency;[111] proposals for the establishment of commodity buffer stocks and an international food reserve;[112] proposals for disaster relief arrangements;[113] and, in the broadest sense, collective security arrangements under the U.N. Charter and other collective security arrangements.

Risk-pooling arrangements also have their limitations, however. In general, they are useful only with respect to risks which are broadly shared by a substantial number of nations to a relatively equal degree; nations with a relatively small exposure to a particular risk would have little reason to join in such a risk-sharing arrangement. Moreover, such arrangements are useful only when the resources needed to cover or respond to such risks are essentially fungible—money, grain, oil, perhaps military power—and can be pooled.

15. Controlling Risk in Multilateral Agreements

While many of the general and special risk-management devices discussed in this and the following chapters are applicable or adaptable to multilateral as well as bilateral agreements, in certain cases the nature of multilateral arrangements calls for special techniques.

Multilateral agreements pose several kinds of problems. For one thing, a nation may not be certain at the time of entering into a multilateral arrangement who its partners in the arrangement may eventually be, and it faces the risk that it may have to cooperate with nations with whom it would prefer not to cooperate, or that nations with whom it wishes to cooperate will not in fact participate or will even work to frustrate the achievement of the objectives of the agreement. Second, as the number of a nation's potential partners increases, it may have more difficulty predicting how each of the other parties is likely to behave and what its eventual outcomes from participating in the agreement are likely to be. Third, it is typically more difficult to find mutually acceptable compromises among a large number of nations having very different interests and views than between only two or a few nations. Sometimes the only way to reach agreement among many nations on a single text may be through acceptance by all of a "lowest common denominator" agreement, in which the obligations of all of the parties are limited to those minimal commitments which even the most intransigent or risk-averse nations will accept. Alternatively, if wide participation is desired, it may be necessary to find some way of relieving one or a few nations from particular obligations which, while generally acceptable to most states, are not acceptable to those particular nations. Conferences such as the Third U.N. Law of the Sea Conference, involving a great many nations with a number of different views on a large number of issues, often face this dilemma. Finally, many of the most significant multilateral cooperative arrangements establish continuing organizations or institutions—such as the United Nations, the European Economic Community, the Organization for Economic Cooperation and Development, or the International Whaling Commission—which are typically vested with some kind of collective recommendatory or decisionmaking powers. The United Nations General Assembly and Security Council, for example, are empowered to make a wide variety of recommendations, and the Security Council can in certain situations make decisions binding on all U.N. members;[114] under Article 25 of the U.N. Charter, "the Members of the United Nations agree to accept and carry out the decisions of the Security Council in accordance with the present Charter." Again, under Article 15 of the International Coffee Agreement, 1976, "members undertake to accept as binding all decisions of the Council under the provisions of this Agreement."[115] Where the organization has authority to make recommendations or decisions without the agreement of a particular nation, that nation faces the risk that subsequent decisions or activities of the organization may turn out to be inconsistent with its interests.

Several of the more important techniques used to deal with these types of risks in multilateral arrangements are discussed below.

a. Protecting against Undesired or Inadequate Participation by Other States

In bilateral arrangements, each nation is certain at the time it enters into the arrangement what nation it will be cooperating with; nation A knows it is agreeing with B, and vice versa. But in multilateral arrangements a nation may have no such assurance, since participation by particular other nations will depend on their subsequent ratification and accession, which may be uncertain or delayed.

This type of situation may pose problems for a nation for several reasons. First, nation A may be prepared to have treaty relations with nation B, but not with nation T. If T is likely to participate in the arrangement, A may not wish to. For example, for many years the United States refused to participate in any multilateral agreement with the People's Republic of China, on the grounds that such participation might imply its recognition or acceptance of the legitimacy of the Chinese Communist regime, as opposed to that of the Chinese Nationalist regime. Second, where an agreement is designed to accomplish certain special purposes, the nations considering agreement may be concerned that participation by nations not sharing these concerns or objectives may frustrate accomplishment of the agreement's purposes. For example, a defensive alliance such as the NATO Treaty requires participation only by nations having a common view as to a military threat posed by the Soviet Union and its allies, and the Antarctic Treaty is likely to be most effective if nations with genuine interests and activities in the Antarctic region participate. Third, the value to a nation of participating in a particular agreement may be closely related to the number or identity of the other nations participating. In some cases the objectives of the proposed agreement cannot be achieved unless most other nations, or at least certain other nations, participate. For example, a collective security arrangement may be ineffective, or even dangerous, unless nations with sufficient strength to deter or repel a potential aggressor participate. In 1945 there was a broad consensus that a new United Nations organization could not hope to achieve its collective security and other purposes unless all the great powers having the principal capacity to maintain peace participated. Likewise, there may be little point in a coffee-exporting nation's participating in an international agreement designed to stabilize or raise the world price of coffee through mutual restrictions on each nation's coffee exports unless most of the world's important coffee-exporting nations also join. If one coffee-exporting nation joins and restricts its exports, but its competitors refuse to join and maintain or raise their exports, the agreement will have little effect in controlling world coffee exports and prices; the only result of the nation's participation in this case will be that its competitors will secure a greater share of the market and higher profits at its expense. In other cases, a nation may fear that it will be placed at a competitive disadvantage vis-à-vis one or more other nations unless they also join and assume the obligations of an agreement. For example, a nation, such as Pakistan, might be reluctant to ratify a nuclear nonproliferation treaty renouncing the development of atomic weapons unless its neighbors and potential adversaries, such as India, ratify it as well.

One way in which a nation can try to deal with this problem is by delaying its decision as to acceptance of an agreement until it sees which other countries also accept and whom its treaty partners will in fact be. But if all nations adopt this wait-and-see approach, the agreement will obviously never take effect; not every nation can go last! Consequently, nations have developed other ways of protecting themselves against this type of risk.

First, a nation can obtain protection against the risk of participation in multilateral agreements by other nations unacceptable to it through provisions expressly restricting participation in the agreement.[116] Thus, participation may be limited to nations invited to and participating in the conference preparing the agreement, particular specifically named nations, nations having specific characteristics or meeting certain criteria, nations presently members of some other related agreement or organization, nations specifically invited to participate by the original participants, or some combination of these requirements. For example, the North Atlantic Treaty of 1949 was initially open only to the fifteen European nations which formulated the treaty; however, "[t]he parties may, by unanimous agreement, invite any other European State in a position to further the principles of this Treaty and to contribute to the security of the North Atlantic area to accede to this Treaty."[117] The World Meteorological Convention is open only to nations having their own meteoro-

logical services.[118] The Organization for Economic Cooperation and Development is open to parties other than the original
parties only by unanimous decision of the existing parties.[119]

The membership provisions of the U.N. Charter illustrate a
combination of these techniques, as Articles 3 and 4 demonstrate:

Article 3

The original Members of the United Nations shall be the states which, having
participated in the United Nations Conference on International Organization at
San Francisco, or having previously signed the Declaration by United Nations
of 1 January 1942, sign the present Charter and ratify it in accordance with
Article 110.

Article 4

1. Membership in the United Nations is open to all other peace-loving states
which accept the obligations contained in the present Charter and, in the
judgment of the Organization, are able and willing to carry out these obligations.

2. The admission of any such state to membership in the United Nations will
be effected by a decision of the General Assembly upon the recommendation
of the Security Council.[120]

For many years the United States implemented its policy of
excluding the People's Republic of China and certain other
states it disapproved of from participation in multilateral agreements in which the United States participated by obtaining final
clauses in such agreements restricting participation to "States
members of the United Nations or its Specialized Agencies."[121]
Since the United States during this period was able to muster
sufficient political support to exclude the People's Republic and
these other states from participating in the United Nations and its
specialized agencies, this formula also effectively excluded
them from participation in these other multilateral agreements.
In contrast, the Soviet Union and other supporters of the excluded nations advocated a provision under which participation
would be open to "all states." This "all states" formula was in
fact applied in agreements such as the Nuclear Test Ban

Treaty,[122] which everyone, including the United States, agreed required the widest possible participation.

In some cases, a nation may be permitted to join an existing agreement only on conditions or terms set in each case by the existing parties or agreed upon between them and the new nation party on an *ad hoc* basis. For example, accession to the General Agreement on Tariffs and Trade is a valuable privilege, since it carries with it rights to the most-favored-nation tariff treatment granted in the GATT schedules. Consequently, under Article XXXIII of the GATT, nations which desire to become parties must negotiate with the existing parties the terms of their accession, including tariff concessions they will offer as part of the deal.[123] Moreover, under Article XXXV of the GATT, at the time a state is admitted as a contracting party, it has a one-time option for any reason to opt out of contractual GATT relationships with any designated party, in which case the agreement will not apply between them; and any existing party has a similar right to opt out of any relationship with the newly admitted state.[124]

Second, a nation can protect itself against the risk of inadequate participation by other nations through provisions that the agreement will not take effect unless and until what that nation regards as sufficient participation is in fact achieved. Sufficient participation may be measured by such criteria as acceptance by particular expressly named nations, acceptance by a certain number of nations, acceptance by some number or proportion of nations having particular characteristics, or some combination of these. For example, the U.N. Charter provided for its entry into force upon ratification by the Republic of China, France, the Soviet Union, the United Kingdom, the United States, and a majority of other signatory states.[125] The Nuclear Nonproliferation Treaty provided for its entry into force upon ratification by the United States, the Soviet Union, the United Kingdom, and forty other states.[126] The Warsaw Pact and the Antarctic Treaty provided for entry into force upon ratification by all of the named signatory nations participating in its negotiations.[127] The International Coffee Agreement, 1976, provided for entry into force upon ratification by at least twenty exporting nations holding at least 80 percent of the votes of exporting members and at least ten importing nations holding at least 80 percent of the votes of importing members, as set out in a special annex to the agreement.[128] And the 1973 Convention on the Prevention of Pollution from Ships will enter into force only following ratification by fifteen nations whose combined merchant fleets constitute at least 50 percent of the world's gross merchant tonnage.[129] An agreement may also contain provisions protecting against the risks of inadequate participation subsequent to its entry into force—as through withdrawals of denunciations. For example, the Genocide Convention provides that the convention shall cease to be in force if, as a result of denunciations, the number of parties becomes less than sixteen.[130]

Third, nations negotiating an agreement may seek to protect themselves against the risk that nonparticipating states may behave in ways which interfere with the purposes of the agreement. It is not easy to achieve such protection. An international agreement normally establishes legal obligations only between or among its parties and is not in itself binding upon states which are not parties.[131] Nonparties will be obligated to respect a particular treaty regime only if it can be established that that regime, or particular elements of it, has become broadly accepted by the international community as general or regional international law, or if a particular state which is not a party has arguably, by some conduct on its part which acknowledges or acquiesces in that regime, estopped itself from denying that it should be considered bound by the regime. Consequently, the parties can only attempt to influence outsiders not to obstruct their cooperative efforts. One way of doing this is through provisions making it clear that the parties will exert and combine their political influence to discourage nonparties from engaging in inconsistent actions. For example, Article 2, paragraph 6, of the U.N. Charter provides that "[t]he Organization shall ensure that states which are not Members of the United Nations act in accordance with these Principles so far as may be necessary for the maintenance of international peace and security." Again, Article X of the Antarctic Treaty obligates each of the parties "to exert appropriate efforts, consistent with the Charter of the United Nations, to the end that no one engages in any activity in Antarctica contrary to the principles or purposes of the present Treaty." But while a variety of political pressures may be available to the parties to implement such provisions, a use of coercive measures for this purpose would presumably be barred by the prohibitions against the threat or use of force in the U.N. Charter, except as authorized by the U.N. Security Council under Chapters VII or VIII of the U.N. Charter. Alternatively, it is conceivable that the parties could seek to obtain the cooperation of nonparties by offering them incentives, such as payments or rewards of some kind or a share in the benefits achieved through the agreement. This issue is of current significance in relation to the proposed formulation by the parties to the Antarctic Treaty of a regime to govern the possible exploitation of Antarctic resources, in which a principal question is likely to be how to make any such regime effective with respect to nations not parties to the Antarctic Treaty.[132]

b. Reservations to Multilateral Agreements

As we have seen, in the case of a bilateral agreement, the potential treaty partners must reach complete agreement on a mutually acceptable single set of provisions in order to reach any agreement at all. If one nation refuses to accept a particular provision which the other insists must be included, or if one attaches a reservation to its approval and the other refuses to accept it, there will simply be no agreement.

More difficult problems can arise, however, with respect to

agreements negotiated by a large number of nations in multi-lateral conferences. In this case, while there may be broad agreement among most nations on the provisions of the agreement, one or more nations may have special problems with particular provisions. The provisions and kinds of risks which cause difficulty may in themselves be relatively minor, and they may be different for different states. For example, the United States appears prepared in general to ratify the Racial Discrimination Convention, but has First Amendment constitutional difficulties in accepting the particular obligations of Article IV of that convention, which, *inter alia*, requires the parties to outlaw organizations that advocate racial discrimination—a requirement that would arguably violate constitutional guarantees of free speech.[133] And while other nations may not have problems concerning Article IV of the convention, they may have difficulties with some other article or articles. Thus, even though most nations may agree with the general objectives and almost all of the provisions of a particular agreement, if every nation is required to accept each and every provision in the agreement in order to participate, comparatively few nations may eventually participate.

In order to permit wider participation in multilateral agreements under these circumstances, nations have developed special rules concerning reservations to multilateral agreements which permit a nation in certain cases to enter into a multilateral agreement with a reservation expressly limiting its obligations in one or more respects below those generally applicable to other parties to the agreement.[134] This reservation technique reflects a judgment that in certain types of agreements, such as human rights agreements, it may be better to have many nations bound to most of the obligations of the agreement than to have fewer nations accepting every one of its obligations. Of course, where reservations are permitted, a nation making a reservation cannot hold other nations parties to the agreement to a level of obligation greater than it has itself assumed.

The circumstances under which reservations can be made to multilateral agreements and the legal consequences of such reservations raise complex legal issues.[135] It is possible, of course, for the nations participating in an agreement to cover these questions expressly in the agreement itself. For example, an agreement may expressly state that reservations are *not* permitted; that is, a nation wishing to participate in the agreement must accept all of its provisions without exception. The International Coffee Agreement, 1976, and the Universal Copyright Convention contain provisions barring reservations.[136] Or the agreement may expressly provide that reservations are permitted, or that they are permitted except with respect to specific articles, or that they are permitted only with respect to specific articles. Many agreements, however, are silent on the question of reservations. In this case, the relevant law and practice is still uncertain. The Vienna Convention on the Law of Treaties establishes certain rules relevant to such situations—most significantly, that a state may not make a reservation which "is incompatible with the object and purpose of the treaty."[137] These rules are expressed in general terms, however, and as indicated, the convention has only recently entered into force and is as yet binding only among comparatively few nations.

The technique of reservations is clearly useful in that, by permitting each nation to control particular risks with which it may be especially concerned, it facilitates broader participation in multilateral cooperative arrangements. On the other hand, reservations can also complicate treaty relations and, in some cases, increase the parties' risks by creating uncertainties as to the existence or extent of treaty relationships between nations which have made reservations and other nations which have not expressly accepted these reservations.

c. Protecting against Collective Decisionmaking

As previously indicated, multilateral agreements sometimes

establish continuing organizations or institutions with collective recommendatory or decisionmaking powers. Where this is the case, a nation must consider the risk that, by entering into the agreement, it may subject itself to recommendations or decisions contrary to its interests.

Decisionmaking in international organizations and institutions is a complex subject which has been extensively discussed elsewhere.[138] It is sufficient here to note that there are a variety of devices through which a nation contemplating participation in an organization may attempt to protect itself against the risk of undesired or adverse organizational decisions. First, a nation may seek provisions in the agreement establishing the organization which expressly limit the subject matter or scope of any collective decisions or actions. For example, the U.N. Charter provides that "nothing contained in the present Charter shall authorize the United Nations to intervene in matters which are essentially within the domestic jurisdiction of any state."[139]

Second, a nation may seek to limit the legal effect of any such actions by making it clear that they are solely nonbinding "recommendations" rather than binding "decisions."[140] This is the case with the actions of the U.N. General Assembly except with respect to certain internal matters (such as assessments and elections).[141]

Third, a nation may seek to ensure that important recommendations or decisions will be adopted only by vote of a special majority of the parties, such as by a two-thirds or three-quarters majority vote, or by vote of a specially qualified majority, which must include certain designated nations or a certain proportion of particular types of nations. Thus, decisions of the U.N. General Assembly on "important questions"—including recommendations with respect to the maintenance of international peace and security, the expulsion of members, and budgetary questions—require a vote of a two-thirds majority of the members present and voting.[142] The Statute of the International Atomic Energy Agency provides that decisions of the plenary General Conference of all members shall be made by a simple majority, except that a two-thirds majority is required for financial questions, amendments to the statute, suspensions of members, and such other questions as the conference by a simple majority vote decides should be decided by a two-thirds majority.[143]

Fourth, a nation may seek a "weighted voting" formula, whereby its votes, and perhaps also the votes of certain other states, are given a greater weight than the votes of certain other states in reaching decisions. Under such a formula, the weights accorded the votes of different participating nations may be based on factors such as size, population, national income, financial contribution to the cooperative organization or venture, economic or technical stake in the cooperative enterprise, or some other criteria. Weighted voting formulas are frequently used in multilateral commodity organizations, like the International Coffee Council, and in financial institutions such as the International Bank or International Monetary Fund.[144]

Fifth, a nation may seek a requirement that no action shall be effective in the absence of its approval—either that any decision, or particular types of decisions, be approved unanimously, or that the nation have a special veto power over decisions. The provision in the U.N. Charter that decisions on other than procedural matters by the U.N. Security Council be made by an affirmative vote of nine members, including the concurring votes of China, France, the Soviet Union, the United Kingdom, and the United States—the so-called veto power of the five permanent Security Council members—is an example.[145]

Sixth, particularly in situations where a nation or group of nations fears that it may consistently be outvoted by a majority or even by a qualified majority of other nations with generally opposing interests, it may seek some type of conciliation procedure which requires a time interval for negotiation and compromise before a decision adverse to its interests takes effect.

The group of developed countries (numbering fewer than twenty nations) have consistently faced problems of this type in negotiating cooperative economic arrangements with the much more numerous group of developing countries (the so-called Group of 77, now numbering well over 100 nations). The conciliation procedure approved by the U.N. General Assembly for use in voting by the U.N. Conference on Trade and Development (UNCTAD) is one effort to find a compromise solution to this difficulty.[146]

Seventh, a nation may wish to provide that it or any other state party to an organizational agreement may opt out of any decision, or of certain kinds of decisions, made by the organization if it disapproves of them, and that these decisions shall not then have any effect with respect to it.[147] For example, the 1946 International Whaling Convention permitted any contracting state to avoid being bound by a regulation adopted by the International Whaling Commission by lodging an objection with the commission within ninety days of notification of the adoption of the regulation.[148] In 1973 the two major whaling states, Japan and the Soviet Union, invoked this provision to opt out of regulations which would have lowered quotas and phased out the killing of fin whales.

Finally, a nation may wish to provide that it, or any party, will have the right to withdraw from the agreement if a decision, or certain kinds of decisions, of which it disapproves is adopted.[149]

The Antarctic Treaty of 1959 illustrates a particularly interesting technique designed to reserve control over decision-making to an "insider" group of nations. Pursuant to Article IX of the treaty, meetings are held periodically by representatives of certain of the parties to consider and recommend to their governments measures in furtherance of the objectives of the treaty. The treaty distinguishes between parties which are entitled to participate in these meetings and those which are not. The so-called "consultative parties" are the original twelve states which participated in the 1959 Conference on Antarctica and became the original parties, as well as any subsequently acceding state party "during such time as that contracting party demonstrates its interest in Antarctica by conducting substantial scientific research or activity there, such as the establishment of a scientific station or dispatch of a scientific expedition." Any measure recommended by the consultative meeting becomes effective when approved by all of the consultative parties. Consultative parties also have other special privileges with respect to amendment and review of the agreement. Thus, while the agreement provides that almost any state may become a party, it in effect establishes a two-tiered system of participation, under which the twelve original parties and any other subsequently acceding state which can also qualify as a consultative party—as of 1979, only one of the eight states acceding to the treaty since 1959—have substantially greater privileges and control over decisionmaking than others.[150]

CHAPTER 3

Protecting Against a Change in the Value of the Agreement

One specific type of risk a nation must consider in deciding whether to enter into an international agreement is the risk that, even if the other nation fully performs its side of the bargain, the agreement may turn out intrinsically to be a bad deal. That is, a nation's performance of its own obligations under the agreement may prove more costly than it presently expects, or the value to it of the other nation's performance may prove less valuable than it presently expects, leaving it with a net loss from the bargain.

While each nation obviously wants to protect itself against a substantial reduction in the value to it of participation in the agreement, its treaty partner will often also have an interest in ensuring that the agreement continues to be perceived by all parties as fair. Norms of reciprocity, and related norms of equity, are powerful forces in human interrelations. Nations (and individuals) want to feel that what they receive is equal to what they have given, and will feel injured if they perceive this not to be the case.[1] The Soviet Union, for example, has continually emphasized the importance of reciprocity in international relations. Indeed, there is considerable evidence that any cooperative agreement which is perceived as unfair, exploitative, or imbalanced is likely to prove unstable over time. If a party comes to believe that an agreement is unfair, that party is likely to seek to escape from the agreement or to change it so as to produce reciprocity or equity, or, if it cannot otherwise legally protect itself, to resort to self-help, breach, or cheating in an attempt to restore the balance.

Two sociologists, Marwell and Schmitt, have recently conducted experimental research on the effects of inequity in the benefits received from cooperation on the continuation of cooperation in two-person interactions.[2] Their conclusions may be summarized as follows:

(1) Inequity had significant effects in destroying cooperation. Underpaid participants withdrew, in at least a significant minority of cases, from an inequitably rewarded cooperative task to a less profitable individual one. The number of instances and extent of such withdrawal increased with the size of the inequity. The data for moderate and large nonrectifiable inequity conditions indicated that the longer the time spent under the inequity condition, the more disruption of cooperation tended to occur and the longer each interruption tended to become.

(2) Withdrawal occurred despite the fact that cooperation even with the inequity was more profitable to the underpaid partner than was noncooperation. That is, some underpaid subjects were willing to forego the greater rewards produced by cooperation if they were accompanied by inequity. Moreover, withdrawal from the inequitable situation occurred despite the fact that the source of the inequity was impersonal rather than the result of action by the overpaid partner, and despite the fact that the inequity was seemingly random in the selection of who was favored and who was disfavored. Removal of the inequity generally led to a resumption of cooperative behavior.

(3) Provision of a means through which rewards could be transferred or distributed in a more equitable way, either by one party's giving or the other party's taking, had differing effects. With respect to participants who were not cooperative under

conditions of inequity, the provision of such a transfer mechanism and its use to transfer rewards to the underpaid partner generally led to high rates of cooperation. On the other hand, with respect to participants who remained cooperative under conditions of inequity, provisions of such a transfer mechanism led, if no transfers in fact took place, to a disruption of cooperation. The likelihood of withdrawal appeared to be greatest if the overpaid subject could permit transfer of rewards but refused to do so.

(4) When the opportunity to take a large amount was present, combined with a large inequity, the underpaid participant generally took from the overpaid participant as a means of transfer to remove the inequity, but the cooperation continued without disruption. When the inequitable differences were small, some overpaid subjects would permit taking and forego additional rewards to produce equity. Marwell and Schmitt comment that ''taking became a means of rectifying inequities rather than a mode of conflict. It may well be that analogous, often more subtle, compensating behaviors are common in other enterprises where one member feels he has a better 'deal' than his partner[s].''[3]

These experimental results in the context of interpersonal cooperation tend to support concern as to the long-term stability of international cooperative agreements perceived as inequitable. They suggest further that where cooperation continues despite an apparently inequitable agreement, it may be because the nations participating in the cooperation have in practice, through their own actions, interpretations, and reciprocal tolerances, informally adjusted the balance of the arrangement in the interest of achieving greater equity.[4]

In sum, experience indicates that there are practical limits on the extent to which it is useful to one nation to try to ''win'' a negotiation or get the better of another in an agreement. An international cooperative arrangement is likely to be most stable when it provides all the participating nations the greatest mutual benefit. As Nierenberg suggests, "In a successful negotiation *everybody* wins."[5]

There are several ways a nation can attempt to deal with this type of risk. First, it can seek through various techniques to ensure that the agreement will not decline in value. Second, it can seek to provide a means for revision or amendment of the agreement if a decline in value in fact occurs. Third, it can seek to provide a means to withdraw or escape from the agreement if a decline in value occurs and satisfactory revision or amendment is not possible or practicable.

1. Controlling the Value of the Agreement

A nation can seek to protect itself against a decline in the value of an agreement either by (1) protecting itself against an increase in its costs, which consist of the value of its own performance toward the other nation plus any preparation or transactions costs related to that performance; (2) protecting itself against a decline in value of the benefits it hopes to receive, which consist of the performance of the other nation toward it; or (3) attempting to ensure that the ratio between the value of its own and the other nation's performance will remain constant or within certain parameters. Devices to achieve these ends are most useful when the respective performances of the parties are capable of some objective evaluation. They are generally less useful in protecting a nation against a decline in subjective value alone—as when one nation subsequently decides that it is less interested in the other nation's performance than it had originally thought, or simply wishes it had done something else. Some possible techniques follow.

a. Warranty by the Other State of the Value of Its Performance

A nation may protect the value to it of another nation's performance by obtaining the other nation's promise not only that it will render a particular performance but that this performance will have a given value or fulfill a certain purpose. For example, in connection with an agreement under which nation B is to furnish nation A technical or financial assistance to construct a dam, A might require B to furnish assistance "sufficient to permit the construction" of the dam, rather than simply requiring B to furnish a certain sum of money, which may, because of inflation or other reasons, prove insufficient to build the dam. Or two nations might provide in their pollution control agreement that each "will take whatever measures are necessary to end pollution" of an international river or lake, rather than that each will take only certain specified pollution control measures, which may or may not prove sufficient to deal with the problem. This technique is analogous to a seller's warranty of "fitness for use" in commercial transactions.[6]

b. Guarantee of Value by Third Party

As a condition of its participation in an agreement, a nation may seek a guarantee by some third nation or international organization that, if the other party's performance does not turn out to be of a certain value, the third nation or organization will agree to furnish an additional performance equal to the deficiency or will otherwise compensate it in an amount equal to the deficiency. For example, in connection with an agreement between nations A and B under which each is to furnish a particular amount to construct a dam, one or both nations may seek guarantees from the International Bank for Reconstruction and Development (either in the agreement or in a collateral agreement) that, if this amount proves insufficient to construct the dam, the International Bank will furnish whatever additional funds are reasonably required. International Bank guarantees played a key role in achievement of the India-Pakistan Indus River agreement.[7]

c. Tying the Level of One State's Performance to the Cost of the Other State's or a Joint Performance

A nation may attempt to protect itself against excessive unforeseen costs in an agreement through provisions which tie the other nation's payment or level of performance to the first nation's costs. For example, the United States might not be willing to agree to construct and sell a broadcasting satellite to Brazil at a fixed price, since it may not be able accurately to predict this price. But it may be willing to construct and sell the satellite if Brazil agrees to pay a price equal to the United States' actual cost, computed by agreed accounting methods or formulas. This is analogous to commercial contracts providing for payment of costs plus a fixed figure or plus a percentage of costs. A well-recognized problem with this technique is that under such a formula the United States may have less incentive to control its costs, and Brazil faces the risk that it may have to pay for what it regards as excessive costs. On the other hand, Brazil will benefit from any savings in costs the United States achieves.

Agreements for sharing costs in a common enterprise according to a fixed ratio or agreed formula can be used both to establish an equitable division of presently uncertain costs and to provide a tie-in between the parties' performances. Examples of cost-sharing arrangements include the Agreement Regarding Financial Support for the North Atlantic Ice Patrol,[8] under which maritime nations establishing the patrol allocate the costs of this enterprise, and certain agreements between the United States and Mexico providing for the construction of works to control the flooding of boundary rivers.[9]

Such arrangements are also, of course, typically included in agreements to establish international organizations.[10] Various possible formulas for contributions include (1) equal shares, as in the North Pacific Halibut Convention;[11] (2) a fixed scale of assessments established in the agreement, as in the Treaty Establishing the European Economic Community;[12] (3) an assessment based on some index relevant to the purpose of the agreement, as in the Inter-American Tropical Tuna Convention, in which members' costs are assessed in proportion to their tuna catches;[13] (4) assessments set by an organ of the organization based on some index of capacity to pay, as in the U.N. Charter;[14] or (5) optional contributions.[15] Thus, under Article 17, paragraph 2, of the U.N. Charter, "[t]he expenses of the Organization shall be borne by the Members as apportioned by the General Assembly." Pursuant to General Assembly resolutions, this apportionment is broadly based on national income statistics, with other factors also being taken into account.[16] Sometimes an agreement will expressly establish a floor or ceiling on the share of contributions of any single member, as in the case of the Charter of the Organization of African Unity.[17]

While cost-sharing formulas subject each nation to the risk that it will have to share any excessive costs of the enterprise resulting from the actions of others, each also has an incentive to reduce the total costs of the enterprise, since it will have to pay part of them. Cost-sharing plans may present particular risks to a nation which is responsible for a large share of costs but does not have power to control decisions which can result in the incurring of costs. The United States, for example, which exercises only one vote among the over 150 votes in the U.N. General Assembly, has relatively little formal power to control U.N. expenses, but is responsible for paying about 25 percent of those expenses.[18] Most U.N. members, in contrast, are each responsible for less than 0.1 percent of these expenses and consequently have less incentive to control them.[19] Indeed, where some nations involved in a common enterprise receive disproportionately large benefits from its programs in relation to their share of its costs, they will have an obvious incentive to expand its programs. The desire of the developing nations, which constitute by far the majority of states in the United Nations, to expand its economic programs, which benefit the developing nations but are largely paid for by developed nations, is an example of this tendency. This can be avoided by arrangements under which decisionmaking powers regarding costs are weighted according to the share of the costs borne, or under which cost-sharing is related to the share of benefits received.

Analogous types of arrangements can be used to ensure that each nation will receive at least a certain share of benefits arising from an agreement, similar to commercial profit-sharing or production-sharing agreements. The issue of how any profits derived from deep-sea-bed mining will be shared has been an issue of negotiation at the Third U.N. Law of the Sea Conference,[20] and will undoubtedly also be a key issue in proposed negotiations regarding the possible establishment of a regime to govern the exploitation of Antarctic mineral resources.[21]

d. Setting Floors or Ceilings on Performance

A nation may limit its costs by providing that its performance under an agreement need occur only under certain conditions or within certain limits related to its costs. For example, the U.S.–Austrian Atomic Energy Agreement provides that "[t]he adjusted net quantity of U-235 in enriched uranium" transferred from the United States to Austria under the agreement "shall not exceed in the aggregate 12,000 kilograms."[22] Or a producing nation might agree that it will sell a consuming nation wheat at an established fixed price, but only if the world price does not exceed that price by more than a certain amount or percentage. The various International Wheat Agreements impose obligations on the parties only when wheat prices rise above or fall below certain levels.[23] Or a nation might agree that it will furnish agricultural commodities assistance to another country only if its own annual harvest or stores exceed or do not fall below a given level or are in excess of its own needs.[24] Or the United States may agree that it will obligate itself to share in the expenses involved in a cooperative arrangement or in financing an international institution such as the United Nations according to an agreed formula, but only to the extent that its share does not exceed a certain figure or a certain percentage of the total.[25]

The establishment of a floor or ceiling on particular kinds of national actions can also, of course, be the central purpose of the agreement, designed to avoid or stabilize competitive behavior. Arms limitation agreements typically set such ceilings. For example, the 1972 U.S.–Soviet ABM Treaty established a ceiling of 200 launchers for each side's defensive or antiballistic missile systems, and stipulated that neither side would try to build a comprehensive system of this type.[26] SALT I established an interim agreement on offensive systems that froze the number of land-and-submarine-based intercontinental ballistic missiles at then-existing levels. The presently proposed U.S.–Soviet SALT II Agreement would attempt to establish basic parity between the two countries by placing equal ceilings on the number (although not the power) of their nuclear delivery vehicles. Under the agreement, each side would be limited to 2,400 strategic weapons launchers until the end of 1981, and to 2,250 launchers from 1981 to the treaty's expiration date at the end of 1985.[27] The concept of setting ceilings on overall military expenditures has a similar objective.[28] Such ceilings can work only when the competitive situation can be defined in terms of numbers alone. If a nation can, through qualitative improvements, put more or more powerful weapons in each launcher, or find a way to get "more bang for the buck," a situation of unstable competition will continue, and the agreements will not be effective.

e. Setting the Level of Performance by a Specific Objective Standard, Index, or Ratio

A nation may seek to establish the level of either its own or its treaty partner's level of performance under an agreement, or both, in relation to some objective standard, index, or ratio, rather than in specific terms.[29] For example, in their 1972 Great Lakes Water Quality Agreement, the United States and Canada agreed that each nation will take whatever pollution-control measures are required to achieve certain specified and objective levels of water quality in the Great Lakes.[30] The 1929 Warsaw Convention limiting the liability of air carriers for the accidental death of passengers in international air transportation expresses these limits in francs, which "shall be deemed to refer to the French franc consisting of 65½ milligrams of gold at the standard of fineness of nine hundred thousandths."[31] An oil-consuming nation and an oil-producing nation might reach a long-term agreement for the sale of oil with a provision that the price of the oil will be at the market price at the time of delivery; or that it will be at a stated price which will be periodically adjusted to reflect changes in the general price level or changes in an index of the ratio of prices between commodities and industrial goods; or that it will be at a price reflecting the value of a "basket" of currencies, such as the Special Drawing Rights (SDRs), the medium of monetary exchange established by the International Monetary Fund on the basis of an assortment of sixteen currencies.[32] Or a group of nations might agree that their respective numbers of naval vessels, aircraft, or troops should be maintained at a certain ratio;[33] or, as under the International Coffee Agreement, 1962, and its successor agreements, they might agree that their allocations or quotas in a commodities or fisheries agreement should be in an established ratio.

The use of an objective standard (or "pegging") is, of course, a familiar technique in collective bargaining agreements, where escalator clauses are increasingly used to adjust wages to fluctuations in the Consumer Price Index. Problems raised by the use of standards, indexes, or ratios include choice of the relevant standard or index, negotiation of the appropriate ratio or quota, and the possibility of difficulties if one or more parties come to regard the particular standard, index, ratio, or allocation formula as no longer fair. For example, while the traditional large coffee exporters such as Brazil and Colombia demanded and obtained provisions ensuring them a fixed major share of coffee export quotas in the International Coffee Agreement, 1962, increasing market demand for African-grown coffees resulted in growing pressures by African producers for a more flexible quota system giving them a larger share in overall exports. Because of the threat of withdrawal of the African nations and collapse of the agreement, these pressures ultimately proved successful, and the quotas were in effect revised.[34]

If a nation wishes to prevent discriminatory treatment of its nationals or property while in another nation's territory, it may use a standard tied to the level of that other nation's treatment either of the latter's own nationals or of the nationals of a third state to which the other nation accords its most favorable treatment. For example, Article XIV, paragraph 5, of the 1954 commercial treaty between the United States and the Federal Republic of Germany provides: "Nationals and companies of either Party shall be accorded national treatment and most-favored-nation treatment by the other Party with respect to all matters relating to importation and exportation."[35] A "national treatment" standard requires that Germany treat U.S. nationals in like situations no less favorably than Germany does its own nationals, and vice versa.[36] A "most-favored-nation" standard requires that Germany treat U.S. nationals in like situations no less favorably than Germany treats nationals of the most-favored third state, and vice versa.[37] Again, the provisions requiring unconditional most-favored-nation treatment contained in Article I of the General Agreement on Tariffs and Trade are the cornerstone of the agreement's system for reducing tariff and other trade barriers.[38]

These types of standards are widely employed in commercial, trade, and other types of international agreements. They assume, however, that nondiscriminatory treatment, rather than special treatment, is really all that one nation is entitled to ask from another, and that nations will generally be willing to grant such nondiscriminatory treatment. For one nation to seek special privileges for its citizens better than those the other nation grants its own citizens or other aliens might be resented by that other nation's citizens and smack of the kinds of privileges coerced by imperialist nations in the era of colonialism. But while "national" and most-favored-nation treatment standards may afford a nation considerable protection, there is still the risk that the way the other nation treats its own nationals or nationals of other states may prove to be grossly inadequate and not constitute a fair exchange to a nation for its own higher performance under the agreement. For example, an agreement between the United States and another nation guaranteeing U.S. nationals "national treatment" in the other nation's prisons or with respect to takings of property may be of little value if the other nation treats its own nationals very badly in its prisons or seizes their property arbitrarily and without compensation. Moreover, as in the case of many disputes involving alleged discrimination, there can be differences of view as to whether cases in which aliens are treated differently from citizens do in fact involve comparable or "like situations" to which the standard is properly applicable, and governments intent on evading such a standard can deliberately seek to establish some kind of differences which will provide them with such arguments.

f. Setting Levels of Performance by a General Standard

Where the performances required of the parties may apply to a variety of situations, a nation may seek to set either its own or the other nation's level of performance by some general standard.

For example, the 1956 U.S.–Netherlands commercial treaty provides that "[e]ach Party shall at all times accord fair and equitable treatment to the nationals and companies of the other Party"; that "[n]either Party shall take unreasonable or discriminatory measures that would impair the rights or interests within its territories of nationals and companies of the other"; and that "[p]roperty of nationals and companies of either Party shall not be taken . . . without the prompt payment of just compensation."[39] Again, nations sharing in the costs of construction or the use of an international canal might agree with the nation through whose territory the canal runs that the charges imposed for passage through the canal will be "reasonable"; or nations which fish in each other's fisheries zones might agree that any conservation regulations which one establishes in its coastal fishery will be designed to protect the "maximum sustainable yield" of the fishery and will have "due regard" to the others' interests; or nations sharing an international river basin might agree that each be entitled to "equitable utilization" of the waters of the river.

In view of their generality, broad standards offer less protection than more specific standards of performance. Often, the nations concerned will have to rely on mutual good faith, precedent, or the aid of third parties in interpreting the meaning of such standards. But general standards do provide at least broad parameters for measuring performance, while permitting the parties flexibility to deal with a varied range of situations. In many cases, appeal to general standards may be the only way of controlling the value of the agreement that the parties can practically achieve.

g. Level of Performance Determined by an Expert Body or Third Party

A nation may seek to have the agreement provide that the level of its own or the other nation's performance shall be established by a third state or individual, or by a public or private international organization or institution. For example, nations participating in fishing operations in a high seas fishery may agree that the level of their respective permitted shares or quotas of catches in that fishery shall be set by an impartial technical secretariat on the basis of its expert estimate of the maximum sustainable yield of the fishery and certain other objective factors. Or two nations may agree that the measures each must take to prevent pollution of a particular international river or lake shall be determined by an expert joint commission or technical board.[40] The agreement may give the expert body or third party broad discretion as to its judgment, or the expert body or third party may in turn be required to make its determination in accordance with certain criteria or objective standards. Sometimes the expert body or third party may be entrusted only with the making of some broad determination, such as the appropriate amount of overall coffee exports or "global quota" which the parties to an international coffee agreement should establish and seek to maintain, or the total figure representing the overall maximum sustainable yield of a particular species to which the parties to an international whaling agreement or fisheries agreement should limit their catch, with the respective quotas or shares in that global figure then to be allocated among the parties in accordance with terms, procedures, or a ratio previously fixed in the agreement.[41]

Third parties can also, of course, be used to settle disputes between the parties as to levels of performance. For example, the General Agreement on Tariffs and Trade provides that if one of the contracting parties withdraws a tariff concession, it must give some equivalent compensatory concession to other parties affected and, if a dispute arises as to the level of such compensation, the other parties to the agreement may determine the amount to be paid.[42] Again, two nations may agree that, while one's liability to pay the other compensation for any damage caused by transboundary flooding resulting from the construction of a dam is admitted, the fact of causation and amount of money it should pay should be determined by an arbitral tribunal.[43]

h. Hedging

A nation might in certain circumstances be able to protect the value of its agreement with one nation by entering into a related collateral agreement with another nation, along the line of "hedging" arrangements commonly employed by commodity traders.[44] There appears to be little international experience in such arrangements, and examples do not come readily to mind. Nonetheless, the rich experience of futures markets in managing risk through devices such as hedges, options, straddles, and so forth might suggest analogous techniques relevant to international arrangements.

2. Providing for Revision or Amendment of the Agreement

A second way a nation can attempt to guard against the risk of a decline in the value of an agreement is to provide expressly for the possibility of revision or amendment of the agreement.[45] Of course, the participating nations can always agree at any time to change the agreement even in the absence of specific amendment provisions. However, provisions for revision or amendment provide formal opportunity for the parties to examine together how the agreement has operated in practice and to discuss any need for change. More specifically, such provisions may ensure a party the right legitimately to raise questions as to the continued balance and equity of the agreement. Most agreements—particularly those contemplating cooperation over an extended period—include at least some provisions for the possibility of revision or amendment. A provision requiring the parties to consider the possibility of revision or amendment need not require, however, that they ultimately agree on such revision or amendment.

Amendment provisions can differ in a variety of respects— for example, as to whether negotiation for revision or amendment is automatic or must be invoked by a party; the circumstances under which such negotiations must be undertaken; and the consequences in the event the parties cannot agree whether or not, or how, to revise the agreement. Where a nation is permitted to withdraw from an agreement if its proposals for revision are not accepted, it has considerable control over risks. But even more limited provisions for revision may have value to a party in indicating clearly that the nations involved contemplate the possibility of a need for change and undertake in good faith to consider adjustments as a means of continuing their cooperation.

The nations concerned might decide to entrust the determination that conditions warrant a reexamination of their relationship, or even the power to revise the terms of their relationship in certain respects, to a third party, such as an international organization or international tribunal. For example, the nations parties to an agreement on exploitation of the resources of the deep-sea bed might decide to leave the decision as to the calling of a conference for revision of the agreement to the United Nations, or the nations parties to a fisheries agreement might decide to delegate a decision as to the need to consider changes in certain technical provisions of the agreement to a regional fisheries organization.

There are three principal types of provisions for review and revision or amendment of agreements.

a. Review or Revision Following Joint Agreement

At a minimum, a nation may wish the agreement to mention the possible need for revision and provide a procedure through which revision can be requested. For example, U.S. air transport agreements with other nations typically include a provision like the following: "Consultation between the competent authorities of both Contracting Parties may be requested at any time by either Contracting Party for the purpose of discussing the interpretation, application or amendment of the Agreement or Route Schedule. Such consultation shall begin within a period of sixty (60) days from the date of the receipt of the request by the other party."[46] In the case of a bilateral agreement, both parties must, of course, agree on an amendment for it to take effect. Consequently, such a provision gives a nation little protection other than the placing of some obligation on the other nation to consider its request for revision in good faith, unless the agreement expressly permits the first nation to withdraw in the event its request for amendment is not accepted.

In the case of multilateral agreements, including agreements establishing international organizations, provisions for review and amendment differ widely. Some agreements expressly provide for a review conference. For example, Article 109 of the U.N. Charter provides that:

1. A General Conference of the Members of the United Nations for the purpose of reviewing the present Charter may be held at a date and place to be fixed by a two-thirds vote of the members of the General Assembly and by a vote of any nine members of the Security Council. Each Member of the United Nations shall have one vote in the conference.

2. Any alteration of the present Charter recommended by a two-thirds vote of the conference shall take effect when ratified in accordance with their respective constitutional processes by two-thirds of the Members of the United Nations including all the permanent members of the Security Council.

3. If such a conference has not been held before the tenth annual session of the General Assembly following the coming into force of the present Charter, the proposal to call such a conference shall be placed on the agenda of that session of the General Assembly, and the conference shall be held if so decided by a majority vote of the members of the General Assembly and by a vote of any seven members of the Security Council.

While the United Nations has established a Committee to Study

Charter Review, no decision to hold a review session has as yet been reached. The 1952 Universal Copyright Convention provides that a revision conference can be called at the request of at least ten contracting states.[47]

Again, conditions for the acceptance of amendments are different under different agreements. Some require unanimous consent, either for any amendment or at least for amendment of particularly important provisions. For example, the International Monetary Fund Agreement requires that any change in the provisions of the agreement guaranteeing the members the freedom to withdraw, to determine changes in their quotas, and to initiate par value changes requires approval of all fund members.[48] The General Agreement on Tariffs and Trade similarly provides that any amendment to Part I of the agreement, which contains the general most-favored-nation clause and provisions on tariff schedules, must be agreed to by all contracting parties.[49] Other agreements provide for acceptance of amendments by a simple majority, a qualified majority, or a certain number of parties. For example, Article 108 of the U.N. Charter provides: ''Amendments to the Present Charter shall come in force for all Members of the United Nations when they have been adopted by a vote of two-thirds of the members of the General Assembly and ratified in accordance with their respective constitutional processes by two-thirds of the members of the United Nations, including all the permanent members of the Security Council.''[50]

The effect of amendments, once accepted, also varies. Some agreements, such as the U.N. Charter and the Statute of the International Atomic Energy Agency, provide that the amendment when accepted is binding on all members.[51] Other agreements, such as the 1944 Civil Aviation Convention and the Charter of the Organization of American States, provide that an amendment is binding only on those parties expressly accepting it.[52] Still others, such as the Convention on the Intergovernmental Maritime Consultative Organization, provide that an amendment is binding on all parties which do not expressly declare their disapproval.[53] In some agreements, such as the International Coffee Agreement, 1976, a party is permitted or even required to withdraw if an amendment to which it objects and which it will not accept takes effect.[54]

Choice among these provisions involves a variety of considerations. A unanimity requirement for amendments may make revision too difficult, driving out dissatisfied participants who are unwilling to remain parties unless the agreement is changed. On the other hand, few nations will be prepared to agree in advance to be bound by amendments which they have not specifically accepted, at least if these involve important obligations. Nor can an agreement function effectively if amendments concerning significant obligations or procedures, such as those affecting the structure of an international organization, are binding on only some participants but not others. In some cases, where it is important that all of the present parties remain in the agreement and that they all have exactly the same obligations, a lowest-common-denominator type of agreement may be the best that can be maintained, and relatively inflexible amendment provisions may be necessary. In other cases, where it is less important exactly which nations participate in the agreement, where the obligations involved are less significant, or where diversity of obligation will not create difficulties, greater flexibility of amendment may be useful.

b. Automatic Review or Revision after a Certain Period

In order to ensure the possibility of review of an agreement, the parties may provide that, after the agreement has been in force for a certain time, a review conference shall be called at the request of any one of them. For example, the 1949 North Atlantic Treaty provides that, after the treaty has been in force for ten years, a review conference shall be held at the request of any party, and the Antarctic Treaty provides that, after the treaty has been in force thirty years, a formal review conference will be called at the request of any party.[55] To protect any party against the onus of initiating the call for such review, an agreement may provide that a review conference shall automatically be held after the elapse of a certain period. For example, the International Coffee Agreement, 1962, provided that the International Coffee Council was to hold a special session during the last six months of the coffee year ending September 30, 1965, in order to review the agreement, and the Nuclear Non-Proliferation Treaty required the parties to meet together five years after its entry into force in order to consider revision or amendment.[56] A nation might further protect itself through insisting on a provision either that the agreement shall terminate in the event the parties do not agree on revision at such a review session, or at least that it will have the right to withdraw if the other nation or nations do not agree to its proposals for revision made at this time. In this case, the provision is analogous to a limit on the duration of the agreement.

In some cases, a provision for review after a certain period may be employed, in effect, as a device for ensuring a temporary status quo to a minority group of nations during the period prior to review. For example, the Law of the Sea Conference negotiations, still in progress as of 1980, include proposals that a mixed system of exploitation of seabed minerals, both by an international enterprise and by state and private enterprise, be permitted for twenty years, at which time a review conference would be held.[57] This review conference, dominated by developing nations favoring a completely international system of exploitation, might then, if the conference decided, terminate exploitation other than by the international agency alone.

c. Review or Revision Following the Occurrence of Certain Circumstances

A nation may seek a provision requiring that the parties review the agreement, or at least particular obligations of a party under an agreement, in the event that certain circumstances occur. This provision is narrower than one providing generally for revision or amendment but may be sufficient to meet that nation's most important concerns. For example, if a nation is concerned that a proposed air transport agreement with another nation might result in the other nation's airlines depriving its own airlines of a fair share of passengers on the routes granted, it might insist on a provision in the agreement requiring that the parties consult and review the agreement if the capacity offered or number of passengers carried by the other nation's airlines exceeds a certain level or a certain proportion of the total carried by both nations' airlines. In some cases, negotiations for revision may be made subject to approval by a third party, such as the collective decisionmaking body of an international organization.[58]

A nation may find a provision of this type useful, even if not coupled with a right of withdrawal, in that it shows that the parties are entering into cooperation with certain conditions in mind and recognize that, if these conditions change, fairness may require a change in the parties' undertakings under the agreement. In this sense, such a provision is analogous to the general international law doctrine of *rebus sic stantibus*, or "changed circumstances," which suggests that a nation may legitimately terminate or withdraw from an agreement if a fundamental change of the circumstances on which the agreement was based occurs, a change unforeseen by the parties at the time of conclusion of the agreement and radically altering the extent of that party's obligations.[59] Again, such a review may be requested by the nation wishing review itself, or it might be left to initiation by an impartial third party.

3. Providing for Release from the Agreement

A third way a nation can protect itself against the risk of a decline in value of an agreement is through provisions which permit it to withdraw or escape from the agreement, or at least from the particular obligations it considers oppressive, if such a decline occurs. Such provisions share most of the characteristics and problems of the broader provisions for unilateral withdrawal previously discussed.[60] Thus, they may differ with respect to which nation can trigger the release, under what circumstances, and subject to what conditions. Such provisions may also differ as to whether the release is effective immediately or only after some time interval, such as six months; whether the release applies to all of a nation's obligations under the agreement or only to some of them (a waiver); and whether the release is only temporary (a suspension) or is permanent.

If an agreement includes general provisions permitting easy and unilateral withdrawal, special provisions concerning withdrawal may be superfluous. Even so, a nation may nevertheless wish to include such special provisions for withdrawal in order to make clear its right to escape from all, or at least some, of its obligations under particular circumstances relating to a decline in the value to it of the agreement. Release or waiver provisions can also be used to protect a nation against the risks of nonperformance by another party or of having to render its own performance.

Some types of release provisions include the following.

a. Release Contingent on Agreement of the Other State (Waiver)

A nation may seek to include in the agreement a right to withdraw from the agreement, or at least escape from certain obligations, with the other nation's or nations' approval. Of course, the parties may, in any case, mutually agree at any time to suspend or terminate the agreement or any of its obligations. A specific release or waiver provision, however, indicates that the parties expressly contemplate that contingencies may arise in which one nation may properly seek release from obligations which have turned out to be very burdensome or inequitable, establishes a specific procedure under which a nation can seek and be granted such relief, and places some moral pressure on the other parties to consider its request for relief in good faith.[61]

Multilateral agreements establishing continuing institutions, such as the General Agreement on Tariffs and Trade and the Articles of Agreement of the International Monetary Fund, frequently contain such waiver provisions, and they are occasionally invoked. For example, Article XXV, paragraph 5, of the General Agreement on Tariffs and Trade provides that

> 5. In exceptional circumstances not elsewhere provided for in this Agreement, the CONTRACTING PARTIES may waive an obligation imposed upon a contracting party by this Agreement; *Provided* that any such decision shall be approved by a two-thirds majority of the votes cast and that such majority shall comprise more than half of the contracting parties. The CONTRACTING PARTIES may also by such a vote
>> (i) define certain categories of exceptional circumstances to which other voting requirements shall apply for the waiver of obligations, and
>> (ii) prescribe such criteria as may be necessary for the application of this paragraph.[62]

The contracting parties have in fact granted such waivers in over fifty cases.[63] Again, Article 60 of the International Coffee Agreement, 1962, provided that

> The [International Coffee] Council may, by a two-thirds distributed majority vote, relieve a Member of an obligation which, on account of exceptional or emergency circumstances, *force majeure*, constitutional obligations or international obligations under the United Nations Charter for territories administered under the trusteeship system, either:
>> (a) constitutes a serious hardship;
>> (b) imposes an inequitable burden on such Member; or
>> (c) gives other Members an unfair or unreasonable advantage.[64]

A nation seeking a waiver or *ad hoc* exemption must usually apply for a waiver from and justify its request to the membership or governing council of the organization; and the granting authority can, if it wishes, grant the waiver on particular terms and conditions, such as a limitation on the duration of the waiver or a requirement for continuing reports or review. Sometimes an agreement may imply rather than expressly provide for the possibility of waiver or assistance in meeting obstacles to performance. For example, Article 50 of the U.N. Charter provides that ''[i]f preventive or enforcement measures against any state are taken by the Security Council, any other state, whether a Member of the United Nations or not, which finds itself confronted with special economic problems arising from the carrying out of those measures shall have the right to consult the Security Council with regard to a solution of those problems.''

b. Release upon Unilateral Determination

A nation may seek the right unilaterally to withdraw from an agreement, or at least from particular obligations under the agreement, if it alone decides that the value of the agreement has fundamentally changed and that its important interests are jeopardized. As previously indicated, the parties to the Nuclear Test Ban Treaty have expressly retained such a right of unilateral withdrawal.[65] Or, in connection with an agreement providing for compulsory third-party settlement of disputes, one nation may insist on retaining the right not to submit such disputes for settlement whenever it unilaterally determines that such disputes are ''with regard to matters that are essentially within its own jurisdiction'' or involve its ''national security.'' For example, under the terms of the controversial so-called Connally reservation to the U.S. acceptance of the compulsory jurisdiction of the International Court of Justice under Article 36, paragraph 2, of the Statute of the Court, the United States provided that its declaration accepting the Court's jurisdiction would not apply to ''disputes with regard to matters which are essentially within the domestic jurisdiction of the United States of America *as determined by the United States of America.*''[66] Or, as in the case of the General Agreement on Tariffs and Trade, the parties to a tariff reduction agreement may retain the right periodically to unilaterally modify or withdraw tariff concessions granted to another party, subject to the right of other parties affected by the action to withdraw substantially equivalent concessions in order to maintain equity.[67] To the extent that this determination is unilateral, it gives a nation broad protection. As previously discussed, however, a nation is presumably under an obligation to use good faith in making such a determination, and agreements containing such provisions are regularly treated by the parties as reflecting real rather than illusory commitments.[68]

c. Release upon the Occurrence of Particular Circumstances

A nation may seek the right to withdraw from an agreement, or to suspend all or certain of its obligations under an agreement, if its performance becomes physically or legally "impossible," or if there is an adverse change in some condition or circumstance which fundamentally changes the value to it of the bargain. For example, a nation agreeing to sell another a certain quantity of wheat from its next harvest may wish to secure provisions making its obligation conditional upon its next harvest's attaining at least a certain level. Or a nation may wish expressly to condition its agreement to furnish another nation military or other assistance or grant certain privileges upon these obligations not at the time being inconsistent with other obligations it has assumed under the U.N. Charter or certain other agreements. For example, one provision of the General Agreement on Tariffs and Trade exempts from obligations under the agreement actions taken by a contracting party "in pursuance of its obligations under the United Nations Charter for the maintenance of international peace and security."[69] Or, in connection with a nation's agreement to provide financial assistance to another nation, or to reduce its tariffs on imports from another nation, or to construct a dam or enter into some other project with another, or to participate in a particular organization with another, it may wish to include provisions which expressly condition its obligation to perform on the appropriation of necessary funds or the enactment of necessary legislation by its legislature. Provisions expressly conditioning obligations upon legislative approval are very common, particularly in U.S. agreements. For example, the 1964 U.S.–Spain Tracking Stations Agreement provides that "it is understood that, to the extent the implementation of this agreement will depend on funds appropriated by the Congress of the United States, it is subject to the availability of such funds."[70]

Again, nations participating in tariff reduction agreements frequently provide escape clauses that permit any nation to withdraw from or suspend its obligations under the agreement if relevant imports from another nation or nations exceed a certain quantity or value, or if they cause injury to its domestic industries, or if its balance of payments is in persistent disequilibrium. For example, Article XIX of the General Agreement on Tariffs and Trade, entitled "Emergency Action on Imports of Particular Products," provides in part:

If, as a result of unforeseen developments and of the effect of the obligations incurred by a contracting party under this Agreement, including tariff concessions, any product is being imported into the territory of that contracting party in such increased quantities and under such conditions as to cause or threaten serious injury, . . . the contracting party shall be free, in respect of such product, and to the extent and for such time as may be necessary to prevent or remedy such injury, to suspend the obligation in whole or in part or to withdraw or modify the concession.

If a party wishes to take advantage of this procedure, it must consult with other interested parties, and it usually will offer compensatory tariff reductions on imports of other products imported from affected countries. If such reductions are not offered, any interested contracting party is authorized by the agreement to suspend "substantially equivalent obligations or concessions, as applied to the trade of the party invoking the escape clause, provided that the GATT Contracting Parties do not disapprove.'' This escape clause has been invoked on a number of occasions.[71]

One problem with such withdrawal or partial release provisions is identifying the circumstances which trigger release. Another problem is deciding who is to determine whether these circumstances have occurred and how such a determination is to be made. Possibilities include permitting the nation seeking to withdraw to make this determination unilaterally; agreeing on some objective index to establish the existence of the relevant circumstances, such as reliance on certain objective international statistics or other criteria; or referring the determination to the membership of an international organization or to a third party, which is expressly given authority to grant a waiver. The International Sugar Agreement, 1958, provides that

> If, during the period of this Agreement, by action of a non-participating country or by action of any participating country inconsistent with this Agreement such adverse changes occur in the relation between supply and demand of the free market as are held by any Participating Government seriously to prejudice its interests, such Participating Government may state its case to the Council. If the Council declares the case to be well-founded, the Government concerned may give notice of withdrawal from this Agreement.[72]

Again, the Agreement Establishing the International Monetary Fund provides that a nation can suspend its obligations under the agreement if the governing board of the fund finds that the nation's balance of payments is in persistent disequilibrium.[73]

Risks of this type can be dealt with to some extent, even in the absence of specific provisions, through general legal rules concerning release from obligations, such as contract doctrines of frustration or the analogous treaty doctrine of *rebus sic stantibus*, or "changed circumstances," previously referred to. But where a nation expressly contemplates the possibility of such contingencies, it can reduce its risk by spelling out in the agreement itself its right to secure, or at least request, release.

d. Rescission in the Event of Fraud, Mistake, or Impossibility

Certain risks concerning the value of an agreement raise special problems. Thus, a nation may be concerned with the possibility of fraud—that the other nation may deliberately be misrepresenting the value of its performance. Or a nation may be concerned that it is entering into agreement with another nation in a mistaken belief as to some essential fact. Or it may be concerned that circumstances may arise which will make it impossible for it to perform its part of the bargain. In the event of these contingencies, it may wish the right to rescind or withdraw from the agreement and, if it has already rendered its performance, recover that performance.

The nations concerned may, of course, seek specifically to protect themselves against these kinds of risks in their agreement. In practice, however, these kinds of problems arise only infrequently and are awkward to deal with in a negotiating context; thus, the parties to an agreement will usually leave them to be dealt with—if they should arise—through doctrines of general treaty law. [74] Resolving these situations may involve the difficulties of defining the contingencies warranting such rescission   the familiar contract problem of defining fraud, mistake, or impossibility—and of recovering a performance which has been rendered.

4

Protecting Against Nonperformance or Inadequate Performance by the Other State

A second and very important type of risk which each nation must consider in deciding whether to enter into an agreement is the risk that the other nation or nations involved will not perform their part of the bargain at all, or will render a performance less valuable than promised. A nation may incur losses as a result of another's nonperformance or inadequate performance of an agreement in several ways: First, if nation A gives the performance it promised, without receiving nation B's full performance in return, A will have given something for nothing or for less than it expected, and may experience a net loss. Second, even if A has not yet given its performance, it may have incurred costs or changed its position in anticipation of and reliance on B's performance, for which it will obtain nothing or an inadequate return. Moreover, in some cases, A's change of position may expose it to the risk of additional loss.

A lack of confidence that the other nation or nations involved will perform their obligations in good faith is frequently a major obstacle to the achievement of international agreement. This concern over the risk of nonperformance is apparent in recent negotiations for arms control, such as the U.S.–Soviet SALT II negotiations;[1] in truce, armistice, and peace agreements, such as those reached in the Vietnam conflict and reached and proposed in the Middle East conflicts;[2] and in nuclear nonproliferation agreements.[3] A similar concern is, of course, pervasive in private, personal, and business relationships; indeed, much of private contract and commercial law and practice involves ways of handling the problems which the risk of nonperformance poses for private cooperation. Illegal private arrangements—such as arrangements involving prostitution, bribery, espionage, kidnapping, or the holding of hostages—may offer particularly interesting analogies to international agreements in this respect. The parties usually cannot rely on official devices such as the law, courts, police, or even on normative social pressures to make sure that each keeps its promises, and consequently must often employ special types of techniques to provide sufficient assurance of performance to permit agreement. Schelling suggests:

[W]here trust and good faith do not exist and cannot be made to by our acting as though they did, we may wish to solicit advice from the underworld, or from ancient despotisms, on how to make agreements work when trust and good faith are lacking and there is no legal recourse for breach of contract. The ancients exchanged hostages, drank wine from the same glass to demonstrate the absence of poison, met in public places to inhibit the massacre of one by the other, and even deliberately exchanged spies to facilitate transmittal of authentic information. It seems likely that a well-developed theory of strategy could throw light on the efficacy of some of those old devices, suggest the circumstances to which they apply, and discover modern equivalents that, though offensive to our taste, may be desperately needed in the regulation of conflict.[4]

Broadly speaking, a nation considering entering into agreement can attempt to protect itself against the risk of nonperformance or inadequate performance by another nation party to the agreement by either increasing the probability that the other nation will perform, or reducing its own vulnerability in the event the other nation does not perform.[5] In turn, the best way of increasing the probability that the other nation will perform is by structuring the agreement so that the other nation both can perform, and believes that it will be better off, or at least not worse off, by performing than by not performing. Over the course of many thousands of years of social interaction, human beings have devised a number of techniques to protect their stake in an agreement by increasing the probability of the other party's performance, and it is consequently necessary to deal with these at some length. While the problem of reducing one's own vulnerability to nonperformance by another nation is conceptually distinct from that of increasing the probability of the other nation's performance, efforts to deal with it involve many of the same techniques, and these are discussed briefly in the final section of this chapter.

As previously indicated, many of these techniques can serve several purposes, some are closely interrelated, and a single agreement may combine a number of techniques. For example, the 1975 Egypt-Israel Agreement on the Sinai and Suez Canal, concluded following the 1973 Yom Kippur War, and the 1979 Egypt-Israel Peace Treaty each contain a variety of devices to protect the parties from the risk of each other's nonperformance, including timing of performances, breakdown of overall performances into reciprocal step-by-step performance, buffer and demilitarized zones, early warning systems, third-party interposition, third-party guarantees, and so forth.[6] Tuchman, describing the Treaty of Bretigny of 1360 between England and France during the Hundred Years' War, gives an interesting example of the use of a complex combination of risk-management techniques in an international agreement some six centuries earlier. The treaty provided for the ransom of King Jean of France, who had been captured by Edward III, for the sum of 3 million gold écus and the cession of large portions of southwestern France to England, and for the renunciation by Edward of all claim to the throne of France and territorial claims in France not covered by the treaty. The treaty was guaranteed by the delivery of forty royal and noble hostages. Tuchman writes:

King Jean was to be returned as far as Calais, where he would remain until a first payment of 600,000 écus was made on his ransom and a preliminary transfer of territories had taken place. He would then be liberated with ten of his fellow prisoners from Poitiers and replaced by forty hostages of the Third Estate—the real source of money—four from Paris and two from each of eighteen other towns. Thereafter, sovereignty of towns and castles was to be transferred, and the remainder of the ransom paid, 400,000 at a time, in six installments at six-month intervals, with one fifth of the hostages released upon each delivery.[7]

Nations concerned with performance risks generally prefer techniques which depend only on their own actions, or "self-help." While the meaning of "self-help" in international relations is less than clear, it is frequently used to suggest that a state may in certain situations properly act unilaterally—that is, without the need for prior resort to international procedures or institutions—in order to prevent or redress certain violations of international law.[8] While the international legal system does allow states to engage in a considerable range of self-enforcement actions in this sense, whether such unilateral enforcement is in fact permissible in any given case will depend on the relevant circumstances.[9] Consequently, where self-help is not practically possible or politically feasible, or is subject to legal repercussions, nations must often look to third parties, whether another state or an international organization, for assistance. But such third-party techniques will generally be acceptable and useful only when all of the nations negotiating an agreement have confidence in the ability and willingness of the third party to perform impartially and effectively its risk-management role. And this, of course, may not be the case. Clearly, the best and most effective way of ensuring that the nations parties to an agreement perform their obligations is to make sure that the agreement is a fair one, is in all of their interests, and is one with which all will wish voluntarily to comply.

The way in which nations attempt to manage risks of non-performance in a particular agreement can suggest much about both their attitudes towards each other and towards compliance with the agreement. Nations which trust each other will typically deal with risks of nonperformance principally by relying on their mutual trust, and will consider it unnecessary to use complex risk-management techniques in their agreement. Nations which distrust each other, on the other hand, may be able to overcome their perceptions of risk only by employing an extensive panoply of specific risk-management techniques—as in the case of the 1975 Egypt-Israel Sinai Agreement and the 1979 Egypt-Israel Peace Treaty.

Indeed, where nations which clearly distrust each other deliberately fail to include in their agreement provisions capable of effectively controlling the performance of particular obligations, one may question whether they seriously intended that these obligations be complied with. The 1973 U.S.–South Vietnam–North Vietnam Truce Agreement is an example.[10] The Truce Agreement included detailed risk-management provisions only with respect to two sets of related obligations—first, the obligation of North Vietnam to release some 600 U.S. prisoners of war, and, second, the obligation of the United States to withdraw its 25,000 troops from Vietnam and to remove its mines from North Vietnamese harbors. These obligations were spelled out in clear and unambiguous language, together with provisions establishing a detailed and timed schedule of staged reciprocal performances, each step of which was conditioned on performance by the other side, designed to ensure that these obligations were in fact carried out.[11] Yet with respect to many other provisions, such as those dealing with the cessation of hostilities, the agreement was much more ambiguous, and credible surveillance or compliance-inducing mechanisms were lacking.[12] Thus, the overseeing of the cease-fire obligations was entrusted to the International Commission of Control and Supervision (composed of Hungary, Poland, Canada, and Indonesia), which required unanimity for action and had long had a questionable record of effectiveness. Again, while Secretary of State Kissinger asserted that the agreement obligated North Vietnam to withdraw its troops from South Vietnam, the agreement was at best ambiguous as to any such commitment, and no specific provisions were included to guard against the risk that North Vietnam would not withdraw. Indeed, the reasoning upon which Secretary Kissinger appears to have based his assertion that North Vietnamese withdrawal was seriously intended as an integral part of the agreement was rather complex. In a press conference at the time, he explained that, while there was no mention in the agreement of a withdrawal of North Vietnamese troops from South Vietnam, neither did the agreement recognize the right of North Vietnamese troops to remain in the South, and it was his belief that, "if this agreement is implemented," these troops should over time be substantially reduced. He reasoned that, first, the introduction of new troops was prohibited; second, the use of normal infiltration corridors through Laos and Cambodia was prohibited; third, military movements across the Demilitarized Zone were prohibited; and fourth, forces on both sides were to be reduced and demobilized. He concluded:

Therefore, it is our judgment that there is no way that North Vietnam can live up to that agreement without there being a reduction of the North Vietnamese forces in South Vietnam, without this being explicitly stated.

Of course, it is not inconceivable that the agreement will not in all respects be lived up to. In that case, adding another clause which will not be lived up to, specifically requiring it, would not change the situation.

It is our expectation that the agreement will be lived up to and therefore we believe that the problem of these forces will be taken care of by the evolution of events in South Vietnam.[13]

Several other provisions, such as the commitment in Article IV obligating South Vietnam to observe human rights, were also not supported by any meaningful risk-management techniques.

Thus, from the way these clearly distrustful parties dealt with these various risks in the agreement, it could be inferred that, while both the United States and North Vietnam took the basic exchange of the U.S. prisoners of war for withdrawal of U.S. forces and removal of mines very seriously, each party was prepared to accept greater uncertainty as to the other's compliance with other obligations in the agreement. The absence of effective risk-management techniques with respect to those obligations, it might be argued, lends some support to the contention that these long-bargained-for other provisions, additional to the basic exchange, were primarily intended to serve an internal or face-saving function for the U.S. government—to allow the Nixon administration to claim to have achieved its proclaimed goal of "peace with honor"—rather than establishing substantial obligations on the part of North Vietnam.[14] In fact, the cease-fire did not hold, and North Vietnamese troops did not withdraw. Following a sometimes tense reciprocal performance by each party of the basic exchange—North Vietnam's release of U.S. prisoners of war and the United States' removal of U.S. troops and mines—each party accused the other of numerous breaches of the agreement and asserted its own consequent freedom of action, and the truce agreement soon broke down.[15]

Let us now examine the most important types of techniques which nations use to deal with risks of nonperformance in agreements.

1. Ensuring that the Other State Can Perform

A nation considering entering into an agreement with another may be concerned that the other nation will not be capable of performing the obligations it is undertaking. That is, one nation may fear that, even if its treaty partner is in good faith as to its intention to perform, its partner may be incorrectly assessing or unduly optimistic about its capacity to meet its proposed commitments. For example, the United States may doubt that Panama has sufficient military capability to meet its obligations under a mutual defense treaty for defense of the Panama Canal; or the United States may doubt that the Soviet Union has adequate technological capability to design, construct, and launch a vehicle capable of rendezvous in space; or China may doubt that Canada will have sufficient grain above its own needs to fulfill an obligation to make certain amounts available to China; or the Soviet Union may doubt that, despite a commitment by the executive branch of the U.S. government, the U.S. Congress will enact legislation permitting the U.S. government to implement a tariff reduction agreement.

The other nation may be similarly concerned that it may not be able to meet its own commitments and may be placed in a position of breach of the agreement. Thus, it will normally also have an interest in any techniques which ensure that it will be capable of rendering any performance agreed to, or conversely, that it will not find itself bound to perform obligations which it cannot meet.

A nation may attempt to satisfy itself as to its treaty partner's capability of performing by obtaining and evaluating available information regarding this question, including any difficulties that the other nation may have experienced in the past in relevant respects. But it may also seek to protect itself against this risk by other means.

a. Demonstration of Capability

Before a nation enters into an agreement with another, it may require the other to demonstrate that it has the capacity to perform. For example, before the United States enters into a proposed atomic energy agreement with another nation conditioned on the other's undertaking to use nuclear materials supplied only for peaceful purposes and not to allow any diversion to weapons uses, the United States may wish to inspect the other nation's existing nuclear facilities, talk with relevant officials, scientists, and technicians, and examine its relevant records in order to ensure that it will be able to provide such safeguards. Or, the United States may wish to defer agreement with another nation for a joint space program pending the other nation's successful launching of an experimental or prototype model of the type of spacecraft required for the cooperative project. Or, before entering into a mutual security agreement with another nation, the United States may first wish to observe the performance of the other nation's forces in war games that demonstrate its military capacity, including its capacity to coordinate its forces usefully with those of the United States against a common enemy.

b. Earmarking Relevant Resources

If a nation is concerned that its potential treaty partner may not have relevant resources available to meet its commitments under the agreement, or that these resources may be diverted to other purposes, it may seek provisions in the agreement which require the other nation to establish, maintain, and segregate these necessary resources. For example, the United Nations might require its member nations to establish and specially train separate military units earmarked for use for collective security or peace-keeping purposes. Or nation A might, as a condition of an agreement to purchase grain or oil from nation B, require B to set aside and earmark reserves of grain or oil sufficient to meet its supply obligations to A. Or A may require B to establish and maintain special restricted accounts for the accumulation of funds to repay loans which A is extending to B. To the extent that A has some direct claim on these resources in the event of breach by B, such earmarking may serve also as a security device. The primary function of earmarking in this context, however, is to ensure that B itself maintains the capacity to perform.

c. Ensuring Legal Capacity

If one nation is concerned as to its potential treaty partner's legal capacity to perform, it may make the entry into force of the agreement contingent on the other nation's prior enactment of any constitutional amendments, legislation, or regulations necessary to implement the agreement. For example, if Canada has doubts as to whether the U.S. Congress is prepared to implement an agreement reducing tariffs on automotive parts by enacting legislation reducing relevant duties, it may wish to provide that the agreement will take effect only upon enactment by the U.S. Congress of the necessary implementing legislation. The United States will, of course, also wish to ensure its legal capacity to carry out the agreement prior to undertaking an international commitment with Canada to do so. Thus, the two nations may expressly provide, as they in fact did in the 1965 U.S.–Canadian Automotive Products Agreement, that the agreement will definitively enter into force only upon exchanges of notes giving notice that appropriate implementing action in each state's respective legislatures has been completed.[16] Indeed, it is the usual practice of the United States government to defer ratification of international agreements until necessary authority or implementing legislation has been obtained or assured.[17]

d. Ensuring Technical or Financial Capacity

If a nation is concerned whether its potential treaty partner has the technical, financial, or institutional capacity to perform its obligations, it may, as a condition of its agreement, require the other nation to take steps to improve its capabilities in this respect, either through wholly internal measures or by accepting assistance from the first nation, third countries, or international organizations. For example, some U.S. atomic energy cooperation agreements contain provisions permitting the United States to review the design of any reactor or other equipment and devices which it determines may be relevant to the application of safeguards,[18] or requiring U.S. approval of facilities for the storage of material that is not being used in the recipient's nuclear reactors.[19] The 1978 U.S Nuclear Non-Proliferation Act requires further assurances in such agreements concerning the physical security of materials furnished, confirmed by a U.S. review of such arrangements.[20] Or, in connection with a fisheries conservation agreement under which nation A agrees to permit trawlers of nation B to fish in waters under A's jurisdiction, A may ask B to establish a special government bureau with responsibility for gathering necessary information on and monitoring its fish catches, and enforcing necessary conservation regulations on its trawlers. Or, in connection with a collective security agreement between nation A and nation B, A may ask B to send key personnel to A for training or to accept a military assistance training team from A. Or, in connection with an agreement under which each party is to construct works relating to the management of a common river basin, one nation may require another's commitment that it will obtain and accept loans from some third party, such as the International Bank, in amounts sufficient to carry out its part of the project.

Of course, even in the absence of express provisions in an agreement, one nation may choose to assist its treaty partner to meet its commitments. Moreover, its treaty partner, in order to ensure its own capacity to perform, will usually accept such help, and indeed may wish provisions in the agreement specifically requiring the first nation to do so. For example, under the World Meteorological Organization's technical assistance program, WMO experts assist in the establishment within member developing countries of national meteorological services that ultimately have responsibility for fulfilling those nations' obligations under the regime established by the organization.[21] And nations participating in atomic energy peaceful cooperation and nonproliferation agreements have, as a matter of mutual cooperation, arranged for exchanges of visits by physical security review teams to provide information and assistance in upgrading their physical security measures for special nuclear materials.[22]

Where an agreement includes certain special obligations which one or more of the parties will need some time to develop the capability to meet, the parties may provide that these provisions will not take effect until a period sufficient for their doing so has elapsed. For example, Annex II of the 1978 Protocol to the London Marine Pollution Convention requires that the parties establish reception facilities at their ports to hold noxious liquid substances which might otherwise be discharged into the ocean by ships. Article II of the convention permits states ratifying the protocol to delay entry into force of this annex for three years after their date of acceptance, or for a longer period with the consent of a two-thirds majority of the parties to the protocol.[23]

2. Making Nonperformance or Inadequate Performance Clear

A nation can increase the probability of another nation's adequately performing its obligations under an agreement by techniques which make any failure to perform by the other nation clear. These techniques can be useful in several ways. First, even if the other nation seriously intends and is prepared to perform its commitments in good faith, it may have an honest misunderstanding as to what those commitments are or whether it has in fact performed them; if its commitments are made clear, it will comply with them. Second, prompt detection and clear determination of breach are often crucial components of an effective risk-management system designed to prevent cheating. If the other nation is considering deliberately violating its obligations under the agreement, it will be less likely to do so if it realizes that its nonperformance will be readily apparent and clearly labeled as a violation, legitimizing whatever sanctions its treaty partner or third parties are in a position to impose. Conversely, if the other nation believes that its obligation is ambiguous or uncertain, it will see itself as in a better position to justify or excuse nonperformance or inadequate performance and to resist any application of sanctions, particularly by third parties. Moreover, if the other nation believes that its failure to perform will not be quickly apparent, it may hope to gain some advantage in the interval before discovery. In his study of arms control agreements, Chayes suggests that a nation, in deciding whether to violate an agreement, "will first discount the absolute value of the applicable sanction by the likelihood that [it] can avoid detection (or at least conviction), and then weigh this result against the gains to be expected from the conduct."[24] Since one nation's ability to establish clearly and promptly the fact of its treaty partner's nonperformance or breach may be a precondition of its ability to employ effectively other protective or compliance-inducing devices, nations frequently pay particular attention to devices intended to achieve this objective.

a. Description of Performance in Specific and Unambiguous Terms

A nation may seek to describe the performance expected of the other nation as clearly and precisely as possible in the agreement.[25] As might be expected, the proposed 1979 SALT II Treaty between the United States and the Soviet Union contains elaborate provisions attempting to define the obligations of each party in the most careful and precise terms. For example, the definition of ''intercontinental ballistic missile launchers'' in Article II of the treaty is followed by two ''agreed statements'' and three ''common understandings'' further refining this definition,[26] and the definition of ''heavy bombers'' is followed by five agreed statements and three common understandings.[27] Overall, the treaty includes ninety-six agreed statements and common understandings designed to clarify any possible misunderstanding.

Nevertheless, there are practical limits to the effectiveness of this technique. First, even the most careful drafting may not prevent ambiguity and disputes as to interpretation. Language is inherently ambiguous, more than one language may be used in negotiating and recording the arrangement, and new or unanticipated situations may arise to which this language must be applied. Moreover, the "rules" of general contract and treaty law reflect and permit a variety of approaches to the interpretation of agreements.[28] Some emphasize the "plain meaning" of the language and literal textual construction, while others emphasize the purpose of the agreement and are more liberal in permitting evidence as to negotiating history and context. A nation cannot be sure which of these rules and approaches the other party or a third party will apply. Second, excessive specificity in an agreement may lead to undesirable rigidity in application of the agreement and an inability of the parties to adjust their arrangement readily to changing circumstances.[29] Often, the parties may not yet be sure precisely what they wish to cover and will wish to leave some leeway. Third, attempts to achieve a high degree of specificity may unnecessarily complicate and delay negotiations and give rise to needless disputes and difficulties. At the extreme, attempts by lawyers to "nail everything down tight"—to dot every *i* and cross every *t*—may suggest distrust, irritate the other party, and threaten the momentum and success of the negotiation. It may simply not be worthwhile to try to define carefully everything in an agreement.

b. Provisions for Verifying Performance

A nation may seek to include in the agreement devices intended to give it and possibly interested third parties prompt notice of its treaty partner's nonperformance, or it may seek to establish such devices outside the agreement. Whether a nation believes it needs such devices, and which type of device is appropriate, will depend on the subject matter of the agreement and the nature of the other nation's expected performance. In the case of an agreement for the sale of commodities, it will probably be immediately obvious to each nation whether the other is performing. In the case of an arms control agreement banning underground nuclear tests or the production of biological weapons, nonperformance by one of the parties may be less visible, leading the other, or both, to seek special verification devices.

Verification can be defined as the totality of means—including intelligence, open sources and "common knowledge," voluntary reporting, and monitoring and inspection—by which one nation can determine whether another nation is complying with its obligations under an agreement between them.[30] The purposes of verification include (1) inducing compliance with obligations by creating a credible likelihood that violations will be detected and result in undesirable consequences for the party that breaches the agreement, (2) enabling the other party to take timely and appropriate action in response to any violations to protect itself and deter further violations, and (3) building confidence among the parties by establishing a record of demonstrated compliance.

A thoughtful 1962 Arms Control and Disarmament Agency study of verification in disarmament agreements suggests that decisions as to the use of verification techniques should take into account the following general propositions:

1. Verification acts as a deterrent to evasion only to the extent that a potential violator is concerned with the risks of exposure. . . .

2. National self-interest, rather than fear of detection, will remain the principal inducement to compliance. . . .

3. The successful operation of verification procedures builds confidence in the disarmament process. . . .

4. Verification to support responses is less essential for informal arrangements than for long-term, formal commitments.[31]

Commenting on verification requirements, the study points out:

Since absolute verification can never be achieved, the level of verification to be sought becomes a matter for military and political decision. The need for verification varies from measure to measure, agreement to agreement, and context to context.

. . . .

3. *Political verification requirements.* The assurance of compliance demanded for any particular measure depends in part upon the mutual distrust of the parties involved. That is, at the present time verification requirements for an agreement between the United States and the Soviet Union are obviously higher than those relating to an identical agreement concluded with, say, Canada. Verification will be demanded by the United States and its allies to the extent that there is reason to be fearful of the intentions as well as the capabilities of the Soviet Union.

Verification requirements will not necessarily increase as disarmament progresses. While it is true that in later stages of disarmament the parties become more vulnerable and the need for confidence is greater, increased verification alone cannot supply that confidence. Indeed, unless increased confidence is generated in other ways, it is doubtful that advanced stages of disarmament will be reached. In view of these considerations, verification requirements may well be greater at earlier stages than at later ones which, if they occur at all, will be preceded by an increase in the level of trust. The inability to predict levels of trust or distrust in advance suggests that the verification requirements for each stage should be determined only in the light of the political conditions existing at that time.[32]

The study further suggests that verification techniques must be designed with the kinds of responses to violations contemplated in mind.[33] Thus, verification procedures should provide information in a form useful to those who will decide on responses and persuasive to a nation's own public and, if international support for response is desired, to the broader international community. The procedures should also be designed to minimize disputes over the operation of the verification system itself and to deal with obstructions that undermine the verification process. Finally, a verification system should give a sufficiently accurate picture and provide necessary further procedures to avoid error or overresponse to apparent violations. Verification can at best only answer the question, Is the other party cheating? It cannot answer the questions, Does it make any difference? and What should we do about it?

The concept of verification has received particular attention in recent years in the context of the negotiation of arms control and disarmament arrangements. A principal tenet of U.S. arms control doctrine has been "no disarmament without inspection and control."[34] In 1970 Gerard Smith, then head of the U.S. Arms Control and Disarmament Agency (ACDA), stated: "We will not conclude an agreement that relies on good faith and trust. . . . In other words, we are not basing our confidence on what we hope the Soviets would do under an agreement but on our ability to verify what they actually do."[35] Again, in 1977 hearings before the Senate on his confirmation as head of the ACDA, Paul Warnke commented: "An agreement which is not verifiable is worse than no agreement."[36] During the last several decades, discussions of various arms control agreements have often focused on the acceptability and reliability of possible verification techniques, such as on-site inspection—which the Soviet Union has usually opposed as both unnecessary and a subterfuge for espionage[37]—and aerial or satellite reconnaissance.

The issue of verification has most recently been raised in the context of negotiations for the proposed U.S.–Soviet SALT II Treaty.[38] In his 1979 State of the Union Address to the Congress, President Carter, urging support for the SALT II Treaty, said: "SALT II will not rely on trust. It will be verifiable. We have very sophisticated proven means—including our satellites—to determine for ourselves whether or not the Soviet Union is meeting its treaty obligations. I will sign no agreement which cannot be verified."[39] But at the end of 1979, the debate on the effectiveness of the verification techniques provided in SALT II continued, particularly in view of the loss of U.S.

surveillance facilities in Iran in 1979.[40] In the course of the debate it became apparent that the question of verification inevitably involved matters of judgment, on which honest people might disagree. The U.S. Administration was not claiming that SALT II was "foolproof"—that is, that the United States could assuredly detect any Soviet violation, no matter how small—but only that it was "adequately verifiable" in the sense that any significant Soviet cheating would be deterred. A 1978 Administration report to the Senate Foreign Relations Committee concludes: "[A]lthough the possibility of some undetected cheating in certain areas exists, such cheating would not alter the strategic balance in view of U.S. programs. However, any cheating on a scale large enough to affect the strategic balance would be discovered in time to make an appropriate response. For these reasons, and others noted in this paper, we believe that the SALT II agreement, taken as a whole, is adequately verifiable."[41]

The concept of assured verification in disarmament agreements has been criticized by a number of commentators. For example, Alva Myrdal, a prominent Swedish participant in disarmament negotiations, has suggested that it is futile to demand verification techniques which would give 100 percent assurance that no violation of an agreement would ever go undetected.[42] In a thoughtful discussion, she contrasts "after-the-fact" approaches to verification, which emphasize a legalistic interest in proving violation of treaty obligations and holding the party accountable, with "before-the-fact" approaches, which are intended to prevent violations by establishing a sufficient risk of disclosure that these risks themselves act as a deterrent against any nation's attempting to violate a treaty obligation. Stressing the role of mutual confidence and trust, as contrasted with detailed verification techniques, as an essential component of such agreements, she comments:

The degree of trust is always of the essence when an agreement is contemplated. The before-the-fact deterrence approach presupposes a climate of confidence, but it has the comparative merit of motivating a willingness to take a first step on somewhat shakier groud, since it then allows confidence to grow gradually as it is tested by experience. To demand foolproof methods for after-the-fact verification is to impose an impossible requirement. . . .

Verification is no substitute for trust. The question of trust in a disarmament agreement remains preeminently a political problem, but verification can obviously contribute to trust and thus to a buttressing of international agreements. . . .

. . . Speaking generally, the imperative task for practical policy should be to reduce the margins of uncertainty in order to change the demand for control from an impossible absolute requirement to a manageable relative requirement. [43]

It is an interesting question whether verification techniques are likely to make much difference in a nation's decision to perform or not to perform its obligations under an agreement. While verification techniques in arms control agreements have differed widely, there is little evidence that clandestine violations have occurred in any of them. [44] Many commentators have pointed out that nations do not usually accept such agreements unless they intend to comply with them, and that the political commitment which binds a nation to performance is more important in its decision to perform its obligations than its fear of being detected in a violation. Where a nation decides not to perform its obligations under an agreement, it is more likely simply to denounce the agreement than to try to cheat on it. [45] Nevertheless, nations—or at least many of their citizens—continue to believe that verification is important, and this in itself may make such techniques significant to the achievement of agreement. Former Secretary of State Rusk has observed: "[The] political aspect of verification is at least as important as the technical. If the public and the Congress can be assured of a reasonable degree of verification, they'll feel reasonably secure about the agreement." [46]

While techniques for verification or for more general third-party supervision of an agreement can help directly to meet the parties' concerns for performance risks involved, they may also serve broader functions in facilitating cooperation. James, in his study *The Politics of Peacekeeping*, suggests several of these. First, a nation's acceptance of verification or supervision techniques may in itself serve as a demonstration of its good faith: "[A] readiness to accept supervision can generally be taken as an indication that the parties are moving towards an agreement in good faith, and are not thinking of anything other than the execution of its terms. The establishment of a supervisory presence, therefore, by producing evidence of the conciliatory disposition of the parties, can play a notable part in reducing suspicion and so can help to obtain an agreed settlement."[47] Second, clear evidence of any breach, particularly evidence secured by third parties which will be broadly accepted by the international community as credible, may serve to protect a nation against international criticism if the other party in fact fails to perform and the first nation feels compelled to withdraw from the agreement or take other measures to protect itself.[48] That is, it may help to legitimate "self-help" actions in the event of breach. Finally, such techniques may be useful as a political face-saver, enabling a nation to meet internal or foreign objections to entering into an agreement with another party which is a traditional enemy or distrusted by the public. James comments:

If, for example, one party has consistently depicted the other as untrustworthy or aggressive, a sudden change of policy which makes an accommodation with him most desirable can cause the first party considerable embarrassment. One way of resolving this problem would be to make arrangements for an international watch on the execution of the agreement. This could carry the suggestion that the other state, while now a necessary treaty partner, could not be safely let out of sight, and also that the international community shared this view of his reliability. Of course, this could lead to a problem with the second party, but if he could be persuaded to accept supervision, the device, although strictly superfluous, might play the important role of making an agreement palatable.[49]

There are various ways in which one nation may seek to

monitor or verify another's performance of its obligations under an agreement.

(i) *Reports to the state concerned or to a third party.* A nation may attempt to monitor another's performance of its obligations under an agreement by requiring that the other make reports or furnish information or data to the first nation concerning its compliance. For example, in the 1973 fisheries agreement between Iceland and the United Kingdom, Iceland required the United Kingdom to furnish reports of the position of British trawlers fishing in Icelandic waters and of landings in British ports by British trawlers with fish caught in Icelandic fisheries.[50] Military assistance agreements between the United States and other nations typically require the recipient nation to report to the United States on the use made of such assistance.[51] U.S. atomic energy agreements with other nations typically require the other nation to maintain and produce operating records and give reports to assist the United States in assessing accountability for special nuclear materials and equipment furnished under the agreement.[52]

Alternatively, particularly in the case of multilateral arrangements, an agreement may require that each nation party give reports on matters relevant to its compliance to a third party, such as an international organization. For example, the International Coffee Agreement, 1962, requires that all coffee-exporting countries report their coffee exports and other relevant data to the Council of the International Coffee Organization.[53] The 1972 London Ocean Dumping Convention requires each party to report periodically to the Intergovernmental Maritime Consultative Organization on "the nature and quantities of all matter permitted to be dumped and the location, time and method of such dumping."[54] The International Whaling Convention requires that all parties report their whale catches to the International Whaling Commission.[55] The Convention on Forced Labor requires that all the parties report on their compliance to the International Labour Organization,[56] and a number of other human rights and other treaties contain other general reporting requirements.[57] Other types of self-policing techniques are also possible. In U.S.–Soviet negotiations on banning chemical weapons, the Soviet Union has proposed a verification system based on self-inspection by "national citizens' committees."[58]

While reporting techniques are widely employed, they have several limitations. They depend for their efficacy on the good faith of the reporting state, on the administrative ability of the reporting nation to collect the relevant information, and on the ability of the receiving nation or organization to interpret and assess the information presented. Without independent means of verification, it may be impossible for one nation to discover whether another is honestly in error in or deliberately falsifying its reports. Moreover, reporting techniques may be burdensome and expensive for the reporting nation. Indeed, reporting or self-policing requirements are perhaps most useful as a means of requiring a nation that wishes to comply with its obligations to monitor and pay more attention to its own performance. For example, a nation which is required to report on its compliance with a human rights agreement may, as it comes to compile the report, realize that it has human rights problems of which it was honestly unaware, or it may undertake internal reform measures that it might otherwise have not bothered with, in order to be able to "beef up" its report.

In some situations, certification techniques or techniques utilizing "tickets" or stamps can be used to police or verify performance. For example, Annex I of the 1973 London Convention for the Prevention of Pollution from Ships requires the parties periodically to survey their fleets and issue "International Oil Pollution Certificates" attesting to the fact that the ships flying their flags meet the standards established in the annex.[59] The International Coffee Organization at one time utilized a system of stamps to ensure that member nations did not cheat by exporting amounts of coffee in excess of their allowed quotas.[60] Under this system, each exporting member nation received a certain number of stamps corresponding to the amount of its allowed quota. Importing member nations permitted coffee imports only when the relevant import documents had these stamps attached. Thus, in theory, a nation could not export more coffee than the stamps representing its quota covered. However, such a system will depend for its efficacy on the difficulty of counterfeiting the necessary stamps or certificates, on the diligence of the importing state in requiring the stamps, and on nondiversion of exports to or through third nations not party to the agreement and consequently not covered by the system.

(ii) *Inquiry, surveillance, or inspection by the state concerned.* A nation may seek to monitor another's performance of an agreement through techniques which permit it either directly or indirectly to check the fact of the other's performance. Such inspection or surveillance procedures may be obligatory and based on free access, or they may be based on special consultation and invitation. They may also be either continuing or periodic and limited in number. Since surveillance and inspection by another state touches sensitive issues of national sovereignty and pride, a system of this sort should ideally involve minimal interference with the other nation and be as unobtrusive as practicable.

There are a number of examples of the use of these types of techniques in international agreements. Article VII of the Antarctic Treaty provides in part that

(3) All areas of Antarctica, including all stations, installations and equipment within those areas, and all ships and aircraft at points of discharging or embarking cargoes or personnel in Antarctica, shall be open at all times to inspection by any observers designated [by any of the contracting parties].
. . .

(4) Aerial observation may be carried out at any time over any or all areas of Antarctica by any of the Contracting Parties.

A number of inspections have been conducted under this provision, and no violation has ever been found.[61]

Fishing agreements, such as the 1972 U.S.–Brazilian Shrimp Agreement, the 1976 U.K.–Icelandic Fishing Agreement, and the North Atlantic Fisheries Convention, permit boarding and inspection to ensure that conservation provisions regarding catches are adhered to;[62] and procedures for boarding and inspection by observers and inspectors designated by members of the Commission for the Conservation of Antarctic Marine Living Resources are established by the recently concluded Antarctic Marine Living Resources Convention.[63] Under the International Observer Scheme associated with the International Whaling Agreement, foreign observers may sail on whaling ships to ensure that they observe International Whaling Commission regulations.[64] The negotiating text for the proposed Law of the Sea Treaty presently being negotiated at the Third U.N. Law of the Sea Conference would similarly permit a coastal state to "take such measures, including boarding, inspection, arrest and judicial proceedings" as might be necessary to ensure compliance with its laws and regulations in its exclusive economic zone.[65]

Atomic energy agreements typically provide that the donor nation may "observe from time to time the condition and use of any source or special nuclear materials . . . and . . . observe the performance of the reactor in which such materials are used" in the receiving nation.[66] Truce or peace agreements frequently expressly provide that each nation may conduct aerial or satellite surveillance over certain portions of the other's territory in order to ensure compliance. For example, the 1975 Israel-Egypt Sinai Agreement provides that "[r]econnaissance aircraft of either party may fly up to the middle line of the buffer zone . . . on an agreed schedule."[67]

Finally, verification by inspection or satellite surveillance may, as previously indicated, play an important risk-management role in arms limitation agreements. Thus, Article XV of the SALT II Treaty, substantially repeating similar provisions in the SALT I Agreements,[68] would provide:

1. For the purpose of providing assurance of compliance with the provisions of this Treaty, each Party shall use national technical means of verification at its disposal in a manner consistent with generally recognized principles of international law.

2. Each Party undertakes not to interfere with the national technical means of verification of the other Party operating in accordance with paragraph 1 of this article.

3. Each Party undertakes not to use deliberate concealment measures which impede verification by national technical means of compliance with the provisions of this Treaty.

This article is followed by two agreed statements and three common understandings further defining the parties' relevant rights and obligations.

The efficacy of one nation's inspection or surveillance in reducing the risk of nonperformance by the other will, of course, depend in large part on the technical ability of its inspectors or surveillance devices to detect noncompliance, particularly where the other nation is attempting to cheat or conceal its violation. Where a nation has confidence in particular techniques, it may be willing to accept fewer types of techniques or to accept more risky agreements. Thus, technological improvement of reconnaissance satellites, such as the development of the U.S. "Big Bird" satellite, reduced the pressure for direct on-site inspection in arms control agreements and was an important factor in the achievement of both the 1972 U.S.–Soviet SALT I Interim Agreement and Protocol on Strategic Offensive Missiles and the Treaty on Anti-Ballistic Missile Systems.[69] On the other hand, loss of U.S. surveillance facilities in Iran raised additional questions about U.S. ability to verify Soviet compliance with the proposed SALT II Treaty and has been used by opponents of the treaty to argue against its ratification.[70] Clearly, even good verification techniques may not work. An example is India's apparent bypassing without detection of

Canadian safeguards on Canadian-supplied nuclear materials, and its explosion of a nuclear device in 1974.[71]

Verification techniques such as surveillance or inspection serve an additional protective function for one nation in that any attempt by the other at concealment or interference with the operation of such techniques may in itself serve as an indication or advance warning of its prospective noncompliance.[72] For example, in February 1979 the United States warned the Soviet Union that any attempt to impede American efforts to monitor Soviet missile tests by encoding test data signals, as the Soviet Union did in a series of SS–18 missile tests, would be considered a serious violation of the proposed SALT II Treaty.[73] Building on this concept, the Swedish government, in the context of disarmament negotiations, has suggested a technique of "verification by challenge" as an alternative to on-site inspection.[74] Under this type of arrangement, a nation suspected of having violated an agreement and "challenged" in this respect by another nation would be expected voluntarily to offer clarifying information or an invitation for inspection in order to allay suspicion and establish innocence. If it refused to respond to a challenge, the other nation would then be entitled to withdraw from the agreement.

(iii) *Inquiry, surveillance, or inspection by a third party.* In some cases, arrangements for inspection or surveillance by a third party, such as a nation outside the agreement or an international organization, may be preferable to an "adversary" verification system involving inspection or surveillance by the parties themselves. This may be because the parties do not themselves have the technical means for adequate verification, because they distrust each other and fear that such techniques will somehow be used to secure an advantage, because inspection by the other party is considered inconsistent with national dignity, because an impartial and widely acceptable determination of breach is particularly desirable in terms of the responses contemplated, or because (particularly in the case of a technical kind of multilateral agreement) third-party inspection is simply less costly and more efficient.[75] The efficacy of third-party verification techniques will again depend on such factors as the availability to the third parties of technical means for determining noncompliance and the competence and trustworthiness of the third party. While international organizations can often play a useful role in this respect, they are not immune from political influence, and certain nations may be unwilling to trust them with such functions. For example, Israel and South Africa are clearly concerned as to the ability of the United Nations to act impartially in situations involving their interests. Thus, the choice between an international or an adversary inspection system will have to take account of the particular agreement and context. The 1962 Arms Control and Disarmament Agency study of verification previously referred to comments:

It is true that international inspection systems making use of either impartial civil servants or neutral-nation inspectors may be more acceptable to some nations than adversary systems. International inspectors are less likely to encounter interference, their findings may be more widely regarded as authentic, and their numbers can be easily expanded to include nationals of additional countries. However, experience has shown the difficulties of negotiating with an international organization, finding competent impartial personnel, and developing and meeting a budget. International or neutral personnel may frequently err on the side of finding no violation in order to forestall crisis or recrimination, or they may regard their role as mediators rather than as judges. By comparison, adversary systems, involving mutual inspection of each party by other parties to the agreement, require a minimum of negotiation, have few personnel and budgetary problems, give a greater sense of security to the inspecting country, and require only that the population of the host country accept the inspectors as partisan observers, not as legitimate authorities.[76]

One context in which provisions for verification by third parties have been widely used in recent years is in truce and demilitarization agreements.[77] For example, the 1975 Egypt-Israel Sinai Agreement includes extensive provisions for aerial reconnaissance by the United States and for inspection by the

U.N. Emergency Force. One paragraph of the annex to the agreement provided that in the demilitarized area established by the agreement, "the United Nations Emergency Force will assure that there are no military or paramilitary forces of any kind, military fortifications and military installations; it will establish checkpoints and have the freedom of movement necessary to perform this function."[78] Another paragraph provided that "[t]he United Nations Emergency Force will conduct inspections in order to ensure maintenance of the agreed limitation within these areas [of limited armaments]."[79] Still another paragraph provided:

> There shall be a continuation of aerial reconnaissance missions by the United States over the areas covered by the Agreement . . . , following the same procedures already in practice. The missions will ordinarily be carried out at a frequency of one mission every 7–10 days, with either party or the United Nations Emergency Force empowered to request an earlier mission. The United States Government will make the mission results available expeditiously to Israel, Egypt and the chief coordinator of the United Nations peace-keeping missions in the Middle East.[80]

The 1979 Egypt-Israel Peace Treaty substantially continues these arrangements for the performance of verification functions by the United States and by the United Nations or an "acceptable alternative" multinational force.[81] Difficulties in implementing this provision arose in July 1979, when the Soviet Union, to demonstrate its opposition to the treaty, indicated that it would veto in the Security Council any resolution extending the special U.N. Middle East peacekeeping force established following the Yom Kippur War. The force was not extended, and Israel pressed the United States to fulfill an alleged commitment to provide an alternative force to police the treaty.[82] By late 1979, these difficulties were apparently being dealt with by the use of U.N. truce supervision observers, who were not withdrawn, and by other arrangements between Egypt, Israel, and the United States.[83]

It is difficult to think of ways of verifying compliance with agreements intended to apply between nations in conflict, such as those providing for the protection of war victims, other than through the use of third parties. The 1949 Geneva Conventions provide for inspection of prisoner-of-war camps by the International Red Cross, which is a nongovernmental international organization.[84]

Another significant example of the use of third-party verification techniques is the international safeguards system established under the Statute of the International Atomic Energy Agency (IAEA).[85] The statute provides that, pursuant to special agreements with nations, the agency can inspect nuclear facilities and take other measures to ensure nondiversion of nuclear materials to weapons or other prohibited uses. Moreover, it can apply sanctions in the event of noncompliance. Article XII of the statute, which is entitled "Agency Safeguards," establishes one of the most developed systems of third-party verification of international obligations yet attempted and warrants setting out in full:

ARTICLE XII

Agency safeguards

A. With respect to any Agency project, or other arrangement where the Agency is requested by the parties concerned to apply safeguards, the Agency shall have the following rights and responsibilities to the extent relevant to the project or arrangement:

1. To examine the design of specialized equipment and facilities, including nuclear reactors, and to approve it only from the view-point of assuring that it will not further any military purpose, that it complies with applicable health and safety standards, and that it will permit effective application of the safeguards provided for in this article;

2. To require the observance of any health and safety measures prescribed by the Agency;

3. To require the maintenance and production of operating records to assist in ensuring accountability for source and special fissionable materials used or produced in the project or arrangement;

4. To call for and receive progress reports;

5. To approve the means to be used for the chemical processing of

irradiated materials solely to ensure that this chemical processing will not lend itself to diversion of materials for military purposes and will comply with applicable health and safety standards; to require that special fissionable materials recovered or produced as a by-product be used for peaceful purposes under continuing Agency safeguards for research or in reactors, existing or under construction, specified by the member or members concerned; and to require deposit with the Agency of any excess of any special fissionable materials recovered or produced as a by-product over what is needed for the above-stated uses in order to prevent stockpiling of these materials, provided that thereafter at the request of the member or members concerned special fissionable materials so deposited with the Agency shall be returned promptly to the member or members concerned for use under the same provisions as stated above;

6. To send into the territory of the recipient State or States inspectors, designated by the Agency after consultation with the State or States concerned, who shall have access at all times to all places and data and to any person who by reason of his occupation deals with materials, equipment, or facilities which are required by this Statute to be safeguarded, as necessary to account for source and special fissionable materials supplied and fissionable products and to determine whether there is a compliance with the undertaking against use in furtherance of any military purpose referred to in sub-paragraph F-4 of article XI, with the health and safety measures referred to in sub-paragraph A-2 of this article, and with any other conditions prescribed in the agreement between the Agency and the State or States concerned. Inspectors designated by the Agency shall be accompanied by representatives of the authorities of the State concerned, if that State so requests, provided that the inspectors shall not thereby be delayed or otherwise impeded in the exercise of their functions;

7. In the event of non-compliance and failure by the recipient State or States to take requested corrective steps within a reasonable time, to suspend or terminate assistance and withdraw any materials and equipment made available by the Agency or a member in furtherance of the project.

B. The Agency shall, as necessary, establish a staff of inspectors. The staff of inspectors shall have the responsibility of examining all operations conducted by the Agency itself to determine whether the Agency is complying with the health and safety measures prescribed by it for application to projects subject to its approval, supervision or control, and whether the Agency is taking adequate measures to prevent the source and special fissionable materials in its custody or used or produced in its own operations from being used in furtherance of any military purpose. The Agency shall take remedial action forthwith to correct any non-compliance or failure to take adequate measures.

C. The staff of inspectors shall also have the responsibility of obtaining and verifying the accounting referred to in sub-paragraph A-6 of this article and of determining whether there is compliance with the undertaking referred to in sub-paragraph F-4 of article XI, with the measures referred to in sub-paragraph A-2 of this article, and with all other conditions of the project prescribed in the agreement between the Agency and the State or States concerned. The inspectors shall report any non-compliance to the Director General who shall thereupon transmit the report to the Board of Governors. The Board shall call upon the recipient State or States to remedy forthwith any non-compliance which it finds to have occurred. The Board shall report the non-compliance to all members and to the Security Council and General Assembly of the United Nations. In the event of failure of the recipient State or States to take fully corrective action within a reasonable time, the Board may take one or both of the following measures: direct curtailment or suspension of assistance being provided by the Agency or by a member, and call for the return of materials and equipment made available to the recipient member or group of members. The Agency may also, in accordance with article XIX, suspend any non-complying member from the exercise of the privileges and rights of membership.

Many bilateral atomic energy agreements for the supply of nuclear materials and technology require that recipient states either accept special safeguards administered by the supplying state,[86] or, more typically, enter into collateral "trilateral" agreements between the two parties and the IAEA for the application of agency safeguards to special nuclear materials and equipment furnished under the agreement.[87] By entering into a safeguards trilateral agreement, a recipient agrees not only to agency inspection but also to the imposition of agency sanctions in the event of noncompliance. For example, the 1969 U.S.–Austria–IAEA Agreement on Application of Safeguards provides:

If the [IAEA] Board determines that there has been any noncompliance with this Agreement, the Board shall call upon the Government concerned to remedy such noncompliance forthwith and shall make such reports as it deems appropriate. If the Government fails to take fully corrective action within a reasonable time:

(b) The Board may take any measures provided for in Article XII.C of the Statute.[88]

Similar provisions requiring each nonnuclear state party to accept agency safeguards on all of their nuclear facilities are contained in the Nuclear Non-Proliferation Treaty.[89]

International safeguards have assumed a major role in global efforts to prevent nuclear proliferation. Pursuant to such safeguards agreements, in 1977 the IAEA's eighty-five inspectors made 700 trips to some 500 nuclear facilities in forty-five countries.[90] In April 1977, President Carter proposed that all nuclear materials and equipment in states not presently having nuclear weapons be subject to IAEA safeguards, that fulfillment of this requirement be a condition of continuing U.S. nuclear supply, and that U.S. law and relevant agreements provide stronger sanctions against any recipient of American nuclear fuel or hardware that sets off a nuclear device or violates IAEA or U.S. safeguards.[91] U.S. legislation implementing these proposals—the U.S. Nuclear Non-Proliferation Act—requires the inclusion of such safeguard provisions in new or amended U.S. atomic energy cooperation agreements.[92] Moreover, to deal with the risk that a receiving nation may, after acquiring U.S. materials or equipment, seek to escape safeguards by terminating the agreement, the act requires that such agreements expressly provide that safeguards will continue to apply to U.S.–supplied materials and equipment and material produced through their use indefinitely, irrespective of the duration of the other provisions in the agreement or whether the agreement is terminated or suspended for any reason.[93] (Under general treaty law, the parties may specifically agree that certain provisions of their agreement will continue, even if the rest of the agreement is for any reason terminated or suspended.)[94] In January 1978, fifteen nations supplying nuclear fuel and technology agreed on a code requiring the application of safeguards to ensure that future exports would not be used for military purposes.[95] The code, *inter alia*, permits the sale of nuclear equipment only if the customer nation agrees to accept international safeguards, including periodic inspections of facilities covered by the agreement, and agrees that any export or sale to a third nation of imported nuclear materials will also be covered by international safeguards.[96]

The effectiveness of IAEA safeguards is a subject of debate. Thus far, there have been no reported cases of noncompliance with IAEA safeguards, and the system is frequently cited as one of the most impressive examples of the efficacy of international verification techniques.[97] Some commentators are skeptical, however. For example, one recent article suggests that there are serious questions as to the system's reliability. The author asserts that agency inspectors often base their reports on educated guesses rather than on hard facts because their equipment breaks down or plant operations provide faulty data that can't be checked; that there is a lack of foolproof safeguards for certain kinds of facilities, such as reprocessing plants, enrichment facilities, or fast-breeding reactors; that there are too few well-trained inspectors; that there are sometimes restrictions on where inspectors can go; and that inspected nations continue to fear that inspection will result in disclosure of secret information.[98] In a more comprehensive recent study, Sanders points out that the effectiveness of safeguards depends heavily on the cooperation of the state to which the restrictions apply:

An essential conclusion to be drawn from the experience gained so far with Agency safeguards—using the term ''safeguards'' to cover a range of activities, from the negotiation of the underlying agreement to the verification of a physical inventory in a facility at the end of a material balance period—is that the effectiveness of the entire exercise depends on the cooperation of the state concerned and each of the authorities involved: from the civil servant negotiating the agreement to the facility operator who has to make his inventory accessible to IAEA inspectors. This cooperation will continue to be needed wherever and as long as safeguards will be applied. The Agency has to earn it constantly, by employing a professionally competent approach, tact, discretion and—perhaps most importantly—by never asking for more information than it demonstrably needs. *Safeguards cannot be imposed.* They can only be made possible by continuing mutual agreement at every level.[99]

(iv) *"Tripwires," or early warning devices.* In some situations, a nation may be able to utilize devices which, by virtue of their relation to certain preliminary activities of the other nation's performance, serve automatically to give early notice of the other nation's intent not to perform its obligations under the agreement. For example, one nation may seek to protect itself in a ceasefire or truce agreement with another through provisions for an advance line of warning stations placed in a neutralized buffer zone between the two. In theory at least, the other nation's armed penetration of the zone, in breach of its obligations, would trigger a warning of noncompliance in time for the first nation to take protective measures. The "tripwire" may be either automatic or manned by the first nation or some third party. This technique was employed in the 1975 Egypt–Israel Sinai Agreement, which established an early warning system consisting of two surveillance stations to provide strategic early warning, one operated by Egyptian and one operated by Israeli personnel, and three watch stations operated by U.S. civilians in the Mitla and Giddi passes to provide tactical early warning, supported by three unmanned electric sensor fields at each end of the passes.[100] The U.S. civilian personnel manning the watch stations were required to "immediately report to the parties . . . and to the United Nations Emergency Force any movement of armed forces, other than the United Nations Emergency Force, into either pass and any observed preparations for such movement." The agreement provided that United States personnel serving the system were to "be allowed to move freely within the area of the system." Or, a strategic arms limitation agreement between nation A and nation B may provide that the construction of sites suitable for the installation of prohibited weapons will be considered a violation of obligations.

c. Unilateral Determination by One State of the Adequacy of Performance by the Other State

A nation may insist on the right to itself be the sole judge of the adequacy of the other nation's performance. For example, a military assistance agreement might specifically provide that the donor nation may unilaterally terminate such assistance if it considers that the recipient nation is employing the assistance for improper purposes or purposes detrimental to the donor's national security or foreign policy interests. Of course, if the agreement makes clear that the furnishing of assistance by the donor is simply discretionary, rather than a continuing legal obligation, specific provisions for termination will not be necessary. Thus, U.S. mutual defense assistance agreements do not contain provisions expressly providing for termination in the event of a recipient nation's violation of its commitments, since the United States apparently takes the position that it is not obligated in any event to continue such assistance and may clearly exercise its right of discontinuation in the event of violation. In August 1978 the United States warned Israel that it might have violated the provisions of a U.S.–Israel 1952 military aid agreement by using American-supplied jets in raids on southern Lebanon,[101] and Turkey's alleged use of American-supplied arms in its intervention in Cyprus in 1974 led to the enactment of U.S. legislation terminating U.S. aid to Turkey, a ban which continued in force for four years.[102]

But while such express provisions for unilateral determination give a nation considerable control over risks, they are on their face unequal in giving one party the right to judge the other, and consequently may not be acceptable to the other nation unless it considers the arrangement highly desirable for other reasons. Of course, as will be discussed in Section 6(a)(iii), general treaty law may in any event permit one party to an agreement to withhold further performance in the event of a material breach by the other party; in the absence of express provisions requiring third-party determination of the existence of breach, one party may itself decide that it is entitled by the situation to exercise such a right, and the other party may in practice have no recourse. Presumably, under either express treaty provisions or general treaty doctrine, such a right must be exercised only in good faith.

d. Determination of Adequacy of Performance by Third Parties

Alternatively, the parties to an agreement may expressly provide that questions as to the adequacy of either nation's performance will be determined by the sole judgment of some third party. They may particularly wish to do so where the possibility of dispute about the adequacy of a particular performance is to be anticipated. For example, one nation's obligation to pay for a dam designed and constructed by another nation might be conditional on approval of the design and construction by the International Bank. This is analogous to the role of the architect under many American construction contracts.[103] More typically, however, agreements will contain general provisions under which, in the event of dispute as to the adequacy of either nation's performance, the matter shall be referred for determination to third parties in accordance with some type of adjudicatory process. For example, many U.S. commercial treaties provide that any dispute as to the interpretation or application of the treaty shall, at the request of any party, be referred for binding settlement either to an arbitral tribunal or to the International Court of Justice.[104]

Third-party dispute settlement techniques are in themselves a major subject of study and have been extensively discussed elsewhere.[105] Provisions for third-party settlement in international agreements may, of course, vary extensively—for example, with respect to how a party may invoke such procedures; the nature of the adjudicatory body or tribunal and how it is selected; its procedure; whether its function is primarily mediation or conciliation between the parties, or whether it can reach a decision on the merits of their dispute; and whether any such decision is simply advisory or is binding on the parties. Thus, dispute settlement provisions in agreements may provide for submission of the dispute to an adjudicatory body such as the International Court of Justice, a specially established tribunal, or some other arbitral or advisory body only upon agreement of both or all parties to the dispute (which the parties can always agree to do in any case on an *ad hoc* basis even in the absence of such a provision);[106] for *compulsory* submission to the International Court, arbitration, or some other body by *any* party to the dispute;[107] for reference of the dispute to a permanent political or administrative organ, such as the assembly or council of an international organization for conciliation, mediation, or advisory or binding decision;[108] for reference of the dispute to an arbitral tribunal or body of experts for an advisory opinion;[109] and so forth. The innovative dispute settlement provisions proposed for the Law of the Sea Treaty under negotiation (as of 1980) at the Third U.N. Law of the Sea Conference would provide the parties a choice of several compulsory dispute settlement techniques; each nation has an option as to which one or more of these compulsory techniques it accepts, although each will be obligated to accept at least one such technique.[110]

Each kind of third-party dispute settlement arrangement has its own advantages, disadvantages, and problems; and techniques appropriate to one agreement may not be appropriate to another. Among the more frequent problems are lack of confidence of one or more of the parties in the third party; delay and cost in securing a relevant recommendation or determination; and questions as to the ultimate effectiveness and enforceability of any recommendation or determination.

Indeed, enforcement problems may arise even where the parties have agreed to compulsory submission of their dispute to the International Court of Justice. However, since nations have in almost all cases complied with final decisions of the International Court,[111] there is little experience as to whether or how these decisions would in practice be enforced if a party failed to comply. Under paragraph 1 of Article 94 of the U.N. Charter, each member state undertakes to comply with the decision of the International Court of Justice in any case to which it is a party. Paragraph 2 provides that in the event any party fails to perform the obligations incumbent upon it under a judgment rendered by the Court, the other party may have recourse to the Security Council, which may, if it deems necessary, make recommendations or decide upon measures to be taken to give effect to the judgment. It is not yet clear whether provisional measures of protection indicated by the International Court under Article 41 of the Statute of the Court pending its final decision in a case are embraced in paragraph 1 of Article 94 of the U.N. Charter.[112] In several recent cases—the 1972 *Fisheries Jurisdiction* cases (U.K. v. Iceland; Federal Republic of Germany v. Iceland); the 1973 *Nuclear Test* cases (Australia v. France; New Zealand v. France); and the 1979 *United States Diplomatic and Consular Staff in Tehran* case (U.S. v. Iran)[113]—the Court issued provisional orders which were ignored by the parties against whom they were directed, yet the noncomplying nations were not subjected to further sanctions. It is also not yet clear whether Article 94 endows the Security Council with an independent source of power to decide upon enforcement measures, including measures binding on all members under Article 25 of the Charter, or whether the Council's power to decide upon binding enforcement measures is confined to measures involving threats to international peace under Chapters VI and VII, and particularly decisions pursuant to Article 39, of the Charter.[114]

As has been noted, nations have generally been reluctant to agree to provisions for compulsory third-party settlement of disputes, or to invoke such provisions even when they are present in an agreement. Consequently, there may be many agreements where provisions for compulsory settlement will not be obtainable or, if they are obtainable, are not likely to be useful.

3. Compelling Performance by the Other State

A nation can seek to include in the agreement provisions which permit either it or third parties to take measures which directly compel the other nation to perform. Such techniques differ conceptually from other types of less direct sanctions (which will be discussed later) in that these other types of sanctions seek to control the other nation's behavior not through direct compulsion but rather through threatening disproportionate or punitive increases in the other nation's costs in the event of nonperformance.

a. Compelling Performance by One's Own Actions

A nation may include provisions in the agreement which legitimize its direct supervision or control of the other nation's performance. Thus, an armistice or peace agreement may provide that one nation's troops may enter and remain within the other's territory to supervise the other's destruction of certain military installations or weapons or to ensure that the other does not develop a military capability or build installations in a certain zone. For example, under the Treaty of Versailles, the Rhineland was to be occupied by the armies of the United States, Great Britain, Belgium, and France until 1935, and German troops were to be excluded from that area.[115] The 1921 Treaty of Friendship between Iran and the Soviet Union required each of the parties not to permit within its territory organizations or forces hostile to or menacing the safety of the other, and granted the Soviet Union a discretionary right of military intervention in Iran if the Soviet Union concluded that its interests were menaced.[116]

Again, in an agreement under which one nation agrees to protect certain minorities of another's national origin who reside in the first nation's territory, the second nation may attempt to secure provisions permitting it to intervene militarily if the first fails to provide such protection. For example, the 1960 Treaty of Guarantee between Cyprus, Greece, Turkey, and the United Kingdom, which was part of the London Accords establishing Cyprus's independence, guaranteed "the state of affairs established by the Basic [unamendable] Articles of the [Cypriot] Constitution," which Basic Articles were designed to protect the rights of the Turkish minority. The Treaty of Guarantee provided that, in the event of a breach of the treaty, the guarantor powers were to consult together; however, "in so far as common or concerted action may prove impossible," each reserved "the right to take action with the sole aim of reestablishing the state of affairs established by the present treaty."[117] In 1974, following an assumption of control by the Greek majority, Turkey invoked this treaty as justification for its intervention in Cyprus.

The United States has on several occasions insisted on such a right of direct action in treaties with other countries. In the 1903 U.S.–Cuba Treaty on Relations with Cuba, the United States reserved the right to intervene unilaterally in Cuba "for the preservation of Cuban independence"[118] (this right was abolished in a subsequent 1934 agreement with Cuba). The controversial DeConcini condition, passed by the U.S. Senate as an amendment to its resolution of ratification of the 1977 U.S.–Panama Treaty Concerning the Permanent Neutrality and Operation of the Panama Canal, has been argued to confer a right on the United States to intervene unilaterally to protect the neutrality of the canal following Panamanian assumption of complete control in the year 2000. As previously indicated, the reservation provides, in part: "Notwithstanding the provisions of Article V or any other provision of the Treaty, if the Canal is closed, or its operations are interfered with, the United States of

America and the Republic of Panama shall each independently have the right to take such steps as it deems necessary, in accordance with its constitutional processes, including the use of military force in the Republic of Panama, to reopen the Canal or restore the operations of the Canal, as the case may be."[119] In an attempt to meet Panamanian concern over the DeConcini amendment, the Senate subsequently passed the "leadership amendment" to the 1977 U.S.–Panama Canal Treaty, which purports to restate U.S. adherence to the principle of nonintervention.[120] The net legal effect of these several amendments remains a matter of debate.[121]

As these examples suggest, such techniques raise a variety of problems. They are capable of abuse, may involve humiliation of the nation against whom they are directed, are arguably contrary to alleged international law principles of nonintervention, may not be regarded by other nations as legitimate, and may provide tinder for future conflicts. A nation will obviously be reluctant to accept the right of another to take coercive action against it; indeed, the presence of such provisions may be used as an argument that the treaty was coerced or patently "unequal" and consequently invalid. Provisions of this type in the Versailles Treaty created lasting resentment among Germans and were an important factor in the rise of Nazism in Germany.

b. Compelling Performance through Third Parties

A nation may seek to include in an agreement provisions providing for and legitimizing a third party's assistance in compelling the other nation to perform its obligations. Thus, one nation may be willing to accept a truce or armistice agreement with another only if the other agrees that armed forces of a third party, such as the United Nations, may enter and remain within the other's territory to ensure that it does not build installations in a certain zone or use it to resume hostilities. U.N. peacekeeping forces have performed functions of this type on several occasions.[122]

Alternatively, one nation may insist on provisions in an agreement which vest third parties—such as international organizations, arbitral tribunals, or courts—with jurisdiction or authority
to order the other nation to perform its commitment in the event
it fails to do so. For example, a fisheries agreement granting one
nation the right to fish in another's coastal waters could include
provisions under which the second nation recognized the jurisdiction of the International Court to order it to perform the
agreement if it failed to do so—by, for example, interfering with
fishing by the first nation's vessels. [123] However, the issuance by
international organizations or tribunals of injunctions or orders
for specific performance raises various problems. First, the
authority of international organizations and tribunals to issue
compulsory orders binding upon nations has traditionally been
limited; as previously indicated, the binding effect of provisional orders issued even by the International Court remains
uncertain. [124] Second, such devices again depend for their credibility upon the parties' belief in the capacity and willingness of
the third party to issue such orders or injunctions; experience
suggests that when the chips are down, third parties may be
reluctant to get involved in other nations' disputes, particularly
if such involvement may threaten their own interests. Third, the
issuance of an order may not in any event suffice to make a
delinquent nation perform unless the order is supported by the
probability that, if the order is not complied with, the third party
will be able and willing to impose coercive sanctions capable of
bringing about the delinquent nation's compliance. But the
authority of international institutions to impose and enforce
coercive sanctions in support of such orders is again doubtful,
and in practice, it is questionable that any such authority would
be implemented. [125] As previously noted, in three recent cases in
which the International Court of Justice has issued interim
orders of protection—the Court's 1972 order in the *Fisheries
Jurisdiction* cases ordering Iceland to cease interfering with
British trawlers fishing off Iceland, the Court's 1973 order in the
Nuclear Tests cases ordering France to cease its testing of

nuclear weapons in the atmosphere in the South Pacific; and the Court's 1979 order in the *United States Diplomatic and Consular Staff in Tehran* case ordering Iran to release the American hostages seized in its takeover of the American embassy in Tehran[126]—neither Iceland, France, nor Iran complied with the orders, and no further concerted international action was taken to compel compliance with these orders.

Despite such problems, a nation faced with breach by its treaty partner may find resolutions by international organizations or international court orders supporting its position useful. At the least, they serve to label the other nation's breach as illegal, to place the nation protesting the breach "in the right," and to help to legitimate any further protective or self-help actions which the injured nation may decide to adopt. It was presumably for these reasons that the U.S. government in late 1979 decided to take its dispute with Iran over the holding of American hostages to the International Court, despite the fact that it was unlikely that the Iranian government would, under then-existing circumstances, respect any provisional order or final judgment by the Court ordering their release.

In view of the many practical and legal factors which weigh against third parties using coercion in such situations, nations may lack confidence that they will do so. Moreover, the difficulties of compelling action by an unwilling nation are obvious. This is particularly true where the performance one nation requires from the other is some continuing affirmative action which may vary in quality. As domestic courts have pointed out, it may be possible to compel one party to a contract to go through the motions of a required performance, but not possible to compel it to perform in a way that really provides the benefits the other party anticipated; for example, even if a court tried to order an opera singer to sing in a performance for which she had contracted, it could not compel her to sing well.[127]

4. Making Nonperformance Impossible or Impractical

A nation can increase the likelihood of the other nation's performing its obligations under an agreement by attempting to structure the agreement in such a way that it is impossible or impractical for the other nation not to perform. In some situations, this may be accomplished directly through substantive arrangements which deny the other nation the means to do otherwise than perform its commitments. For example, the Versailles Treaty sought to assure against German aggression against France by permanently demilitarizing the left bank of the Rhine and limiting German armed forces and armaments.[128] The Nuclear Non-Proliferation Treaty requires not only that the nonnuclear powers that are parties agree not to develop or acquire nuclear weapons, but that the nuclear powers that are parties agree not to transfer to other nations material, equipment, or technology capable of use in developing such weapons, except under international safeguards.[129] Conceivably, it may be possible to impose physical barriers between nations to prevent one from encroaching on the other in violation of an agreement—a "Berlin wall" or an impassable buffer zone or a radioactive barrier. Thus, teachers may prevent students from giving each other answers on examinations by putting them in separate rooms. But nonperformance may also be made impracticable through less direct techniques.

a. Dividing the Means Necessary to Accomplish a Mutual Objective

One nation might seek to ensure another's cooperation in an agreement, or at least ensure that the other cannot profit from "going it alone" in trying to attain a mutual objective of the agreement, by dividing between the two countries the means essential to attaining that objective. For example, where two nations join in a military alliance involving the deployment of nuclear weapons, and neither is willing to trust the other with a decision as to their use, they may agree that one will retain control over the nuclear warheads and the other will retain control over the launching missiles; then neither can launch armed nuclear missiles without the other's cooperation. Schelling uses as examples of this technique two people on a treasure hunt tearing the treasure map in half and each keeping one of the halves, or one partner on a hunting expedition carrying the gun and the other the ammunition.[130] "Fail-safe" techniques, which prevent the opening of a safe deposit box or the launching of a nuclear missile unless at least two persons with separate keys independently choose to combine their actions, are further examples. Neither party can attain its objectives unless there is cooperation.

Of course, this technique involves the additional risk that one nation, by refusing to cooperate, can also prevent the other from attaining its objective alone and may improperly exploit this power to extort an additional price for its cooperation. Conceivably, this additional risk could in turn be diminished by giving some trusted third party some measure of final control or a duplicate ''set of keys'' with instructions to release them to the other party under stated conditions or after a given time interval.

b. Institutionalizing ("Internalizing") the Other State's Performance within Its Own Domestic Legal System

A nation may seek provisions in the agreement which require the other nation to, in effect, institutionalize or ''internalize'' its promised performance within its own legal, administrative, or cultural system. Such techniques are among the most powerful and effective ways of increasing the probability of the other nation's performance, since they mobilize all of the pressures of that nation's domestic law and norms, as well as the considerable force of bureaucratic habit and inertia, in the direction of its compliance with its international commitments. For example, the victors in a war, wishing to ensure that the defeated nation will not again undertake aggression, may include provisions in the treaty requiring that the defeated nation amend its constitution to prohibit its government from maintaining a military force or engaging in aggressive war. This technique is suggested by Article 9 of the postwar 1946 Japanese Constitution, which provides that "the Japanese people forever renounce war as a sovereign right of the nation and the threat or use of force as a means of settling international disputes" and that "land, sea, and air forces, as well as other war potential, will never be maintained."[131] In this case, however, the constitutional provision renouncing war was not specifically required by the U.S.–Japan Peace Treaty, which was concluded only later, in 1951; and the idea for the provision originated with the Japanese rather than the American government, although General MacArthur encouraged it.[132] Again, an agreement establishing a new nation which will include ethnically or racially divided groups may require that protections for particular threatened minorities be specifically embodied in the new nation's constitution. The 1960 London Accords establishing the independence of Cyprus provided for the continuing protection of Turkish Cypriot interests through the inclusion of certain entrenched clauses in the Cyprus Constitution requiring Turkish representation at every level of the government and establishing Turkish veto power over critical decisions in most areas; the constitution provided that these key, or "basic," constitutional provisions "cannot, in any way, be amended, whether by way of variation, addition or repeal."[133] The integrity of these provisions was in turn guaranteed by a Treaty of Guarantee between Cyprus, Greece, Turkey, and the United Kingdom, which, as previously indicated, was invoked by Turkey in 1974. The development of imaginative arrangements of this type could be crucial to the solution of difficult ethnic and racial conflicts presently existing in many areas of the world, particularly the Middle East and southern Africa.

Many international agreements include provisions expressly requiring that the parties adopt internal legislation or other internal measures necessary to implement their performance of their commitments under the agreement. For example, the Universal Copyright Convention requires each party to amend its internal copyright laws to implement its obligations under the convention.[134] The 1955 Convention on the Law Applicable to Sales of Goods provides that "the Contracting States have agreed to incorporate the provisions of Articles 1–6 of this convention in the national law of their respective countries."[135] Again, the International Covenant on Civil and Political Rights provides: "Where not already provided for by existing legislative or other measures, each State Party to the present Covenant undertakes to take the necessary steps, in accordance with its constitutional processes and with the provisions of the present Covenant, to adopt such legislative or other measures as may be necessary to give effect to the rights recognized in the present Covenant."[136]

Where one nation has provisions in its internal constitution or domestic law doctrines which require that international agreements shall be treated either as overriding inconsistent domestic law, as self-executing, or as directly enforceable by domestic courts, this may have a similar effect in providing other nations assurance that it will carry out its treaty obligations. For example, Article VI of the U.S. Constitution, which provides that "Treaties . . . shall be the supreme law of the Land," makes certain "self-executing" treaties, such as commercial treaties, directly enforceable in U.S. courts.[137] Constitutional provisions of other countries, such as the Netherlands and Greece, may give international agreements an even stronger effect, in some cases (unlike the situation under U.S. law) superior even to subsequent national legislation.[138] Very far-reaching cooperative arrangements, such as the Treaty Establishing the European

Economic Community, may be interpreted as establishing an overriding, or "community," law, superior in relevant respects to the domestic law of the participating states and in certain cases requiring direct application by their domestic courts.[139]

c. Institutionalizing the Other State's Performance through Third-Party Involvement

A nation may seek to involve third parties in processes related to its treaty partner's performance. For example, in the Third U.N. Law of the Sea Conference negotiations, developing and less technologically advanced nations insisted on an arrangement for exploitation of the minerals of the seabed under which developed nations with the present technology to exploit such resources will be permitted to exploit such minerals only under the aegis of and within a framework of regulations established by an International Seabed Authority, which will be in a position to supervise their performance of their obligations under the treaty.[140] Or, conceivably, in connection with an agreement between nation A and nation B for B's payment of certain funds or furnishing of certain services to A, A might seek an arrangement which permits T, a more trustworthy state which is already obligated to make payments or perform services for B, to deduct certain payments or services from what it owes B and give them directly to A. This device would be analogous to withholding taxes or assignment, deduction, attachment, or garnishment devices in municipal law.

d. Political, Economic, or Social Integration

The most far-reaching technique nations can employ for increasing the likelihood of each other's performance of an agreement is through the establishment of common or joint ventures or supranational institutions which can directly and independently control the required performance. For example, two nations may ensure that neither violates an agreement providing for the division of the profits of an offshore oil or gas deposit lying under both of their continental shelves by providing for their joint exploration and exploitation of the deposit under a unitized management authority or limited condominium arrangement.[141] Or, two nations may attempt to ensure that neither will be in a position to violate a nonaggression agreement between them by merging into a single national entity under joint control, or, as a lesser step, by merging their coal and steel resources, armed forces, or some other resource necessary to conduct an aggressive war, into a common pool subject to joint control. The 1958 merger of Egypt and Syria into the United Arab Republic (subsequently dissolved) and the formation in 1951 of the European Coal and Steel Community are examples of such broad-ranging integration.[142] Such a supranational approach to cooperation, of course, usually involves objectives and raises issues far transcending those of risk management under relatively simple cooperative agreements.

5. Rewarding Full Performance

A nation can attempt to increase the likelihood of another nation's performance by offering it some special gain or bonus—above the gain it would normally expect from the agreement—if it performs in a particularly prompt or satisfactory manner.[143] For example, an agreement for nation A's purchase of grain from nation B may provide that, if B delivers the grain by a certain date, A will pay somewhat more than it has promised (that is, give a bonus); or that B will have to deliver somewhat less grain to A than otherwise promised (that is, receive a discount); or that A will make some additional side payment to B, such as providing B certain favorable credit terms or technical assistance. Or an agreement may provide a special benefit, reward, recognition, or prize for a nation which fully or best performs its obligations under the agreement.[144] Human experience suggests that special recognition or honors may be effective incentives which could be made more use of in international affairs. Or one nation party to an agreement may indicate to another that its willingness to enter into other and perhaps more desired and favorable agreements with the other nation will depend on how well the other nation performs its commitments in the present agreement. As has been indicated, a nation's interest in establishing a general reputation for trustworthiness, as an aid to its ability to negotiate other agreements with either its present treaty partner or others in the future, will, in any event, furnish a strong incentive for it to fully perform its obligations. Finally, a system of future rewards may be built directly into the agreement. For example, the quotas granted to the different nations parties during one period of a fisheries or commodity agreement can be made to depend on each nation's performance during past periods of the arrangement, with a nation being entitled to possible additions to its quota only upon a showing of full compliance. Incentives of all these types are, of course, common in private employment and business arrangements.

6. Decreasing the Probability of the Other State's Gaining from Nonperformance

A nation will have more incentive to perform (or, put otherwise, less incentive not to perform) its obligations under an agreement with another nation if it believes there is little likelihood of its realizing any significant potential gain from nonperformance or breach of the agreement. Consequently, nation A, in negotiating an agreement with nation B, will typically put considerable emphasis on risk-management techniques designed either (1) to ensure that B cannot secure A's performance without giving B's own performance in return; (2) to subject B to collateral equivalent loss if B attempts to retain A's performance without giving B's own performance; or (3) to subject B to penalties for nonperformance or breach which will cancel out whatever gains it may hope to achieve by such nonperformance.

a. Conditioning One's Own Performance on the Other State's Performance

Perhaps the oldest and most common technique human beings have devised for protecting against the risk of nonperformance in a cooperative arrangement is the device of conditioning one's own performance on the other party's performance. This technique serves to protect nation A in an agreement with nation B in that, if B fails to perform, A can simply withhold its own performance. But this technique also increases the probability of performance by B, since, unless B performs, it cannot receive the reciprocal performance it wants from A. Devices relating to the order or timing of performance are the best-known examples of this technique.[145] This technique has the virtue of self-help—that is, it can be implemented by nation A itself. But it also has certain drawbacks.

(i) *Making the other state perform first.* The most obvious and effective way in which one nation can condition its own performance on another nation's performance is by making the other nation perform first. For example, nation A may be willing to agree that it will withdraw from territory of nation B that it occupies only if B agrees first to cease belligerent actions against A. Israel has taken a position similar to this regarding withdrawal from Arab territories it occupies. This technique has several limitations.

First, devices based on the timing of performance cannot protect both parties simultaneously; both nations cannot go last. Thus, in the example above, nation B may respond to nation A's proposal by saying that it is willing to agree to cease belligerent actions against A only if A agrees first to withdraw from B's territory which it occupies. Certain Arab states have in fact taken this position regarding peace negotiations with Israel. Where there is strong initial distrust on each side, this problem of timing may be difficult to resolve, and the two parties may reach an impasse in their negotiations. Thus, the 1967 U.N. Security Council Resolution 242 on the Middle East deliberately left this question of timing of performance between Israel and the Arab countries unanswered, and has spawned continuing debate.[146] The relevant paragraph provides that the Security Council

1. Affirms that the fulfillment of Charter principles requires the establishment of a just and lasting peace in the Middle East which should include the application of both the following principles:

(i) Withdrawal of Israel armed forces from territories occupied in the recent conflict;

(ii) Termination of all claims or states of belligerency and respect for and acknowledgement of the sovereignty, territorial integrity and political independence of every state in the area and their right to live in peace within secure and recognized boundaries free from threats or acts of force.[147]

The resolution is silent as to which of these principles is to be met first. Of course, several parties negotiating a series of continuing transactions with or among each other can achieve a compromise by sharing this risk concerning the timing of performance; that is, they can take turns at going first.

Second, there are many types of agreements in which it is not practical to control risk by making the other party go first. For example, where one nation agrees to help another to construct a dam on condition that the other will thereupon furnish the first nation a portion of the power generated or water resources made available by the dam, performance by the first nation in helping to construct the dam must obviously come first. Again, if one nation agrees to furnish another nuclear material to fuel a power reactor on the condition that this material not be diverted to weapons purposes, performance by the supplier nation must obviously precede performance by the recipient nation. Moreover, many types of arrangements contemplate a number of complex and continuing performances by both nations in which it is impossible to say which nation goes first and which goes last. While in some cases it may be possible to segment such arrangements into a series of discrete transactions with a specific order of performance, in many cases it may not.

(ii) *Simultaneous exchange.* Simultaneous exchange is also a venerable technique for dealing with the risks of performance where the parties distrust each other and cannot agree on which will go first or last. Deutsch notes: ''Simple examples of simultaneity of giving and receiving are to be found in the actions of children exchanging toys. Typically, each child holds onto his own toy as he takes the toy of the other child. He releases his toy gradually (i.e., he can grab it again) as he feels the other child releasing his toy. The process is reversible until the exchange has been completed. When the objects to be exchanged are divisible, simultaneity of exchange is often achieved by exchange of one unit at a time.''[148] In international dealings two nations, each of which holds hostages or prisoners of war belonging to the other, may agree to exchange these prisoners through arrangements under which the group held by each nation will at a given time and location move simultaneously to the control of its own government or a third party across a common bridge or border. This type of technique was employed in the prisoners-of-war exchange at Panmunjom following the 1953 Korean armistice between the United Nations Command and North Korean and Chinese People's volunteer forces.[149] It is also illustrated by the exchange between Israel and the Popular Front for the Liberation of Palestine of sixty-six Palestinian prisoners held by Israel for one Israeli soldier captured by the Popular Front, which took place at the Geneva Airport in

July 1979 under the auspices of the International Committee of the Red Cross. The *New York Times* reported:

> It took four hours to complete the exchange because of the "deep suspicion" [between the parties]. . . .
>   . . . the two planes . . . were parked out of sight of each other. The prisoner exchange took place shortly after 10 A.M. An airport passenger bus with the Red Cross symbol carried the Palestinians, and a minibus of the International Committee carried Private Amram. The two vehicles passed as they went from one plane to the other. . . .
>   . . . In another sign of mistrust, Palestinian officials did not permit their prisoner to leave their plane to sit in the Red Cross minibus a few yards away to await the exchange until assured by walkie-talkie that half the Palestinian prisoners had been checked out of the Israeli plane onto the airport bus.[150]

If spy novels and movies are to be believed, this technique is also used by governments for exchanges of captured intelligence agents.

One problem with this technique is that exact simultaneity may be difficult or impossible to arrange. Since an untrustworthy partner, once it has what it wants in hand, may try to cheat on the deal by keeping what it wants without paying the agreed price, the timing of exchange must sometimes be very exact. This problem is illustrated in an episode of Gogol's novel *Dead Souls*, where two characters, Chichikov and Sobakievich, are haggling over the amount of an advance on Sobakievich's sale of certain peasants to Chichikov. Chichikov finally offers Sabokievich fifteen more rubles, saying:

> "May I have a receipt?"
> "And why do you want a receipt?"
> "It's always better to have one. In a bad hour anything might happen."
> "Very well, but let me have the money!"
> "Why do you want the money? I've got it here in my hand! As soon as you write out the receipt you will have it immediately."
> "But, pray, how am I to make out a receipt without first seeing the money?"

The problem of mutual distrust is finally solved as follows:

Chichikov let Sobakievich take the notes. Approaching the table and putting the fingers of his left hand over them, he then scribbled with his other hand on a bit of paper a statement to the effect that he had duly received an advance of twenty-five roubles in banknotes for the sale of the souls.[151]

(iii) *Withholding further performance.* Where one nation has already carried out one or more of a series of continuing performances at the time it becomes aware that its treaty partner will not perform, or at least will not perform fully, it can partially protect itself by reciprocally withholding its own further performances. Since many agreements—trade agreements, tax agreements, arms control agreements, and so forth—call for continuing performances, this technique potentially has a wide application.

A right of one party to withhold its performance in the event of the other party's nonperformance of its obligations can be expressly provided for in an agreement. For example, the Universal Postal Convention provides that, when a country fails to observe the provisions respecting freedom of transit of mail, the postal administrations of the other countries may discontinue their postal services with that country.[152] From 1978, U.S. atomic energy cooperation agreements with other nations must, as mandated by the 1978 U.S. Nuclear Non-Proliferation Act, include provisions granting the United States the right to cease cooperation if the president of the United States finds that the receiving state has terminated or abrogated the International Atomic Energy Agency safeguards required by such agreements, or has materially violated an IAEA safeguards agreement.[153]

Again, a tariff agreement may provide that, if one nation party fails to accord the other the reductions it promised, or otherwise nullifies or impairs the other party's rights under the agreement, the nation deprived of such benefits may retaliate by reciprocally suspending its provision of benefits to the non-complying nation, either by its own decision or following a decision by some third party. Article XXIII of the General

Agreement on Tariffs and Trade, which is entitled ''Nullification and Impairment,'' is an interesting example of a provision permitting the suspension or withholding of performance in such cases following a conciliation process and with the approval of the GATT Contracting Parties, acting as a group. Article XXIII provides:

1. If any contracting party should consider that any benefit accruing to it directly or indirectly under this Agreement is being nullified or impaired or that the attainment of any objective of the Agreement is being impeded as the result of

(a) failure of another contracting party to carry out its obligations under this Agreement, or

(b) the application by another contracting party of any measure, whether or not it conflicts with the provisions of this Agreement, or

(c) the existence of any other situation, the contracting party may, with a view to the satisfactory adjustment of the matter, make written representations or proposals to the other contracting party or parties which it considers to be concerned. Any contracting party thus approached shall give sympathetic consideration to the representations or proposals made to it.

2. If no satisfactory adjustment is effected between the contracting parties concerned within a reasonable time, or if the difficulty is of the type described in paragraph 1(c) of this Article, the matter may be referred to the CONTRACTING PARTIES. The CONTRACTING PARTIES shall promptly investigate any matter so referred to them and shall make appropriate recommendations to the contracting parties which they consider to be concerned, or give a ruling on the matter, as appropriate. The CONTRACTING PARTIES may consult with contracting parties, with the Economic and Social Council of the United Nations and with any appropriate inter-governmental organization in cases where they consider such consultation necessary. If the CONTRACTING PARTIES consider that the circumstances are serious enough to justify such action, they may authorize a contracting party or parties to suspend the application to any other contracting party or parties of such concessions or other obligations under this Agreement as they determine to be appropriate in the circumstances. If the application to any contracting party of any concession or other obligation is in fact suspended, that contracting party shall then be free, not later than sixty days after such action is taken, to give written notice to the Executive Secretary to the CONTRACTING PARTIES of its intention to withdraw from this Agreement and such withdrawal shall take effect upon the sixtieth day following the day on which such notice is received by him.

The Contracting Parties have authorized such a suspension in only one instance—an authorization in 1955 to the Netherlands to suspend its GATT concessions for wheat flour to the United States and impose discriminatory quotas in retaliation for U.S. import restrictions on dairy products from the Netherlands. The Netherlands did not actually exercise this authority, however.[154]

Alternatively, a nation may choose to rely on general doctrines of treaty law which permit it either to terminate a treaty or to suspend the performance of its obligations under a treaty in the event of a material breach by its treaty partner.[155] This right is expressly recognized by Article 60, paragraph 1, of the Vienna Convention on the Law of Treaties, which provides that "[a] material breach of a bilateral treaty by one of the parties entitles the other to invoke the breach as a ground for terminating the treaty or suspending its operation in whole or in part." Succeeding paragraphs of Article 60 provide similar rights for parties to multilateral treaties and define the concept of "material breach."[156]

This principle has broad application. For example, if the United States and Mexico have concluded a commercial air transport agreement providing that carriers of each can pick up or discharge passengers at certain designated cities of the other, and Mexico refuses to allow an American carrier to exercise privileges accorded by the agreement, the United States can, even in the absence of any specific provision in the agreement to that effect, refuse to allow Mexican commercial aircraft to pick up or discharge passengers at U.S. airports. Again, if the Soviet Union breached the Nuclear Test Ban Treaty by conducting tests in the atmosphere, the United States would under these doctrines of treaty law, even in the absence of specific provision in the treaty, correspondingly be released from its obligation not to conduct such tests.[157] This principle was invoked by former Secretary of State Kissinger in a July 1977 statement to a congressional committee in which he took the position that

North Vietnam's violation of the U.S.–South Vietnam–North Vietnam Truce Agreement of 1973 had relieved the United States of its alleged promise to provide up to $4.75 billion for the postwar reconstruction of North Vietnam. Dr. Kissinger argued that ''for them to try to hold us to an obligation when they have violated nearly every provision of the agreement strikes me as an absurdity.''[158] (It is interesting that, while it has been common for one nation to suspend the performance of its obligations under an agreement on the basis of alleged breach by the other, the right to abrogate or annul an agreement on these grounds has been exercised rarely, and has apparently never been adjudicated in an international tribunal.)[159]

This technique will clearly be most effective in protecting a nation if it is ahead of the game—that is, if the value of its remaining performances exceed those which its noncomplying treaty partner still has to render. If the situation is the opposite, a nation is likely to incur some losses, though they will be less severe than if it had to complete its performance despite its partner's breach. Moreover, as with many sanctions, this technique may have political and other costs, and nations are not likely to assert a right to suspend performance or abrogate an agreement on grounds of breach lightly.

(iv) *Breaking the arrangement into parts.* As previously indicated, a larger or continuing arrangement can sometimes be segmented or broken down into a series of smaller discrete transactions, with each nation's performance of each segment conditioned on the other's performance of the previous segment. Thus, a truce, armistice, or military disengagement agreement may comprise a series of increasingly significant reciprocal steps by each nation, with performance of each phase by one party contingent on satisfactory performance of the preceding phase by the other. The 1975 Egypt-Israel Sinai Agreement, for example, includes a protocol establishing a detailed day-by-day schedule or timetable for phased withdrawals from occupied land and transfers of territory by Israel, Egypt, and the U.N. Emergency Force.[160] The release by North Vietnam of American prisoners of war and the withdrawal by the United States of American troops from Vietnam under the 1973 Vietnam Truce Agreement followed a similar phased pattern.[161] Under this type of arrangement, a nation will never be far ahead of its treaty partner in its performance, and if its partner fails to comply with a particular segment, its losses will generally be limited to that single segment.

(v) *Performance held by third party (escrow).* One way of dealing with the problem of timing of performance in an agreement is through arrangements for the exchange of one or both performances through a trusted third party which is under instructions to deliver each party's performance to the other only when the other party's performance is received. Deutsch comments:

> Third parties may provide the arrangements by which simultaneity of exchange is achieved. The third party may, for example, serve as a transfer agent who receives the contributions and passes them on to the other person only *after* both parties have contributed. Or, a third party may function as an observer who is able to confirm for each party that the other is not attempting to dupe him. Moreover, the third party may be able to deter violations of an exchange by the penalties and punishments that he is able and willing to employ against a violator. It is evident that for a third party to play a facilitating role in an exchange, he must be viewed as neutral, competent, and motivated to facilitate the exchange.[162]

The use of a third party provides much of the protection of simultaneity without in fact requiring simultaneous performance by the nations concerned. The function of the escrow agent is analogous to that of a stake holder: providing assurance that a nation will actually receive its treaty partner's performance if it performs its own part of the deal and thus becomes entitled to it.

For example, nation A and nation B may be prepared to agree that A will withdraw its military forces from B's territory in exchange for B's return of certain prisoners of war. However, the two nations may distrust each other, and each may believe that, if it performs first, that the other will not carry out its part of the bargain. In this case, the two nations may agree that B will deliver the prisoners to T, a third state or international organization trusted by both parties, with instructions that T deliver them to A only when A's forces are in fact withdrawn. In the agreement between the United States and Iran resolving the hostage situation, signed in Algiers January 19, 1981, the parties dealt with problems of mutual distrust and timing of performance in the exchange of American hostages held by Iran for Iranian assets held by the United States through the two governments' designation of the government of Algeria as intermediary and escrow agent.[163] Algeria's role was a key factor in the success of the negotiations. Again, in the context of an arms control agreement requiring the destruction of certain weapons, nation A and nation B might conceivably agree to deliver the relevant arms to T, which is instructed by both parties to destroy these arms only after both nations have relinquished their arms, but otherwise, to return the complying nation's arms to that nation.

Escrow devices can typically be used only when at least one of the performances involves something discrete and tangible that can be physically transferred through a third party. Analogous devices can be developed, however. Thus, an agreement between two nations involving a transfer of territory can be implemented through a temporary transfer of control of the territory to a third state or international organization, which can assert such control through a temporary stationing of its military or administrative personnel there. Indeed, analogous techniques might be used in attempting to forge agreements to deal with problems involving internal ethnic or racial divisions, as in southern Africa or Lebanon. For example, one potential obstacle to compromise arrangements is that neither whites nor blacks, Christians nor Moslems, may be prepared irrevocably to yield control over military or police forces to each other. But they might be willing to yield such control on a temporary basis to some neutral third party, such as an international organization, under conditions which would allow either party to recall its supporters participating in such forces if the other party failed to live up to the arrangement.

Of course, escrow devices can work only if both parties have trust in the escrow agent's honesty and neutrality, and both believe that the escrow agent will be willing and able to carry out its assignment. Moreover, the role of escrow agent can be demanding and uncomfortable, particularly if the agent must judge whether each of the parties has performed as promised; and third nations or international organizations may be reluctant to accept such an assignment.

b. Providing for the Recovery of One's Own Performance

Where one nation has to perform its part of the arrangement first, it can seek to protect itself against the risk that the other nation may then fail to perform through provisions which permit it, in the event of the other's nonperformance, to recover its performance from the other. Such techniques can ordinarily be used only when the performance given by the nation which performs first is tangible or otherwise of such a nature that it is susceptible of recovery.

For example, many U.S. agreements for atomic energy cooperation give the United States the right to require, in certain circumstances, the return of nuclear material and equipment supplied under the agreement, or of nuclear material produced through their use, when a recipient nation has failed to comply with the safeguards requirement in the agreement;[164] the 1978 U.S. Non-Nuclear Proliferation Act provides more broadly that new or amended agreements must contain a stipulation providing for such a right of return if the recipient nation detonates a nuclear explosive device or terminates or abrogates an agree-

ment providing for IAEA safeguards.[165] Thus, the U.S.–
Austria Agreement for Cooperation Concerning Civil Uses of
Atomic Energy provides: ''In the event of non-compliance with
the provisions of this Article or the guarantees set forth in Article
XI and the failure of the Government of the Republic of Austria
to carry out the provisions of this Article within a reasonable
time,'' the United States shall have the right ''to suspend or
terminate this Agreement and to require the return of any materials, equipment and devices referred to in paragraph B(2) of this
Article.''[166] U.S. atomic energy cooperation agreements also
typically contain provisions requiring U.S. consent with respect
to the retransfer to third countries of supplied items or special
nuclear material produced through the use of supplied items.[167]

Similarly, military assistance agreements might provide for
the return of material or weapons furnished in the event of
misuse in violation of the conditions of the agreement. In practice, however, the United States has not included such a provision in its military assistance agreements, presumably because it
would be both politically awkward and physically difficult to
enforce. While Section 505 of the U.S. Foreign Assistance Act
of 1961, as amended, provides that no defense articles shall be
furnished any country on a grant basis unless it agrees not to use
or permit the use of articles for purposes other than those for
which furnished, and to ''return to the United States Government . . . such articles . . . which are no longer needed for the
purposes for which furnished,''[168] the sanction usually applied
by the United States in cases of misuse of assistance is the
cutting off of further assistance. As indicated, Turkey's alleged
use of American arms in its intervention in Cyprus in 1974 led to
the enactment of legislation terminating military aid to Turkey,
an embargo which was not lifted until late 1978.[169]

However, a nation cannot easily recover its performance
when this performance consists, for example, of special treatment which it has already provided to its treaty partner's nationals under a commercial treaty, or of food furnished to

another nation under an aid agreement which the other nation has already distributed or consumed. Moreover, attempts to recover a performance already in another nation's hands obviously pose particular difficulties and risks and may, if the other nation resists return of the performance, require coercive measures either by the nation seeking to recover the performance alone or with the assistance of third parties. Nevertheless, there are various ways in which a nation can increase the likelihood that it will be able to recover its performance from another nation in the event the other fails to comply with its obligations.

(i) *Retention of rights to the performance despite delivery.* A nation can seek to legitimize its attempt to recover its performance in the event of its treaty partner's default through various devices which maintain its "title" to the performance, either indefinitely or pending full performance by the other nation. Such devices are analogous to such familiar commercial security techniques as conditional sales, trusts, leases, and reversion provisions in concession agreements. For example, one nation may lease rather than sell special nuclear material to another nation for use in nuclear reactors, making clear its claim to recover the nuclear material if the other nation seeks to divert the material to weapons use or otherwise fails to perform the conditions of the lease. This device has been used in some U.S. atomic energy cooperation agreements with other countries.[170]

(ii) *Requiring special measures by the other state to protect or permit recovery of the performance.* A nation may facilitate its recovery of its performance through provisions which require the recipient nation to take special measures to segregate or safeguard that performance pending its own full performance of its side of the agreement. For example, a nation supplying special nuclear material to another under an atomic energy agreement might require that the other nation specifically agree to segregate this material, to utilize it only in a particular reactor in which it is accessible to recovery by the supplier, or to place it under the physical control of some trusted third party which is for this purpose allowed to maintain possession of the material within the other nation's territory.[171]

(iii) *Providing for third-party assistance to compel restitution.* An agreement may specifically provide for the intervention, if necessary, of third parties to assist one of the parties to obtain recovery or restitution of its performance if it has performed its side of the arrangement but the other party fails to do so, and the parties may collaterally obtain third-party guarantees of such assistance. For example, nation A may agree to return to B certain territory of B's which A has occupied in recent armed conflict on the understanding that B will not place military forces in the area and that, if B does attempt to militarize the area, A will be entitled to call on the assistance of third states or an international organization in reestablishing A's control or at least reestablishing a demilitarized buffer zone. Provisions for International Atomic Energy Agency involvement in obtaining return of special nuclear materials from receiving nations not complying with agency safeguards are another example. Article XII of the Statute of the International Atomic Energy Agency provides that if a nation receiving nuclear materials and assistance from a supplying nation under agency safeguards fails to take requested steps to correct a deficiency in its performance of its obligations under the safeguards agreement within a reasonable time, the IAEA may, by a decision of the board of governors, "suspend or terminate assistance and withdraw any materials and equipment made available by the Agency or a member in furtherance of the project."[172] Trilateral agreements providing for the application of IAEA safeguards to special nuclear materials furnished under a bilateral atomic energy agreement typically provide expressly that the IAEA governing board may, in cases of noncompliance, "call for the supplying state to call for the return of the equipment, devices and material which have been made available to the recipient state.''[173] More generally, a nation may simply seek agreement that it can submit the question of its treaty partner's noncompliance to an international organization, international arbitration, or an international tribunal, which can order restitutionary as well as other remedies.

But while third parties may be willing to legitimate and lend approval and moral force to a nation's own attempts to recover its performance in cases of this sort, they will usually be less willing to become directly involved in coercive intervention. As the president of Mexico said in explaining Mexico's refusal in late 1979 to allow the Shah of Iran to return to Mexico from the United States, where he had been receiving medical treatment, despite Mexico's apparent promise to do so, a nation may not want to embroil itself in ''a conflict which is not ours.''[174]

c. Requiring the Other State to Furnish Collateral or Bond

The use of collateral, deposits, or performance bonds as security for one party against another's nonperformance is common in private contracts, but less common in international agreements. The technique involves, of course, one party's placing something equivalent in value to its performance in the custody of the other party, with the understanding that the other party will be able to keep or sell the collateral if it does not perform. Macneil refers to techniques of this type as ''planning to keep ahead of the game.''[175] This type of security device differs from security devices such as hostage, pawn, or pledge in that the latter may involve a loss or forfeiture by a defaulting nation exceeding the value of the performance it agreed to render and thus may have a punitive or coercive influence in discouraging nonperformance or breach. For example, as security for its promise to pay for certain goods which nation A has agreed to supply it, nation B might agree to transfer title to or ''mortgage'' certain property it owns in A's or a third nation's territory, of a value equivalent to the price of the goods, subject to the condition that title will revert to B upon B's full payment for the goods supplied.

One problem with security devices involving collateral is that it may be difficult or impossible to place a monetary or other value on a particular promised performance, and thus to agree on an equivalent value for the collateral. Another problem is that, if the parties distrust each other, the party asked for collateral may be afraid to place it in the other party's control, fearing that the other may retain the collateral even if full performance is made. For example, tenants may have great difficulty in getting landlords to return damage deposits. This difficulty can be met by entrusting the collateral to a mutually trusted third party in an arrangement analogous to that involved in escrow.

d. Providing for Third-Party Assistance to Compel Payment Equivalent in Value to Performance

Nation A may seek to deny nation B the possibility of gaining from nonperformance or inadequate performance through devices which utilize third-party assistance—such as assistance by another state, international organization, or international tribunal—to compel B in the event of its nonperformance to pay A the value of that expected performance. A commodity agreement establishing export quotas may provide that the governing council of the commodity organization may deduct amounts by which a member nation has exceeded its quotas in one period from future quota allocations made to that nation; indeed, the agreement may provide that the council can impose further punitive sanctions on a noncomplying nation in the event of repeated violations. The various international coffee agreements set forth an elaborate scheme of escalating sanctions of this type.[176] Again, a tariff reduction agreement may provide that any party may refer a dispute regarding another party's failure to reduce tariffs to an international organization or institution (such as the Contracting Parties to the General Agreement on Tariffs and Trade, an arbitral tribunal, or an international court), which may require the noncomplying party to pay damages to the injured party equal to the expected value to that party of the tariff reductions or other concessions which it has failed to grant. If a nation party to an agreement believes that it will be required by a third party to give the value of its performance in any case, it will have little incentive not to give the performance in the first place.

This technique has, of course, a number of limitations common to all techniques involving third-party dispute settlement. As has been suggested, a nation may lack confidence in the impartiality, fairness, or competence of the third party; in the third party's willingness or political courage to reach a judgment that a noncomplying nation should pay damages in such a case; in the noncomplying nation's willingness to respond to such a judgment; or in the willingness or ability of the third party to enforce its judgment through coercive sanctions if a noncomplying nation refuses to respect such a decision. Moreover, the value of the prospective performance may be difficult to assess, and the authority of international institutions or courts to order the payment of such expectancy damages is less than clear.

e. Preventing the Other State from Exploiting One's Vulnerability

A nation may be concerned that its performance of its obligations under an agreement may make it especially vulnerable, and that its treaty partner may be tempted to breach the agreement in order to exploit that vulnerability and subject it to loss. This may particularly be so when the agreement is entered into in the context of broader competitive relations, as in the case of an armistice or an arms control agreement. For example, Israel is clearly concerned that its withdrawal from the Sinai, under the terms of the 1979 Egypt-Israel Peace Treaty, will make Israel more vulnerable to attack, and that this increased vulnerability may tempt Egypt to take advantage of the situation by attacking Israel in violation of its commitment to renounce the use of force against Israel. Consequently, Israel has been careful to include in the treaty measures designed to reduce its vulnerability and losses in the event Egypt attacks—not only to protect itself against the risk of such an attack if it does occur, but also because Egypt is less likely to attack in breach of the agreement if it believes that such an attack will gain it little or nothing. These techniques will be separately and more fully discussed in Section 8.

7. Making Nonperformance Costly

A nation will be more likely to perform its obligations under an agreement with another nation if it believes that it will be more costly for it not to perform than to perform (or, put otherwise, less costly for it to perform than not to perform). Consequently, a nation concerned with the risk that its treaty partner may not perform will seek to structure the agreement in such a way, or to provide collateral arrangements, so that the other nation will not only not gain by breach, but will suffer some penalty, detriment, or loss. These techniques will typically consist of provisions for punitive sanctions, imposed either by the injured nation itself, or by or with the assistance of third parties. The effectiveness of any potential sanctions in deterring a nation from deliberate breach of an agreement will depend both on that nation's perceptions of the probable cost to it if sanctions are imposed, as compared with what it believes it can gain from breach, and on its perceptions as to likelihood that such sanctions will in fact be imposed. That is, the prospect of sanctions will deter a nation from deliberately choosing not to perform its obligations only if it considers the loss it will suffer from imposition of sanctions, discounted by the probability of their imposition, as likely to cost it more than it can expect to gain from nonperformance.

There are, of course, a wide range of possible sanctions and sanctioning techniques. The subject of sanctions and deterrence strategies is extensively discussed in other writings;[177] therefore, it will be dealt with only briefly here. However, since popular discussions of techniques for inducing compliance with international treaties and other obligations often focus on the concept of punitive sanctions, it is worth pointing out that the disadvantages of such techniques often outweigh their advantages. Among the problems raised by sanctions are (1) the sanctions may not be credible, in the sense that the target nation does not believe they either will or can be effectively imposed and applied; (2) sanctions may involve costs not only for the target nation but also for the nation or nations imposing the sanctions; (3) sanctions, if imposed, may lead to resentment, increased intransigence, and further breach of international commitments by the target nation, rather than to compliance, making negotiated settlement more difficult; and (4) sanctions, if imposed, may lead to retaliatory action by the target nation, thus escalating the dispute or threatening peace. Indeed, the mere inclusion of provisions for sanctions in an agreement may pose a special kind of dilemma for nations parties: to use them may accomplish little or make matters worse; not to use them may suggest weakness or lack of will and deprive the sanctions of future credibility. If it is unlikely that the nations concerned will be prepared to actually invoke sanctions against a non-complying party, it may be better to omit such provisions from an agreement.

Some principal types of sanctioning techniques include those discussed below.

a. Forfeiture or Loss of Prepayment, Part Performance, or Reliance Costs

Where the agreement is structured so that nation A obtains at least some performance from nation B prior to A's giving its own performance to B, A may wish the agreement to further provide it the right not only to withhold its further performance but also to retain B's partial performance as a penalty if B fails to complete its performance. For example, if the United States is concerned that another nation with which it is entering into an agreement to sell grain may renege on its commitment to take and pay for the grain, the United States might require that the other nation prepay to it as earnest money one-quarter of the total cost of the grain, that the other nation also pay for all shipments as they occur, and that the United States be allowed to retain the other nation's prepayment as a forfeit in the event that it fails to pay for any shipment or otherwise breaches the agreement. In effect, the United States is always "ahead" of the other nation with respect to its position under the agreement, and the other nation will incur a loss by stopping performance.

In some situations a nation may have already incurred substantial preperformance costs in preparing to carry out an agreement, costs which it can recover only through its treaty partner's performance of the agreement. In this case, the threat that it may lose this investment if it subsequently fails to perform and its treaty partner consequently does likewise may similarly deter it from breach, even though no forfeiture to the other party is involved. In general, to the extent that an agreement requires a party to make a substantial investment in preparing for its performance, that party is more likely to carry through on its performance. For example, the United States, as a condition of entering into a mutual defense arrangement with another nation, might conceivably require that the other nation use its own funds to construct substantial military facilities capable of being effectively used only by U.S. or the two nations' joint forces. If the other nation subsequently reneges on the agreement and decides not to permit the United States to use these facilities, it will have wasted these expenditures. Of course, if the other nation believes that it will gain more by escaping from the agreement that it will lose by wasting this investment, it may decide to breach the agreement anyway.

b. Deposit of Collateral, Hostage, or Pawn Greater in Value Than Either State's Performance

Hostage devices were one of the earliest techniques devised to protect against the risks of nonperformance in international agreements.[178] While such devices are rarely expressly included in international agreements, the possibility or implied threat that one party may decide to retaliate against the nationals, property, or interests of the other in the event of the other's breach may play an analogous role. Such techniques are, of course, not uncommon in private transactions and relationships.

The way such techniques work is generally familiar. As part of their agreement, nation A will require nation B to deposit or place within A's control some type of collateral, pawn, or hostage which has a value to B greater than the value to B of either B's or A's performance, with the understanding that A may keep or destroy the collateral, pawn, or hostage if B fails to perform its obligations under the agreement. A may be prepared to let a third party hold the hostage so long as the third party's commitment to transfer the hostage to A or retain or destroy the hostage itself in the event of B's failure to perform is credible. This technique places pressure on B to perform without regard to the order of each nation's performance. That is, regardless of whether A has performed first or not, it is still less costly to B to perform than to lose, by reason of its nonperformance, its collateral, pawn, or hostage. Thus, it is not important that the hostage, collateral, or pawn be of value to the nation holding it, but only that it be of more value to the nation giving it than either nation's performance under the agreement. For example, in connection with an agreement under which one nation agrees to a long-term purchase of oil from another, the purchasing nation might require the supplying nation to make substantial investments in property in the purchasing nation exceeding the value of the oil arrangement, with the understanding that the purchasing nation will be entitled to seize these investments if the supplying nation cuts off the supply of oil. Or, more realistically, a purchasing nation may, outside the terms of the agreement, communicate the threat that it will seize the supplying nation's existing investments in the purchasing nation, which are worth more than the value of the oil supply agreement to either party, if the supplying nation refuses to honor its commitment and cuts off the supply of oil. Again, it has been suggested that one way of making two nations comply with a nonaggression pact would be to have the agreement provide for each to move particular individuals of particular importance to it, or certain numbers of its nationals, to locations where the other could credibly retaliate against them if the first nation attempted to cheat on the agreement by launching an attack.

The efficacy of the device depends, of course, upon the credibility to the nation considering breach of its treaty partner's threat to keep or destroy the hostage. Thus, the technique may be more useful to nations which have a reputation for ruthlessness than to those which can be expected to be "soft-hearted" and observe "civilized" and humanitarian notions. For thousands of years human beings could serve as hostages because nations were generally quite prepared to keep or kill them if the other party broke its agreement. While this practice fell into disuse in more modern times, current developments—such as the holding of the American diplomats as hostage in Iran, the holding of Israeli air passengers at Entebbe Airport by Uganda, and the activities of various "liberation" groups—suggest that use of threats against innocent individuals or groups as an instrument of international political policy is again becoming credible, despite the fact that such acts are now probably in violation of international law.[179] The strategic doctrine of ''deterrence'' through mutual assured destruction assumes that the population centers of the United States and the Soviet Union will in effect serve as hostages for each nation's behavior, since each nation will believe that if it launches a ''first strike'' of nuclear weapons against the other, the other will be both willing and capable of retaliating against it by destroying these ''hostages.''

A nation may be reluctant to supply a hostage or deposit of value to another, even if it intends and expects to perform its obligations in good faith, for fear that the other, once it has the hostage under its control, will use the hostage as the basis for extorting some special advantage beyond what it is due under the agreement. Indeed, even a mutual exchange of hostages of equivalent value between nations may raise certain problems. Conceivably, in this situation nation A might try to use nation B's hostage not only to secure B's performance but also to protect the hostage A has given to B from B's retaliation in the event of A's nonperformance, and vice versa. For example, if A and B exchange hostages to secure their mutual performance of a nonaggression agreement, B may nevertheless feel free to attack A, since it can meet A's threat to punish B's hostage (which A holds) by counter-threatening that, if its hostage is harmed, it will in turn punish A's hostage (which B holds). Mutual deterrence theorists have wrestled at length with analogous ''Mexican standoff'' problems. Once again, escrow third-party techniques may offer a solution to this dilemma.

Various types of ''self-executing'' or ''automatic'' hostage mechanisms have been proposed. For example, Schelling suggests that an agreement between two nations not to use nuclear weapons against each other's capital cities might be made effective through arrangements to exchange certain numbers of their school children, who would be educated for the year in each other's capital cities and would serve as automatic hostages for each other's performance of the agreement.[180] A similar function could be performed by any arrangement under which a nation's breach of an agreement would automatically and necessarily cause it unacceptable loss—for example, a "doomsday" nuclear device positioned in a nation's territory and designed to explode automatically if that nation launched its nuclear missiles. More realistically, a promise by one nation to come to another's assistance in the event of an attack by a third nation will be more credible if the first nation assigns some of its own military forces to the territory of the nation it has agreed to help, since the second nation will assume that the first will not allow its own troops to be sacrificed. The stationing of U.S. troops in Germany and Korea, and of U.S. civilian technicians in the Sinai under the 1975 Egypt-Israel Sinai Agreement, probably serves this kind of "hostage" function as well as other purposes.

More generally, any property or nationals of one party physically located within its treaty partner's territory or control may serve as hostages for its compliance. Thus, even in the absence of any specific provisions for sanctions in an agreement, one party will have to consider the possibility that the other will find some way of effectively retaliating in the event of its breach. Few nations are either invulnerable or indifferent to the possibility of such retaliation. During the 1979–80 U.S.-Iranian hostage crisis, the United States eventually reacted to Iran's seizure and holding hostage of U.S. diplomats in Tehran by freezing some $8 billion of Iranian assets in the United States, declaring Iranian diplomats in the United States *persona non grata* and requiring them to leave, and taking steps to revoke the visas of certain Iranian students and other nationals in the United States, as well as by taking other retaliatory measures such as prohibiting most exports to, imports from, travel to, and financial transactions with Iran.[181] It is interesting, however, that Iran was not dissuaded from keeping the fifty-three American diplomats hostage by the fact that there were some one hundred to two hundred thousand Iranian nationals, including sixty to seventy thousand Iranian students, then present in the United States,[182] and that the United States apparently never seriously considered threatening to similarly detain or take direct coercive action against these Iranians as a means of retaliating against or placing pressure on Iran to release the American hostages and cease its illegal action. In view of U.S. law and traditions, such a threat would probably not have been credible.

c. Political, Economic, Military, or Other Sanctions

More broadly, an agreement can specifically provide for the imposition of general political, economic, military, or other punitive sanctions in the event of breach. While a nation or group of nations may in any case threaten to use such sanctions against another nation deliberately violating an agreement, specific provisions in an agreement permitting such sanctions will legitimate their use, make it easier and less politically costly for nations to invoke them, and thus make the threat that they will be invoked more credible. The threat of sanctions can be reinforced and in some cases made more credible by provisions in an agreement permitting the injured party or parties to call upon third parties for assistance in imposing sanctions. While proponents of international order have typically placed considerable emphasis on the concept of punitive sanctions—the need for an "international policeman"—as a way of ensuring compliance with international law and treaties, the usefulness of punishment as a way of making nations behave is less than clear. Indeed, one thoughtful commentator, Roger Fisher, states baldly that "[p]unishing governments has not worked in the past and will not work now."[183]

Provisions for punitive sanctions are most common in multilateral agreements, particularly those establishing international organizations.[184] There is a wide range of possible sanctions, and only the principal types will be suggested.

Some multilateral agreements rely primarily on the threat of public exposure, condemnation, or the "mobilization of shame" to deter violation and induce compliance.[185] Under this type of procedure a charge of violation usually sets in motion an investigation and consultation designed to persuade or exhort the offending nation to cease its violation. Only after informal or formal attempts to bring about compliance have failed will some type of formal criticism of the noncomplying party be issued. The procedures developed by the International Labour Organization for implementation of conventions sponsored by the ILO are an example.[186] Under these procedures, member states are required to make a variety of reports to the organization concerning their compliance with ILO conventions and recommendations. These national reports are examined by an independent committee of experts, which passes its observations on to a committee of the ILO conference, which may in turn discuss its more significant observations with the nations concerned. The ILO committee can also include in its report to the full ILO conference a special list of the most serious "deficiencies" of member nations in this regard. For a nation to be on this list is regarded as a serious criticism, which member nations will seek to avoid. Other specialized agencies, such as UNESCO, and other international agreements, such as the Covenant on Civil and Political Rights, establish similar reporting and monitoring procedures under which criticism may be mobilized against a noncomplying member or party.[187]

"Mobilization of shame" as a sanction has both advantages and drawbacks. Somewhat surprisingly, many nations—even the most unprincipled, ruthless, or totalitarian—are sensitive to international criticism or condemnation, and turning the spotlight on their violations of an agreement may sometimes cause them to change their behavior. Moreover, imposing such a sanction involves relatively little real cost for the nations supporting such a condemnation, which simply join in approving a resolution, or for the nation suffering the condemnation, which simply suffers a loss of pride. On the other hand, such techniques may often prove ineffective or even counterproductive. Some nations may prove immune to and ignore international criticism, shrugging it off as politically motivated or of no importance. Or the target nation may threaten political retaliation against nations joining in the condemnation, influencing many to abstain from doing so and diluting the effectiveness of the sanction. Or the criticism may create deep resentment on the part of the target nation, isolating it and making it even more intransigent and less inclined to respect its commitments. This may be particularly the case if the target nation feels that it is being unfairly singled out for criticism for political reasons, or that the criticism is hypocritical. In some cases, nonpublic techniques, which do not represent so overt a challenge to a nation's dignity, may have more chance of persuading a noncomplying nation to change its behavior than public techniques, which may only result in making it more stubborn and less willing to make any concessions.

Many agreements establishing international organizations provide that parties which violate its provisions may be subjected to specific penalties or be denied certain of the benefits of membership in the organization. For example, under the U.N. Charter, a member of the United Nations which is two years in arrears in its payment of contributions may be barred from exercising its vote in the General Assembly.[188] In 1964, the United States sought unsuccessfully to apply this provision against the Soviet Union.[189] In 1974 the members of the International Civil Aviation Organization successfully applied a similar provision against South Africa.[190] Similarly, the International Monetary Fund may declare a member which has failed to fulfill any of its obligations under the agreement ineligible to use the Fund's general financial resources, or it may penalize a member which makes an unduly protracted use of the Fund's resources by increasing the normal charges for the use of the Fund's resources by that member.[191] The International Coffee

Organization may penalize a member nation which has exceeded its coffee export quota by deducting an amount greater than this excess from that member's future quotas, and the International Tin Agreement permits the International Tin Council to reduce a member nation's production quota in future control periods and confiscate that nation's share in the joint tin buffer stock established by the agreement if that nation fails to abide by the regulations of the council.[192]

Many agreements establishing international organizations permit the members to suspend or expel a member nation which violates important obligations.[193] Under Article 5 of the United Nations Charter, a member against which preventive or enforcement action has been taken by the Security Council may be suspended from the rights and privileges of membership by the General Assembly upon the recommendation of the Security Council.[194] Under Article 6 of the charter, a member of the United Nations which has persistently violated the principles contained in the charter may be expelled from the organization by the General Assembly upon the recommendation of the Security Council.[195] In 1975, the World Meteorological Organization suspended South Africa from membership,[196] and South Africa earlier withdrew from both the ILO and the FAO in the face of threats of suspension or expulsion.[197] Even so, the usefulness of expulsion as a technique for inducing compliance with international obligations continues to be a matter of debate. For example, Schermers comments:

> The expediency of expulsion as a sanction is questionable. It may harm the organization as much as it harms the expelled Member. The Member would only be an outcast if there were no other non-Members. It will suffer somewhat from losing its rights of membership, but it will also be discharged of its obligations towards the organization. For organizations of a universal character an expulsion will be a retrograde step on the path to universality. Expulsion creates a hostile atmosphere between the State and the organization and therefore makes it difficult to restore the co-operation with the State in question, whenever this could be beneficial. When all its ties have been severed, a State will not become more willing to take the wishes of the

organization into account. The possible influence exerted on a State may be much greater when its representatives can be pressed at an international conference than when those representatives are never seen.[198]

Some agreements provide for direct economic or even military actions against a nation that violates its obligations. The Versailles Treaty, for instance, authorized the Allied Powers to reoccupy the Rhineland in the event that Germany at any time failed to meet its obligations to make reparations under the treaty.[199] Since 1925, international narcotics treaties have provided for the imposition of an embargo on imports or exports, or both, of narcotics from or to a country or territory where a situation exists endangering the aims of the international narcotics control system.[200] However, the most important agreement expressly providing for economic or military sanctions is the U.N. Charter. The charter permits the Security Council in the event it determines the existence of a threat to the peace, a breach of the peace, or an act of aggression, to make recommendations or decide upon measures to maintain or restore international peace or security,[201] which measures may, if the council so decides, be binding upon all U.N. members.[202] These measures may include complete or partial interruption of economic relations and of rail, sea, air, postal, telegraphic, radio, and other means of communication; the severance of diplomatic relations; or actions by air, sea, or land forces, including demonstrations, blockade, and other operations by members of the United Nations.[203] A breach of treaty might in certain circumstances be held by the Security Council to constitute such a "threat to the peace."[204] For example, it could conceivably have done so in the 1979–80 crisis arising out of Iran's holding of American diplomatic and consular personnel, which, as the International Court held, was clearly in violation of Iran's treaty commitments. But the U.N. Security Council has to date never imposed mandatory military sanctions, and has imposed mandatory economic sanctions on only two occasions—against Rhodesia in 1966[205] and against South Africa in 1977[206]—neither of which proved very effective. In January 1980, a U.S.–proposed U.N. Security Council resolution which would have imposed economic sanctions against Iran for its continued holding of the American hostages in Tehran, despite a Security Council resolution and International Court order calling for their release, was vetoed by the Soviet Union.[207] In April 1980, the United States acted unilaterally to impose sanctions on Iran, breaking diplomatic relations with that country and imposing a formal embargo on American exports to Iran.[208]

Military and economic sanctions obviously raise many questions. Article 2, paragraph 4, of the U.N. Charter provides that "[a]ll Members shall refrain in their international relations from the threat or use of force against the territorial integrity or political independence of any State, or in any other manner inconsistent with the purposes of the United Nations." The use of military or economic sanctions to coerce compliance with international agreements could, unless authorized by the United Nations, arguably violate this Charter prohibition.[209] Sanctions are unlikely to be very effective in bringing about compliance except where the target nation is weak or—in the case of economic sanctions—especially dependent on international trade. During the U.S.–Iran hostage crisis, for example, Iran apparently did not believe it would be seriously affected by the U.S.–proposed embargo; its response to the threat of sanctions, as reported by U.N. Secretary General Waldheim at the time, was, "We couldn't care less."[210] Such sanctions may polarize a dispute, unite the target nation's citizens against outside "intervention," and result in increased intransigence and unwillingness to compromise. They may cause the target nation to retaliate or take other hostile or illegal measures to protect its interests, further escalating the dispute. Iran threatened to cut off oil sales to any nation supporting the U.S. proposal to impose sanctions against it.[211] Sanctions may create bad feelings between nations supporting such sanctions and nations opposing or failing to participate in them, or may have other indirect costs. The Soviet Union's veto of the U.S.–proposed resolution to impose sanctions, and other actions contrary to U.S. interests in the U.S.–Iran hostage crisis, aggravated U.S.–Soviet tensions. They may impose serious costs on nations imposing the sanctions and on third parties, as well as on the target nation. They may hurt largely innocent groups within the target nation, rather than the political elites controlling its policies.

For all of these reasons, the threat of military and economic sanctions is not usually very credible or useful, and it is not surprising that they have been rarely used as a technique to induce compliance with treaty obligations or, indeed, as a way of exerting pressure against any but relatively weak and politically isolated nations.

Finally, a few agreements, such as some human rights agreements and agreements relating to the laws of war, establish a system under which sanctions may be imposed directly on individuals responsible for violations.[212] For example, under the Genocide Convention, national leaders or others engaging in genocidal acts contrary to the convention may be held personally accountable for these acts and, at such time as an international criminal court is established (which has not yet occurred), could be tried by such a court.[213] The 1973 U.N. Apartheid Convention also contains provisions under which individuals violating the convention's prohibitions against apartheid can be directly tried and punished by states parties.[214] Yet, whatever may be the future potential of this technique as a way of inducing compliance with international agreements, government leaders are clearly chary of the possible abuse of such provisions (which could apply directly to themselves), and it is unlikely to have wide acceptance in the near future.

8. Reducing One's Own Vulnerability in the Event of Nonperformance

A nation can seek to protect itself against the risk of its treaty partner's nonperformance not only by increasing the probability of its treaty partner's performance in the ways discussed in previous sections, but also by decreasing its own vulnerability or exposure to loss in the event that its treaty partner fails to perform. That is, a nation will wish to structure an agreement so that it will, at worst, be able to return as close as possible to the *status quo ante* in the event that the other party fails to comply with the agreement.

As previously indicated, a nation may also be interested in reducing its vulnerability as a way of increasing the probability that the other nation will in fact choose to perform. That is, if the reason nation B considers not performing its obligations is that it hopes to exploit A's vulnerability or otherwise secure a competitive advantage over A, any device which reduces A's vulnerability will also increase the probability of B's performance. But a nation may also wish to be in a position to limit its losses in the event that the agreement does not work out. Yet an excessive concern by one party with reducing its vulnerability may communicate distrust and generate a reciprocal distrust in its treaty partner, damaging the chances that their agreement will prove successful. Commitment to an agreement involves acceptance of at least some measure of risk, and at some point each of the parties will have to place some measure of trust in the other if their cooperation is to prove useful.

Since these techniques have been generally dealt with in previous sections, they will be noted only briefly here.

a. Reducing One's Own Reliance Costs

A nation can reduce its exposure to loss in the event of the other party's failure to perform by reducing its preperformance investment in the proposed agreement. A nation's investment in an agreement will include both any preparation costs it incurs which it can recover only through the successful carrying out of the agreement, and the opportunity costs to it of foregoing possible alternative actions or cooperative arrangements with others. For example, if one nation is uncertain as to the probability of another's fully performing a long-term agreement to supply it large quantities of grain, it may not wish to make a large investment either in special storage facilities for that grain or in special port facilities suitable only for discharging the other nation's cargo vessels. It might also wish to retain contacts with, or even secure options from, alternative suppliers.

b. Preventing Loss of One's Own Performance

A nation can reduce its exposure to loss through techniques which ensure that it will not lose its own performance if its treaty partner does not perform. These include the various devices previously discussed which have the purpose either of timing the respective performances so that one party can withhold its performance in the event of the other's breach, or of facilitating a party's recovery of its performance in the event that it has given that performance to the other prior to the other's breach. Thus, a nation which does not trust its treaty partner may wish to secure provisions in the agreement which require that the other party perform first, or at least which give it ample notice or warning of the other's breach or impending breach in time for it to take steps to protect itself against any further loss of its own performance.

c. Preventing the Other State from Exploiting One's Own Reliance on the Agreement

Nation A may be concerned that its reliance on and performance of its agreement with nation B may place it in a position of relative weakness (in relation to B or to some third party) which

B or the third party, in the event that B fails to perform its obligations, will be in a position to exploit. For example, as previously suggested, A may fear that if it enters into and performs its part of a truce agreement with B which requires A's withdrawal of its forces from a part of B's territory, B, in breach of its commitments, may then use this territory to launch an attack upon A. Or, A may fear that, if it enters into a long-term oil supply agreement with B, B—once A has become dependent upon B—will, in breach of the agreement, increase the price of oil or use the threat of a denial of oil as a means of coercing A to act in certain ways. There are various techniques by which a nation may seek to protect itself against such a contingency.

(i) *Making it impossible or impractical for the other state to exploit one's vulnerability.* One nation may be able to structure the agreement so as to make it impossible or impractical for the other to take advantage of its vulnerability. For example, a truce agreement between two nations may require one to withdraw from certain positions, which withdrawal will leave it exposed to attack by the other nation if that nation decides to break the truce. To guard against this possibility, the first nation may insist on the inclusion in the agreement of provisions for the construction of an impassable barrier on the ceasefire line or in the neutral zone between its own and the other nation's forces, or for the stationing of troops of third parties in sufficient strength to deter any attempt by the other nation to exploit its withdrawal. The 1975 Egypt-Israel Sinai Agreement and the 1979 Egypt-Israel Peace Treaty each provide detailed arrangements of this type, including arrangements for buffer zones, demilitarized zones, and zones of limited armaments, monitored by U.N. or other forces.[215] The United Nations has performed a similar interpository function in truce or armistice situations in the Middle East, Yemen, Cyprus, India and Pakistan, and in certain other situations.[216] The use of third parties, such as the United Nations, to serve an interpository and monitoring role in such truce and armistice agreements may, of course, also serve the additional function of permitting the nations involved to give up territory acquired, or cease attempts to regain it, without losing face.[217]

(ii) *Providing warning.* A nation may also reduce its vulnerability by arrangements ensuring that it will receive warning of any breach or impending breach by its treaty partner in time to take protective measures. Such warning may be provided through reporting, surveillance, or inspection devices, or through the use of buffer zones implemented or controlled either directly by the nation concerned or by third parties. These techniques have been discussed in Section 2(b) of this chapter. Again, the 1975 Egypt-Israel Sinai Agreement and the 1979 Egypt–Israel Peace Treaty provide a variety of such devices.

(iii) *Standby arrangements.* A nation may reduce its vulnerability through arrangements which permit it to return to its former position rapidly if its treaty partner should breach the agreement in an attempt to exploit a vulnerable position the first nation is in because of its performance of the agreement. For example, any disarmament agreement entails the obvious risk that one party, in violation of the agreements, may either secretly conceal arms or quickly make or obtain them, placing it in a position to take advantage of its treaty partner which has complied with the agreement. To guard against the contingency of such cheating, a distrustful nation might conceivably seek provisions in the agreement permitting it to retain a reserve of standby weapons or a ''mothballed'' fleet, which would be subject to third-party inspection or control to ensure that it was solely a reserve and could be used only in the event of the other party's breach. Or a nation may be concerned that, by entering into a long-term oil or food supply agreement with another nation, it will be placing itself in a position of dependence which the other nation can then exploit by threatening to cut off its supply. To guard against this risk, the concerned nation may wish to maintain a substantial reserve of oil or food, perhaps requiring its proposed treaty partner as a condition of the agreement to assist it in building up this reserve. In a related context, an Israel–U.S. Memorandum of Agreement accompanying the 1975 Egypt-Israel Sinai Agreement provides that, in connection with Israeli withdrawal from the Sinai oil fields, the United States will finance "a project for the construction and stocking of the oil reserves to be stored in Israel, bringing storage reserve capacity and reserve stocks now standing at approximately six months, up to one year's need at the time of completion of the project."[218]

(iv) *Third-party guarantees or assistance.* A nation can reduce its vulnerability through arrangements under which a third party or parties guarantee that it will not be exposed to loss as a result of its treaty partner's violation of the agreement or other factors related to its participation in the agreement, or at least agree to assist it in taking measures which will reduce its vulnerability. Examples of this technique are the various assurances given by the United States to Israel to encourage conclusion of the 1975 Egypt-Israel Sinai Agreement and the subsequent 1979 Egypt-Israel Peace Treaty. One memorandum of agreement between the United States and Israel accompanying the signature of the 1979 Peace Treaty (which reflects a similar memorandum accompanying the 1975 agreement) is designed to provide assurances of U.S. support in the event of violations of the treaty. It provides in part:

> Recognizing that the withdrawal from Sinai imposes additional heavy security, military and economic burdens on Israel;
> The Governments of the United States of America and of the State of Israel, subject to their constitutional processes and applicable law, confirm as follows:
> 1. In the light of the role of the United States in achieving the Treaty of Peace

and the parties' desire that the United States continue its supportive efforts, the United States will take appropriate measures to promote full observance of the Treaty of Peace.

2. Should it be demonstrated to the satisfaction of the United States that there has been a violation or threat of violation of the Treaty of Peace, the United States will consult with the parties with regard to measures to halt or prevent the violation, ensure observance of the Treaty of Peace, enhance friendly and peaceful relations between the parties and promote peace in the region, and will take such remedial measures as it deems appropriate, which may include diplomatic, economic and military measures as described below.

3. The United States will provide support it deems appropriate for proper actions taken by Israel in response to such demonstrated violations of the Treaty of Peace. In particular, if a violation of the Treaty of Peace is deemed to threaten the security of Israel, including, inter alia, a blockade of Israel's use of international waterways, a violation of the provisions of the Treaty of Peace concerning limitation of forces or an armed attack against Israel, the United States will be prepared to consider, on an urgent basis, such measures as the strengthening of the United States presence in the area, the providing of emergency supplies to Israel, and the exercise of maritime rights in order to put an end to the violation.

4. The United States will support the parties' rights to navigation and overflight for access to either country through and over the Strait of Tiran and the Gulf of Aqaba pursuant to the Treaty of Peace.

5. The United States will oppose and, if necessary, vote against any action or resolution in the United Nations which in its judgment adversely affects the Treaty of Peace.

6. Subject to Congressional authorization and appropriation, the United States will endeavor to take into account and will endeavor to be responsive to military and economic assistance requirements of Israel.[219]

Egypt objected to this memorandum on the grounds, among others, that it was in effect directed against Egypt, although the United States indicated that it had offered to extend similar assurances to Egypt. Moreover, the question whether these assurances represent legally binding commitments of the United States has been a subject of debate, raising certain issues under U.S. internal law.

Another U.S.–Israel memorandum of agreement accompanying the 1979 peace treaty (which again reflects a similar memorandum accompanying the 1975 Sinai Agreement) is designed to meet Israel's concerns regarding the availability of oil following its withdrawal from the Sinai oil fields, and provides U.S. assurances that, if oil to meet Israel's needs becomes unavailable to Israel, the United States will make oil available for purchase by Israel to meet Israel's "normal," or at least its "essential," requirements, depending upon the ability of the United States to procure oil to meet its own normal requirements.[220] Again, in connection with the 1979 Egypt-Israel Peace Treaty, the United States agreed to provide $4.8 billion in special financial aid to the two countries over the next three years, including special financial undertakings to Israel to help finance the construction of two new airfields in the Negev to replace those from which Israel was withdrawing in the Sinai.[221]

As in the case of all third-party techniques, guarantees raise problems of credibility and reliability, and it is not surprising that some are cynical about the usefulness of this technique. For example, Menachim Begin, present premier of Israel, was said to have argued in 1975 that the breakdown of the Vietnam Accords demonstrated the inadequacy of international guarantees for the security of a nation. He was quoted as stating that "an international agreement guaranteed by both East and West, by both superpowers, was turned into a scrap of paper," adding that the logical conclusion was that "in the whole world there is no guarantee that can guarantee an international guarantee."[222] Again, General Mordechai Gur, former Israeli Army chief of staff, in commenting on the Camp David Agreement, stated: "You're speaking about promises from the U.S., but I want to tell you what Kissinger told me after the breakdown of the shuttle in 1975: 'It's a mistake to think that you can force a big power to do something because of a pact or an agreement. If we want to help you, as we did in the Yom Kippur war, we'll do it. If not, no agreement can force our hand.' "[223] Unlike the parties to most international agreements, who hope directly to profit from receiving each other's performance and thus have a continuing stake in keeping their promises and maintaining the agreement, the third-party guarantor usually has a more tenuous stake, and the strength of its commitment to its promise may weaken as time passes and circumstances change. Nor is it likely that a third party would accept the kind of effective risk-management techniques that might assure its keeping its promise of guarantee. Consequently, as the quotations above suggest, a nation's confidence in such a third-party guarantee must rest largely on trust, which may prove justified or unjustified.

CHAPTER 5

Using Risk-Management Techniques Effectively: Limitations and Possibilities

While specific risk-management provisions can often help nations reach agreement, there will be situations where the use of particular kinds of risk-management provisions is unacceptable or undesirable, or where other approaches to controlling risk, such as trust, make more sense. This final chapter looks more closely at some of the limitations of risk-management techniques, at the role of trust, and at some of the things we might do to make risk management more useful and effective.

1. Some Limitations of Risk-Management Techniques

The fact that risk-management techniques are available does not mean that nations will always choose to employ them, even if such devices offer the only way of dealing with risks that otherwise threaten their achievement of agreement. There are several reasons why these techniques are not more widely used. One is that negotiators and their lawyers are not always sufficiently aware of the possibilities of such techniques or skilled in making the most of them. But a second and more important reason is that risk-management techniques often have their own risks and costs, which may severely limit their usefulness. The added protection such techniques can provide may simply not be worth the added risks and costs they involve. Some of the most significant of these limitations follow.

a. Risk-Management Techniques Cannot Control Risk Completely

As previously noted, a completely risk-proof agreement is usually unattainable. Risk-management techniques can decrease risks, but cannot remove them entirely. Most agreements involve irreducible elements of uncertainty and risk that are beyond the practical ability of the parties to control. There are several reasons for this.

First, nations negotiating an agreement cannot anticipate all contingencies. Every negotiator and lawyer knows that, even in what seems the most carefully drafted and "foolproof" agreement, something may be overlooked. For example, during negotiation of the 1972 U.S.–Soviet SALT I "interim" agreement, which prohibited each side from building additional ballistic missile launchers for five years to ensure that neither side built any more "heavy" missiles, the United States apparently did not anticipate that the Soviet Union would be able to adapt existing silos to a new model of missile which was for all practical purposes a heavy missile. By doing so, the Soviet Union substantially increased its nuclear capability without violating the agreement.[1] In most cases, the consequences and costs of any such mistakes or unforeseen contingencies will be limited and acceptable. But where agreements involve vital national interests—or, as in the case of truce or arms control agreements, national survival—the consequences of any gap in the agreement may be more serious, and nations will be reluctant to take any chance.

Second, even the best risk-management techniques are unlikely to be one hundred percent reliable. Even the most thorough system of aerial surveillance or provisions for on-site inspection cannot completely remove the risk of clandestine evasion of a disarmament or armistice agreement. Thus, the Carter Administration conceded, in the debate on ratification of the SALT II Treaty, that absolute certainty of detecting violations was not in practice attainable.[2] The widest demilitarized or buffer zone may not be sufficient to prevent a determined aggressor from profiting by surprise attack. The firmest guarantees of third-party assistance may, in certain circumstances, prove worthless. The most solemn judgments of an international court may be ignored. The imposition of the severest economic or even military sanctions by an international organization, such as the United Nations, may be ineffective in compelling compliance.

While the use of third parties to implement risk-management techniques may in some cases add to their reliability, it again cannot guarantee their effectiveness. A third party may fail to carry out its assigned job adequately for many reasons—lack of ability, bias, disinterest, or an unwillingness to incur the risks and potential political or other costs of having to take a position favoring one side or the other. As previously noted, many nations are reluctant to accept provisions in agreements for compulsory settlement of treaty disputes by the International Court or other third-party agencies, fearing that such provisions might decrease their flexibility in dealing with treaty problems and that the third party might not act fairly, sensibly, or impartially. Indeed, in some situations, a nation may see third-party involvement as increasing rather than decreasing its risks. Israel, for example, has clearly been suspicious of U.N. involvement in its disputes with its Arab neighbors, fearing that the United Nations could not be trusted to perform its duties impartially. Conceivably, a nation might attempt to cover this risk of inadequate or improper performance of risk-management functions by a particular third party through additional guarantees or a system permitting a decision to be appealed to another third party. But provisions for additional protection would have to stop somewhere, and even a series of such arrangements still could not provide complete assurance.

b. Risk Management Involves Compromises between Certainty and Flexibility

In seeking to manage the risks of their agreement, the nations involved may encounter irreconcilable tensions between their desires for flexibility and freedom of choice regarding their own behavior and their desire for certainty and predictability with respect to the behavior of their treaty partner. In most cases, they will not be able to satisfy both objectives and, if agreement is to be reached, will have to settle for an imperfect compromise.

Ideally, each nation would presumably prefer an agreement which places maximum pressure on its treaty partner to perform its obligations, while leaving itself maximum freedom to escape from the agreement and to choose not to perform its obligations. For example, nation A might most effectively protect itself against the risk of nonperformance or inadequate performance by its treaty partner, nation B, through provisions in the agreement which foreclose B's right unilaterally to withdraw or be released from its performance; set forth B's obligations clearly; provide for A's monitoring or verification of B's performance; permit A to require compulsory third-party settlement of any dispute as to B's performance; provide for effective sanctions in the case of any breach by B; and so forth. But, in order to protect its own flexibility and option not to perform if the agreement declines in value or otherwise turns out to be a poor arrangement, nation A might also wish provisions in the agreement, applicable only to itself, which generally limit its commitments, grant it a broad unilateral right to withdraw or be released from the agreement, and specify its obligations only in equivocal terms; and nation A will correspondingly not wish the agreement to include provisions for verification, compulsory adjudication, or sanctions applicable to its own performance. Yet it is unlikely—at least in any fair and noncoercive negotiation among relatively equal parties—that nation B will consent to an agreement which firmly obligates B to perform its treaty commitments while providing broad flexibility for A to escape its commitments. Norms of reciprocity will typically dictate at least some symmetry among the obligations each party assumes. Consequently, A will usually be able to obtain B's agreement to a particular risk-management system only if that system applies to A as well. In short, the price one nation may have to pay for increased certainty of its treaty partner's performance is likely to be some loss in its own flexibility not to perform, and the price a nation may have to pay for increased flexibility regarding its own performance is likely to be some loss in its certainty as to its treaty partner's performance.[3]

Since different nations face different risks in an agreement, have different perceptions as to those risks, and consequently have different risk-management objectives, there may be some situations where one nation may reasonably agree to assume more rigid commitments than its treaty partner. But in many cases objectives of certainty and flexibility will be inconsistent, and the parties will have to arrive at some mutually acceptable balance which gives each less than it would prefer. In general, nations seem more likely to be worried that they will themselves be rigidly bound to an agreement, without any possibility of escape, than that their treaty partner might somehow escape.[4] Thus, since flexibility will typically represent the least risky compromise acceptable to both parties, agreements will generally tend towards looser rather than more rigid commitments.

c. Risk-Management Techniques May Be Costly

Risk management may involve substantial direct costs for the parties in terms of the money, people, resources, and time required to maintain or implement particular techniques. Verification through surveillance and inspection—for example, the maintenance and operation of the U.S. reconnaissance satellite program, of the IAEA safeguards system and staff of inspectors, of U.N. observer or buffer forces such as those in the Middle East, or of the U.S. civilian technician force manning early warning stations in the Sinai—may cost many millions of dollars. The cost of operating the U.S. Sinai Support Mission during fiscal year 1978 alone was $11.7 million,[5] and the cost of the U.N. Emergency Force assisting in implementing the Egypt-Israel cease-fire and disengagement agreements amounted during the period October 1978 to October 1979 to over $58 million.[6] Resort to international arbitration, conciliation, or adjudication is typically time-consuming and expensive; a case brought before the International Court may be decided, if at all, only after years of litigation and millions of dollars in legal and other expenses. For example, the *Southwest Africa* case took six years from the time of filing to decision, and the *Barcelona Traction* case took eight years to reach decision.[7] Each of these involved scores of lawyers and massive evidence, and in neither case did the Court render a judgment on the merits of the case. Buffer stocks or deposits of collateral may divert resources from productive uses. Dividing larger agreements into smaller ones may be inefficient. Coercive techniques employing military measures or economic sanctions are, of course, particularly likely to involve very large expenditures and other costs.[8]

In deciding whether to use particular risk-management techniques, nations will have to weigh the possible contribution of the techniques against their direct costs and other disadvantages. Where an important agreement clearly cannot be achieved unless provisions for a particular technique are included—as when a nation insists on verification as a condition of its participation in an arms control or armistice agreement—even very costly techniques may be justified. But where less important or less risky agreements are involved, or where risk-management concerns are peripheral to the reaching of agreement, the use of more costly sorts of techniques may simply not be worthwhile. Some interesting experiments by two sociologists, Marwell and Schmitt, on interpersonal behavior in situations involving risk suggest that even a small added cost for avoiding risk may be highly effective in eliminating risk-avoidance behavior.[9]

d. Risk-Management Techniques May Involve Indirect Political or Other Costs

As has been indicated throughout the previous discussion, risk-management techniques may pose serious domestic or international political problems. Invocation of such coercive techniques as military intervention or the imposition of economic sanctions may give rise both to domestic criticism and political repercussions in the nation applying the sanctions and to international criticism or reactions by other nations. The use of coercive techniques may make the target nation more intransigent and solution of problems of noncompliance more difficult. Withdrawal from an agreement or organization may result in a loss of potential international influence and the setting of an undesirable precedent. Invoking compulsory arbitration or dispute settlement may be viewed by the respondent nation as an unfriendly act and damage general relations or lead to retaliatory actions. Surveillance and inspection, the presence of foreign observers or forces, compulsory submission of disputes to third-party settlement, or the use of hostages may offend the sense of dignity of the nation which is the target of such provisions, and consequently be either politically impossible for its government to accept, or, if accepted, give rise to a continuing sense of resentment and frictions.

e. Risk-Management Provisions May Compel Unwise Responses to Treaty Problems

Once included in an agreement, risk-management provisions may have their own dynamic which a nation may not be able to control. For example, if an agreement provides that nation A may suspend its own performance or impose military or economic sanctions in the event of nation B's noncompliance, and B blatantly breaches the agreement, the government of A may feel constrained to stop its performance or invoke such sanctions, even if it does not wish to do so, or else risk losing face, domestically and internationally. Or, if an agreement provides for compulsory reference of disputes to the International Court, a nation's government may come under domestic political pressure to refer a dispute to the Court even if it views such action in the circumstances as unwise and ineffective. It is true that in some cases a nation may wish to have such ''weapons'' available, in the unlikely case it has to use them. But in other cases, it may be better not to have the weapon at all, since simply having it may leave no option but to use it.

f. Risk-Management Provisions Can Be Abused

Risk-management provisions may be used improperly or unnecessarily. A right to invoke third-party settlement of disputes may be used as a means of pressure or an instrument of delay. A right to withdraw or withhold performance may be used without basis to excuse or disguise what is really a treaty breach. A right to use military or economic measures to assure compliance may be improperly used to cloak intervention or aggression. There are few actions a nation may wish to take for which an experienced lawyer cannot think up some colorable legal argument, and risk-management provisions can sometimes be twisted to such ends.

g. Risk Management May Complicate Negotiations

Attempts to control risk can complicate, delay, and bog down negotiations and obstruct the reaching of agreement. Lawyers may understandably have what Macaulay describes as a '' 'craft urge' to see exchange transactions neat and tidy from a legal standpoint.''[10] But negotiators, chiefly interested in achieving a favorable substantive bargain, may be indifferent to risk-management concerns and impatient with what they see as the lawyers' excessive caution. They will expect their lawyers to protect them but will insist on their not getting in the way. To negotiators, the important thing will be getting the agreement; any problems can be dealt with later.

If problems of risk are not crucial to achieving the agreement, this approach may make good sense. For example, where fragile negotiated compromises may fall apart if additional problems are introduced in negotiations and the bargain is not struck quickly, it may be well worth sacrificing risk-management objectives to preserve the forward momentum of negotiation. Macneil, discussing analogous issues in private contracts, comments: ''The costs in time, money and danger to successful negotiation of the basic performance planning arising from the thoroughness of risk planning may often be too high relative to the gains to be thereby achieved.''[11] *Newsweek*'s description of an episode in the 1979 talks in Israel between President Carter and Prime Minister Begin, which paved the way for a break-through in the Egypt-Israel Peace Treaty negotiations, suggests negotiators' ambivalent reactions to the lawyer's role—in this case despite Israel's obvious concern with risk management objectives:

Carter and Vance then began to explain the essence of the new U.S. proposals. . . .

Suddenly, the atmosphere brightened. Begin spoke with a ''cautious kind of optimism'' about one of the changes—and asked Carter's forbearance to discuss the proposals in Hebrew with his delegation. Then Israel's U.N. Ambassador Yehuda Blum, a conservative expert in international law, arrived. ''Here is my great legal mind,'' Begin said. But the U.S. negotiators were not pleased. To some of Carter's aides, ''whiny, goddam lawyers'' on both sides were largely to blame for the snags that had dogged the talks since the once-heralded breakthrough at Camp David. Blum took one look at the new wording and launched a strenuous argument against it. His perturbed tone and expression did not escape Carter, who—without understanding a word that was being said—finally asked, ''Are you trying to *help*?'' The Israelis dissolved in laughter.[12]

h. Risk Management May Lead to Distrust

An attempt by one party to carefully control its risks may be interpreted by the other as a sign of distrust, adversely affecting both their negotiations and the implementation of any agreement they reach. As often noted, attitudes of trust and distrust may be reciprocated and become ''self-fulfilling'' prophecies: trust tends to generate trust and distrust tends to generate suspicion.[13] Former U.S. Secretary of State Stimson, urging after World War II that the United States share its knowledge and control of nuclear energy for peaceful purposes with Russia, told the president that ''the chief lesson I have learned in a long life is that the only way to make a man trustworthy is to trust him.''[14] Thus, if nation A seems to trust nation B, B is likely to respond with similar attitudes and the two nations will require few risk-management provisions in their agreement. On the other hand, if A insists on strong risk-management provisions, such as verification or third-party enforcement, in its proposed agreement with B, B may, perhaps correctly, assume that this is because A expects it to cheat. B's perception that A distrusts it may lead B, in turn, to fear that A will withhold its performance or take other improper actions to protect itself from B's anticipated cheating. And so on! As mutual distrust escalates, each nation may come to see the proposed agreement as more risky, reinforcing its perception of the need for additional protective devices and increasing the chance that they will be invoked. Such situations of reciprocally deteriorating trust are common in personal relationships, such as marriage or homebuilding contracts, where one party's suspicions can lead to reciprocal suspicions and protective measures by the other, and to a cycle of escalating distrust, ultimately damaging or destroying the cooperative relationship.

i. Risk Management Cannot Easily Control the Risk of "Irrational" Behavior

Finally, many risk-management techniques—particularly those designed to protect against the other party's nonperformance—are based largely on the assumption that nations will act rationally and respond to inducements, threats, or sanctions in ways that maximize their gains and minimize their losses. That is, they assume that if a nation is aware that it will lose more by violating an agreement than by complying with it, or at least that it cannot gain from violating the agreement, it will reasonably choose to comply with the agreement. But a nation may, because of a lack of relevant information, misinformation, or deficiencies in its evaluating processes, fail to recognize that its best interests lie in performing; it may not know "what's best for it." Or a nation may, for reasons of bureaucratic inertia, internal politics, pride, emotion, or spite, choose not to perform despite the fact that this behavior is "rationally" contrary to what international relations theorists consider its best interests; it may not do what is best for it. Experience in the Vietnam conflict and the Iranian hostage crisis suggests that even the threat or actual imposition of severe military or economic sanctions may not dissuade a nation from a course of action to which it is emotionally or ideologically committed. Or a nation may rationally reach a judgment that what it will gain from noncompliance outweighs what it will lose, despite its treaty partner's belief that such a judgment is irrational; it may simply differ as to what's best for it. For example, some commentators have questioned whether the Soviet Union fully accepts the U.S. concept of mutual deterrence.[15] U.S. theorists may consider it self-evident that each nation's capability to wreak "mutually assured destruction" on the other makes the use of nuclear weapons unthinkable and the accumulation of nuclear arsenals above this point absurd, but it is possible that Soviet leaders and generals may simply not think the same way and may take the view that more weapons are always better than less and that the nation with the most powerful armaments *can* "win."[16]

2. The Relevance of Trust

While nations rely principally on specific risk-management provisions to control the risks of their agreements, they can also, as discussed in Chapter 1, deal with these risks in other ways. The most significant of these other approaches is trust.[17] Where a nation has a high degree of trust in its potential treaty partner not to cheat or otherwise to take advantage of it, this alone may be enough to meet its perceptions of risk. In most cases, however, trust and the use of specific risk-management techniques do not function as mutually exclusive approaches but often complement or supplement each other, serving together to bring nations to levels of assurance where they are prepared to enter into agreement.

Trust and the use of specific risk-management provisions may interrelate in several ways. To the extent that nations trust each other, they will feel less need for the inclusion of more specific risk-management provisions in their agreement, or will be satisfied with simpler and more general provisions. Conversely, if nations can devise and agree on specific risk-management provisions capable of effectively controlling their risks, they may be able to reach agreement despite distrust. Thus, the fact that the United States and the Soviet Union, or Israel and the Arab nations, distrust each other need not prevent their reaching effective and mutually beneficial agreements, if they can meet their concerns for risk through the inclusion of appropriate risk-management provisions in these agreements. On the other hand, nations which distrust each other are likely to insist on far-reaching risk-management provisions as a condition of cooperation, and will be able to achieve agreement only if such provisions can be successfully negotiated. Similarly, nations which cannot agree on specific risk-management provisions in their agreement will be able to achieve cooperation only if they are willing to trust each other sufficiently to make up for the absence of these provisions.

The role of trust will obviously differ in different circumstances, and it is difficult to say how important trust really is in achieving particular types of international agreements. Studies of private transactions suggests that trust plays a very considerable role in private agreements. Macaulay, on the basis of empirical research concerning contract practices among businesses in one of the states of the United States, notes that "[b]usinessmen often prefer to rely on 'a man's word' in a brief letter, a handshake, or 'common honesty and decency'—even when the transaction involves exposure to serious risks."[18] But transactions between governments are usually very different from transactions between private individuals or businesses. Among other things, they are typically more important, involve longer time periods, and are more bureaucratic. In a context where a number of different government officials will be involved in negotiating, in approving, and in carrying out an agreement, it is not easy to say who is trusting whom. Consequently, for these reasons alone, one would expect governments to be less willing than individuals to rely on trust.

Certainly, there are many types of agreements where trust probably plays only a relatively limited role. It is unlikely to be a significant factor in the reaching of armistice and cease-fire agreements, arms control agreements, or agreements attempting to resolve difficult ethnic conflicts, such as the Cyprus, Namibia, Rhodesian, or Palestinian problems. Where vital national and ethnic interests or survival is at stake, officials are likely to take the view held by President Carter in regard to the proposed SALT II Treaty, that "the stakes are too high to rely on trust."[19] Moreover, negotiations for these types of agreements typically involve circumstances in which the parties strongly distrust each other and their attitudes cannot easily be changed. Consequently, such agreements can usually be reached only where the prospective parties can bring the risks involved within manageable limits through the use of specific risk-management techniques. Again, trust probably does not play an important role in many of the fairly routine and standardized types of agreements which constitute the bulk of international cooperative arrangements—commercial treaties, trade agreements, aviation agreements, tax treaties, postal agreements, and the like. The risks involved in such agreements are usually moderate and well understood, and through long experience nations have developed effective and standardized provisions to manage these risks.

But there are some types of agreements where trust probably plays a more significant role. First, some agreements are of such a nature that it is almost impossible to think of risk-management techniques which will be effective; consequently, the nations involved will have to accept the other party's promises, if at all, on trust. For example, it is difficult to think of ways of keeping nations from cheating in a commodity agreement if they really want to. Second, trust may affect government decisions to enter into agreements which have some risk, but which are not sufficiently important to justify using the risk-management techniques that would be necessary to effectively control such risks. Economic or military assistance agreements are possible examples. While techniques to ensure proper use and to prevent diversion might be devised, such techniques would raise a variety of political and other problems, and few nations bother to insist on the kinds of risk-management provisions which would be required. Third, trust may play a crucial role in a nation's willingness to enter into an agreement where its acceptance is conditioned on a third party's assumption of some risk-management function. Of course, the trust relevant to this situation is that of trusting the third party rather than the treaty partner; indeed, the need for third-party participation in risk management usually suggests less than complete trust between the parties. For example, the U.S. commitment to perform surveillance functions, guarantee Israel's oil supplies, extend military and financial aid to Israel, and otherwise assure Israel against certain risks was clearly a major factor in obtaining Israel's agreement to the 1979 Egypt-Israel Peace Treaty.[20] But this acceptance must necessarily have been based to a considerable extent on Israel's trust in the United States; there were no practicable techniques through which Israel could assure itself that the United States would in fact perform these commitments. Similarly, the acceptability of other third-party techniques—such as the use of a U.N. buffer force, the application of the International Atomic Energy Agency's safeguards program, or compulsory adjudication by the International Court—must rest ultimately on trust. Finally, there may be situations where a nation is teetering on the edge of a decision whether to enter into a particular agreement, in terms of the risks involved, and its broad perceptions of the trustworthiness or lack of trustworthiness of its potential treaty partner may tip the balance.

Even where trust does not play a central role in managing the risks of a particular agreement, it may still facilitate agreement in less obvious ways. Nations that trust each other may be willing to rely on simpler and less costly risk-management techniques in their agreements, while negotiations between distrustful nations may be complicated by their insistence on more complex and burdensome techniques. Trust can reinforce the credibility and usefulness of more specific techniques by reducing concern that they will be improperly or unfairly invoked. Trust can establish a climate in which substantive negotiations are more easily conducted, while distrust may poison the atmosphere of a negotiation. Finally, general public attitudes of trust for a prospective treaty partner may encourage negotiations, while public attitudes of distrust may make even desirable and low-risk agreements, such as human rights agreements, politically impossible to achieve.

3. Towards More Effective Risk Management

Since the ability of nations to deal successfully with the risks of cooperation may be crucial to their achieving international agreement, it is important to try to develop more awareness of risk-management possibilities and improve the usefulness of risk-management techniques. This might be done in several ways.

a. Learning More about Risk Management

First, more research is needed. We need to know more about how nations—or, more concretely, the officials who determine nations' policies—behave in situations involving cooperation under conditions of risk. More specifically, how and why do nations decide to enter or not to enter into international agreements? What are the factors which affect their perceptions of uncertainty and risk, trust and distrust, and how do such perceptions influence their decisions and behavior? What kinds of problems are likely to arise in carrying out an agreement, and how do the parties usually deal with these problems? How and why do nations decide not to comply with treaty obligations, and what factors affect these decisions? How and why do particular risk-management techniques work, and under what circumstances do they work more or less effectively? How can present techniques be improved so as to make them more useful? Are there new or thus far unused techniques which might help nations better deal with problems of risk? Is the kind of inventory and analysis of various techniques presented in this study likely to be useful to officials concerned with these problems, and if so, in what ways should it be expanded and improved? And so on!

There are various ways of seeking answers to these questions—case studies of particular agreements, in-depth analysis of particular techniques, experiments involving simulation or "gaming," attempts to tap the rich practical experience and insights of negotiators and international lawyers through interviews or meetings. Of course, empirical research into these governmental decisions and international processes is not easy.

Foreign policy decisions are frequently shrouded by official secrecy, diplomatic reticence, or bureaucratic complexity; even when officials involved are ready and willing to speak, they may have difficulty in articulating or analyzing the way in which relevant decisions were reached, or in identifying the factors which influenced those decisions. But anything we learn will be a step forward, and we should do what we can. Since problems of risk and risk management are pervasive, affecting cooperation between individuals and groups as well as nations, such research should be cross-disciplinary, drawing not only on the work and experience of diplomats and international lawyers, but also on that of social and political scientists and the broader legal and business community.[21]

Existing international institutions such as the United Nations Institute for Training and Research (UNITAR)[22] and The Hague Academy of International law,[23] and professional societies such as the American Society of International Law and the International Law Association, have conducted excellent research studies of related international problems, such as international dispute settlement, and might find research concerning risk management worth pursuing.

b. Promoting Education and Training in Risk-Management Techniques

Programs might be undertaken to help diplomats and international lawyers become more aware of risk-management problems and possibilities and more skilled in the appropriate use of risk-management techniques. Such programs might also help diplomats and lawyers better understand each other's concerns and approaches and develop better ways of effectively working together in negotiations. This objective could be furthered through broader professional education; discussion and writing concerning risk management; special training programs; seminars or conferences; the preparation of negotiating manuals or aids; and the like. Again, programs of this type could readily be developed through existing institutions, such as the United Nations Institute for Training and Research and The Hague Academy of International Law, and professional schools and professional societies in the field of international law and diplomacy.

c. Improving the Risk-Management Capabilities of Existing International Organizations

As we have seen, such third parties as international organizations and international tribunals can often play an important role in helping nations manage the risks of international agreements. Yet we have also seen that the potential use of third-party techniques may be limited by the doubts of one or more of the nations negotiating an agreement as to a third-party's competence, impartiality, trustworthiness, or effectiveness.

More efforts to meet these concerns and improve the capacity of international organizations such as the United Nations to perform useful third-party roles—such as verification, escrow and trustee tasks, and the offering of credible guarantees—are needed. It is important that the United Nations, the International Court, and other international institutions act impartially and effectively in performing third-party risk-management functions in a given case, not only to meet the demands of fairness in that particular case, but also to establish their credibility and usefulness to nations in future cases. Thus, the entire international community has a stake in developing this risk-management capability of international institutions. Considerable attention is being given to improving the capacity of the International Court to perform its dispute-settlement functions. These efforts should be expanded to improve third-party risk-management techniques more generally.

d. Developing New Techniques and Institutions

We can supplement existing techniques by trying to develop new ways of managing the risks of international cooperation. For example, as Schelling has suggested, a study of cooperative arrangements in earlier or primitive societies, or among criminals or others not subject to formal law, may suggest such innovative techniques.[24] The continuing challenge of risk in private business, commercial, and financial arrangements has spawned a wide variety of sophisticated techniques possibly applicable to international experience. Techniques such as escrow, insurance, condominium, and the like may be more acceptable, relevant, and useful in international dealings than has been assumed.

The concept that officials or others may be individually responsible for certain types of breaches of international law has acquired at least a fragile acceptance with respect to so-called international crimes, such as the planning of aggression, genocide, slavery, piracy, war crimes, and apartheid;[25] but "civil" liability has thus far not been suggested as a sanction for breaches of international agreement more generally, despite the fact that it is, of course, individual officials who are responsible for the decisions which constitute breach. Performance awards, bonuses, and prizes play a significant role in motivating private conduct; but there has thus far been little use of such techniques in seeking to influence governmental behavior in international relations.

Experiments with new kinds of risk-management institutions might also be worth trying. Nations have long accepted the importance of establishing impartial institutions such as international courts to perform international dispute-settlement functions, and there have been a number of interesting innovations and proposals designed to facilitate the use of international adjudicative institutions and strengthen their role.[26] One example is the 1965 Convention on the Settlement of Investment

Disputes, formulated by the World Bank, which establishes an International Centre for Investment Disputes to provide facilities for conciliation and arbitration of investment disputes between contracting states and nationals of other contracting states in accordance with provisions of the convention.[27] But there has been little recognition of the need for establishing specialized institutions to perform other third-party risk-management functions. Consequently (with the important exception of the International Atomic Energy Agency's safeguards system), such tasks have fallen, on an *ad hoc* basis, to political organizations such as the United Nations, which may be ill-equipped to handle them. Proposals have already been made for the establishment of a new specialized international agency to perform verification functions relating to disarmament agreements.[28] This idea could be broadened to suggest the establishment of a new agency capable of performing an even wider range of nonadjudicative third-party risk-management tasks, and perhaps other facilitative or marriage-broker functions, with respect to international agreements more generally. Presumably, such an agency would, like the International Court, operate solely on a consensual basis, performing only such functions as the parties to particular agreements might expressly request it to perform. Clearly, it would be important to organize such an agency in a way that maximized the likelihood that nations would accept it as impartial, to insulate it from political influences, to provide it with a competent staff committed to its purposes, and to give it authority and resources adequate to carry out its risk-management functions. Initial experiments with such an agency might be modest, allowing for growth and an expansion of its functions as its acceptability and usefulness was established.

e. Keeping Risk-Management in Perspective

Finally, effective risk management requires a sense of proportion. The purpose of agreements is to permit the parties to attain the mutual benefits that cooperation makes possible. Risk management is not an end in itself but is relevant and significant only insofar as it facilitates the reaching of substantive agreement. It is important to make sure that the tail not wag the dog.

In most international agreements, significant problems are not likely to arise. A nation will normally not enter into an agreement unless it believes the agreement is in its interest and it intends to keep rather than break it. Once a nation does commit itself to an agreement, many types of influences—normative considerations, a practical interest in maintaining a reputation for keeping one's word, political and bureaucratic inertia, and so forth—will exert powerful pressures upon it to fulfill its commitment, without regard to the presence or absence of risk-management provisions in the agreement. And where problems do arise, the nations concerned will usually be prepared to work out equitable solutions, without regard to what an agreement says. Nations have, in the long run, no choice but to keep doing business with each other, and they are generally aware that their common interest in stable cooperative arrangements can be served only through their mutually trustworthy behavior with respect to agreements that are, and remain, fair and useful to all parties. Indeed, treaty problems are more likely to result from the development of a basic imbalance in the agreement, which may well deserve remedy, than from bad faith.

Except in cases where the parties are especially hostile or competitive, a nation can usually expect its treaty partner to recognize special problems that develop, to refrain from exploiting or taking unfair advantage of such a situation, and to be willing to make such adjustments in the arrangement as may be necessary to restore a measure of equity or prevent one party from incurring substantial unanticipated costs. Some agreements expressly recognize such an obligation. For example, the Treaty of Friendship, Commerce, and Navigation between the United States and West Germany provides: "Each party shall accord sympathetic consideration to, and shall afford adequate opportunity for consultation regarding, such representations as the other party may make with respect to any matter affecting the operation of the present Treaty.''[29] A nation's most important protection in an agreement will usually be, not specific risk-management provisions, but its treaty partner's realization that if the two nations are to continue to do business, as they probably must, it must behave fairly and in good faith.

Effective risk management also requires common sense. This means that nations must have realistic risk-management objectives, reflecting an awareness that it is impossible to eliminate all risks, that partial control of the most significant risks may be the best that can be attained, and that particular techniques may cost more than they are worth or create more risks and problems than they solve. Often it will be simpler and wiser for nations to deal with risk simply by trusting each other, or by leaving problems to adjustment through later negotiation if they arise, than to seek expressly to cover these risks in an agreement. And where express risk-management provisions do prove necessary to agreement, the preference should be for techniques which tend to preserve rather than threaten the agreement and permit the parties to work out their problems and continue their cooperation if they so desire.

The art of negotiating and drafting international agreements will inevitably require good judgment in deciding when risk management is useful and when it is not, when particular techniques can help nations cooperate and when they are more likely to cause problems in reaching or carrying out an agreement. As yet, we have only a general idea of the principles which should guide such judgment and the techniques which might inform this art. But the problems of managing the risks of cooperation are certain to persist as long as human beings live together and work together, and efforts to organize and develop our experience of how best to deal with these problems seem overdue. More effective risk management will not alone achieve greater global cooperation. But it can help.

REFERENCE MATERIAL

Appendix: A Checklist of Risk-Management Techniques

I. General risk-management techniques
  1. Nonbinding arrangements
      a. "Tacit agreements"
      b. Arrangements in a form indicating a nonbinding intent
      c. Agreements expressing nonbinding intent
  2. Agreements to agree
  3. Option agreements
  4. Equivocal agreements
  5. Limiting the importance of the subject matter
  6. Limiting the size or scope of the agreement
  7. Exceptions clauses and reservations
  8. Limiting the duration of the agreement
  9. Providing for a trial period (provisional application)
  10. Providing for unilateral denunciation or withdrawal
  11. Breaking the agreement into parts
  12. Amendment or revision
  13. Dispute settlement provisions
  14. Risk-spreading devices
  15. Controlling risk in multilateral agreements
      a. Protecting against undesired or inadequate participation by other states
      b. Reservations to multilateral agreements
      c. Protecting against collective decisionmaking
II. Protecting against a change in the value of the agreement
  1. Controlling the value of the agreement
      a. Warranty by the other state of the value of its performance
      b. Guarantee of value by third party
      c. Tying the level of one state's performance to the cost of the other state's or a joint performance
      d. Setting floors or ceilings on performance
      e. Setting the level of performance by a specific objective standard, index, or ratio

219

    f. Setting levels of performance by a general standard

    g. Level of performance determined by an expert body or third party

    h. Hedging

  2. Providing for revision or amendment of the agreement

    a. Review or revision following joint agreement

    b. Automatic review or revision after a certain period

    c. Review or revision following the occurrence of certain circumstances

  3. Providing for release from the agreement

    a. Release contingent on agreement of the other state (waiver)

    b. Release upon unilateral determination

    c. Release upon the occurrence of particular circumstances

    d. Rescission in the event of fraud, mistake, or impossibility

III. Protecting against nonperformance or inadequate performance by the other state

  1. Ensuring that the other state can perform

    a. Demonstration of capability

    b. Earmarking relevant resources

    c. Ensuring legal capacity

    d. Ensuring technical or financial capacity

  2. Making nonperformance or inadequate performance clear

    a. Description of performance in specific and unambiguous terms

    b. Provisions for verifying performance

      (i) Reports to the state concerned or to a third party

      (ii) Inquiry, surveillance, or inspection by the state concerned

      (iii) Inquiry, surveillance, or inspection by a third party

      (iv) "Tripwires," or early warning devices

    c. Unilateral determination by one state of the adequacy of performance by the other state

    d. Determination of adequacy of performance by third parties

  3. Compelling performance by the other state

    a. Compelling performance by one's own actions

    b. Compelling performance through third parties

  4. Making nonperformance impossible or impractical

    a. Dividing the means necessary to accomplish a mutual objective

    b. Institutionalizing ("internalizing") the other state's performance within its own domestic legal system

    c. Institutionalizing the other state's performance through third-party involvement

    d. Political, economic, or social integration

  5. Rewarding full performance

6. Decreasing the probability of the other state's gaining from nonperformance
   a. Conditioning one's own performance on the other state's performance
      (i) Making the other state perform first
      (ii) Simultaneous exchange
      (iii) Withholding further performance
      (iv) Breaking the arrangement into parts
      (v) Performance held by third party (escrow)
   b. Providing for the recovery of one's own performance
      (i) Retention of rights to the performance despite delivery
      (ii) Requiring special measures by the other state to protect or permit recovery of the performance
      (iii) Providing for third-party assistance to compel restitution
   c. Requiring the other state to furnish collateral or bond
   d. Providing for third-party assistance to compel payment equivalent in value to performance
   e. Preventing the other state from exploiting one's vulnerability
7. Making nonperformance costly
   a. Forfeiture or loss of prepayment, part performance, or reliance costs
   b. Deposit of collateral, hostage, or pawn greater in value than either state's performance
   c. Political, economic, military, or other sanctions
8. Reducing one's own vulnerability in the event of nonperformance
   a. Reducing one's own reliance costs
   b. Preventing loss of one's own performance
   c. Preventing the other state from exploiting one's own reliance on the agreement
      (i) Making it impossible or impractical for the other state to exploit one's vulnerability
      (ii) Providing warning
      (iii) Standby arrangements
      (iv) Third-party guarantees or assistance

Short Titles and Abbreviations

Treaties and Other International Agreements

ABM Treaty
> Treaty on the Limitation of Anti-Ballistic Missile Systems, signed at Moscow May 26, 1972, 23 UST 3435, TIAS 7503, text also in 11 *ILM* 784 (1972).

Antarctic Marine Living Resources Convention
> Convention on the Conservation of Antarctic Marine Living Resources, concluded at Canberra May 20, 1980, text in 19 *ILM* 841 (1980).

Antarctic Treaty
> Antarctic Treaty, done at Washington Dec. 1, 1959, 12 UST 794, TIAS 4780, 402 UNTS 71, text also in 54 *AJIL* 476 (1960).

EEC Treaty
> Treaty Establishing the European Economic Community, done at Rome March 25, 1957, 298 UNTS 3.

Egypt-Israel Peace Treaty
> Treaty of Peace Between the Arab Republic of Egypt and the State of Israel, signed at Washington March 26, 1979, text in 79 *Dept. St. Bull.* 3 (May 1979), 18 *ILM* 362 (1979).

Egypt-Israel Sinai Agreement
> Egypt-Israel Agreement on the Sinai and Suez Canal, done at Geneva Sept. 4, 1975, text in 14 *ILM* 1450 (1975).

European Human Rights Convention
> Convention for the Protection of Human Rights and Fundamental Freedoms, done at Rome Nov. 4, 1950, 213 UNTS 221.

FAO Constitution
> Constitution of the United Nations Food and Agriculture Organization, done at Quebec Oct. 16, 1945, 12 UST 980, TIAS 4803.

GATT
> General Agreement on Tariffs and Trade, done at Geneva Oct. 30, 1947, 61 Stat. (5),(6), TIAS 1700, 55 UNTS 187, 4 Bevans 639.

Genocide Convention
> Convention on the Prevention and Punishment of the Crime of Genocide,

adopted by the General Assembly of the United Nations Dec. 9, 1948, 78 UNTS 277.

IAEA Statute

Statute of the International Atomic Energy Agency, done at New York Oct. 26, 1956, 8 UST 1093, TIAS 3873, 276 UNTS 3.

IBRD Agreement

Articles of Agreement of the International Bank for Reconstruction and Development, done at Washington Dec. 27, 1945, 60 Stat. 1440, TIAS 1402, 3 Bevans 1390, 2 UNTS 134.

ICAO Convention

Convention on International Civil Aviation, done at Chicago Dec. 7, 1944, 61 Stat. 1180, TIAS 1591, 3 Bevans 944, 15 UNTS 295.

ILO Constitution

Instrument for the Amendment of the Constitution of the International Labour Organization, done at Montreal Oct. 9, 1946, 62 Stat. 3485, TIAS 1868, 4 Bevans 188, 15 UNTS 35.

IMF Agreement

Articles of Agreement of the International Monetary Fund, opened for signature at Washington Dec. 27, 1945, 60 Stat. 1401, TIAS 1501, 3 Bevans 1351, 2 UNTS 39.

International Coffee Agreement, 1962

International Coffee Agreement, done at New York Sept. 28, 1962, 14 UST 1911, TIAS 5505, 469 UNTS 169.

International Coffee Agreement, 1976

International Coffee Agreement, 1976, done at London Dec. 3, 1975, 28 UST 6401, TIAS 8683.

Marine Pollution Convention

The International Convention for the Prevention of Pollution from Ships, done at London Nov. 2, 1973, text in 12 *ILM* 1319 (1973).

NATO Treaty

North Atlantic Treaty, signed at Washington April 4, 1949, 63 Stat. 2241, TIAS 1964, 4 Bevans 828, 34 UNTS 243.

Non-Proliferation Treaty

Treaty on the Non-Proliferation of Nuclear Weapons, done at Washington, London, and Moscow July 1, 1968, 21 UST 483, TIAS 6839, 729 UNTS 161.

Nuclear Test Ban Treaty

Treaty Banning Nuclear Weapon Tests in the Atmosphere, in Outer Space, and Under Water, done at Moscow Aug. 5, 1963, 14 UST 1313, TIAS 5433, 480 UNTS 43.

OAS Charter
Charter of the Organization of American States, signed at Bogota April 30, 1948, 2 UST 2394, TIAS 2361, 119 UNTS 3.
OAU Charter
Charter of the Organization of African Unity, done at Addis Ababa May 25, 1963, 479 UNTS 39.
Ocean Dumping Convention
Convention on the Prevention of Marine Pollution by Dumping of Wastes and Other Matter, done at Washington, London, Mexico City, and Moscow Dec. 29, 1972, 26 UST 2403, TIAS 8165, text also in 11 *ILM* 1291 (1972).
OECD Convention
Convention Establishing the Organization for Economic Cooperation and Development, signed at Paris Dec. 14, 1960, 12 UST 1728, TIAS 4891.
Oil Pollution Convention
International Convention for the Prevention of Pollution of the Sea by Oil, done at London May 12, 1954, 12 UST 2989, TIAS 4900, 327 UNTS 3.
Outer Space Treaty
Treaty on Principles Governing the Activities of States in the Exploration and Use of Outer Space, including the Moon and other Celestial Bodies, done at Washington, London, and Moscow Jan. 27, 1967, 18 UST 2410, TIAS 6347, 610 UNTS 205.
SALT I Agreement
Interim Agreement of Certain Measures with Respect to the Limitation of Strategic Offensive Arms, with Protocol, signed at Moscow May 26, 1972, 23 UST 3462, TIAS 7504, text also in 11 *ILM* 791 (1972).
SALT II Treaty
Treaty Between the United States of America and the Union of Soviet Socialist Republics on the Limitation of Strategic Offensive Arms, signed in Vienna June 18, 1979, text in 18 *ILM* 1138 (1979).
U.N. Charter
Charter of the United Nations with the Statute of the International Court of Justice attached thereto, signed at San Francisco June 26, 1945, 59 Stat. 1031, TS 993, 3 Bevans 1153.
U.S.–German FCN Treaty
U.S.–Federal Republic of Germany Treaty of Friendship, Commerce, and Navigation, signed at Washington Oct. 29, 1954, TIAS 3593, 7 UST 1839, 273 UNTS 3.
Vienna Convention
Vienna Convention on the Law of Treaties, adopted May 23, 1969 by the

U.N. Conference on the Law of Treaties, U.N. Doc. A/Conf. 39/27 (1969), text also in 63 *AJIL* 875 (1969) and 8 *ILM* 679 (1969).

Vietnam Truce Agreement

United States–Democratic Republic of Vietnam–Republic of Vietnam–Provisional Revolutionary Government of Republic of South Vietnam, Agreement on Ending the War and Restoring the Peace in Vietnam, signed at Paris Jan. 27, 1973, 24 UST 1, TIAS 7542, text also in 12 *ILM* 62 (1973) and 68 *Dept. St. Bull.* 169 (Feb. 1973).

Warsaw Pact

Treaty of Friendship, Co-operation, and Mutual Assistance, signed at Warsaw May 14, 1955, 219 UNTS 3, text also in W. E. Butler, *A Source Book on Socialist International Organizations* (Alphen aan den Rijn, The Netherlands: Sijthoff and Noordhoff, 1978), p. 1136.

Whaling Convention

International Convention for the Regulation of Whaling, done at Washington Dec. 2, 1946, 62 Stat. 1716, TIAS 1849, 4 Bevans 248, 161 UNTS 72.

WHO Constitution

Constitution of the World Health Organization, done at New York July 22, 1946, 62 Stat. 2679, TIAS 1808, 4 Bevans 119, 14 UNTS 185.

WMO Convention

Convention of the World Meteorological Organization, done at Washington Oct. 11, 1947, 1 UST 281, TIAS 2052, 77 UNTS 143.

Other Sources and Periodicals

AJIL

American Journal of International Law

Bevans

Treaties and Other International Agreements of the United States of America 1776–1949, compiled under the direction of Charles I. Bevans

Dept. St. Bull.

Department of State Bulletin (published by U.S. Department of State, Washington, D.C.)

ICJ Rep.

Reports of the International Court of Justice

ILM

International Legal Materials (published by the American Society of International Law, Washington, D.C.)

LNTS

League of Nations Treaty Series

Proc. ASIL

Proceedings of the American Society of International Law (at annual meetings of the Society)

Rec. des Cours

Recueil des Cours de l'Academie de Droit International (Leiden: A. W. Sijthoff) (lectures delivered at the annual summer sessions of the Hague Academy of International Law)

Stat.

United States Statutes at Large

TIAS

Treaties and Other International Acts Series, issued singly in pamphlets by the U.S. Department of State

TS

Treaty Series, issued singly in pamphlets by the U.S. Department of State (until replaced in 1945 by TIAS)

UNTS

United Nations Treaty Series

UST

United States Treaties and Other International Agreements (volumes published on a calendar-year basis beginning as of Jan. 1, 1950)

Notes

CHAPTER 1:   Risk as an Obstacle to International Agreement

1   The literature on international dispute-settlement is very extensive. See, generally, *e.g.*, C. Waldock, ed., *International Disputes: The Legal Aspects* (London: Europa, 1972); and the series of studies by the United Nations Institute for Training and Research on dispute settlement, including S. Bailey, *Peaceful Settlement of Disputes: Ideas and Proposals for Research* (New York, UNITAR, 1971). Representative treaty provisions on dispute settlement are collected in United Nations, *A Survey of Treaty Provisions for the Pacific Settlement of International Disputes, 1949–1962*, U.N. Sales No. 66.V.5 (1966). On judicial settlement of disputes, see, *e.g.*, L. Gross, ed., *The Future of the International Court of Justice*, 4 vols. (Dobbs Ferry, N.Y.: Oceana, 1976); C. Jenks, *The Prospects of International Adjudication* (London: Stevens/Dobbs Ferry: Oceana, 1964); H. Mosler and R. Bernhardt, eds., *Judicial Settlement of International Disputes* (Berlin, Heidelberg, and New York: Springer Verlag, 1974); and M. Katz, *The Relevance of International Adjudication* (Cambridge: Harvard Univ. Press, 1968). For discussions of dispute-settlement procedures under agreements establishing international organizations, see, *e.g.*, H. G. Schermers, *International Institutional Law*, 2 vols. (Leiden: A. W. Sijthoff, 1972), Vol. 2, Chpt. 9, and F. Kirgis, *International Organizations in Their Legal Setting* (St. Paul: West, 1977), pp. 290–430; and, with respect to the United Nations more particularly, *e.g.*, K. V. Raman, ed., *Dispute Settlement through the United Nations* (Dobbs Ferry, N.Y.: Oceana, 1977). There are a great many studies covering either particular disputes, particular dispute-settlement institutions, or dispute-settlement mechanisms in particular fields, *e.g.*, Sohn, "Settlement of Disputes Relating to the Interpretation and Application of Treaties," 150 *Rec. des Cours* 195 (1976), and my own, Bilder, "The Anglo-Icelandic Fisheries Dispute," 1973 *Wis. L. Rev.* 37, and R. Bilder, "The Settlement of Disputes in the Field of the International Law of the Environment," 144 *Rec. des Cours* 139 (Vol. I, 1975).

2   Among broader recent studies compiling certain risk-management provisions, see H. Blix and J. H. Emerson, eds., *The Treaty Maker's Handbook* (Dobbs Ferry, N.Y.: Oceana, 1973), a useful compilation of standard treaty clauses; and P. Rohn, *World Treaty Index*, 5 vols. (Santa Barbara: ABC-Clio, 1974), and P. Rohn, *Treaty Profiles* (Santa Barbara: ABC-Clio, 1976), which compile, index, and collate in a variety of ways information concerning treaties from a computerized data bank covering treaties published during the period 1920–70, established by the University of Washington Treaty Research Center, and directed by Professor Rohn. See also U.N. Secretariat, *Handbook of Final Clauses*, ST/LEG/6 (August 5, 1957).

Increasing attention is being paid to problems of risk management and contractual planning in the study of domestic American contract law see, *e.g.*, I. Macneil, *Contracts: Exchange Transactions and Relations*, 2nd ed. (Mineola, N.Y.: Foundation Press, 1978), Part II; and Macneil, "A Primer of Contract Planning," 48 *So. Calif. L. Rev.* 627 (1975), and in international concession and other business arrangements, see, *e.g.*, D. Smith and L. Wells, Jr., *Negotiating Third World Mineral Agreements: Promises as Prologue* (Cambridge, Mass.: Ballinger Pub. Co., 1975).

3   For useful efforts to examine some of these risk-management issues, see, *e.g.*, T. Schelling, *The Strategy of Conflict* (Cambridge: Harvard Univ. Press, 1960); F. Iklé, *How Nations Negotiate*, (New York: Harper & Row, 1964); R. Fisher, *International Conflict for Beginners* (New York: Harper & Row, 1969); T. Franck, *The Structure of Impartiality: Examining the Riddle of One Law in a Fragmented World* (New York: Macmillan, 1968); S. Schwebel, ed., *The Effectiveness of International Decisions* (Dobbs Ferry, N.Y.: Oceana, 1971); Chayes, "An Inquiry into the Working of Arms Control Agreements," 85 *Harv. L. Rev.* 905 (1972); and Heymann, "The Problem of Coordination: Bargaining and Rules," 86 *Harv. L. Rev.* 797 (1973).

A number of studies of particular negotiations and agreements contain useful insights on risk-management problems. See, *e.g.*, H. Nicolson, *The Congress of Vienna: A Study in Allied Unity, 1812–1822* (London: Constable, 1946); E. Stein, *Diplomats, Warriors, Scientists and Politicians* (Ann Arbor: Univ. of Michigan Press, 1966); J. Newhouse, *Cold Dawn: The Story of SALT* (New York: Holt, Rinehart & Winston, 1973); E. Preeg, *Traders and Diplomats* (Washington, D.C.: Brookings Institution, 1970); M. Camps, *The Free Trade Area Negotiations* (Princeton: Woodrow Wilson School, Princeton Univ., 1959); Bilder, "The International Coffee Agreement: A Case History in Negotiation," 28 *Law and Contemporary Problems* 328 (1963).

The extensive literature on arms control theory and deterrence theory is also relevant to certain aspects of risk management, particularly verification and sanctions.

4 For broad discussions of the importance and role of cooperation, see generally, *e.g.*, G. Marwell and D. R. Schmitt, *Cooperation: An Experimental Analysis* (New York: Academic Press, 1975); M. Deutsch, *The Resolution of Conflict* (New Haven: Yale Univ. Press, 1973); M. A. May and L. W. Doob, *Competition and Cooperation* (New York: Social Science Research Council, 1937); P. Blau, *Exchange and Power in Social Life* (New York: John Wiley, 1964); G. C. Homans, *Social Behavior: Its Elementary Forms*, rev. ed. (New York: Harcourt Brace Jovanovich, 1974); Patchen, "Models of Cooperation and Conflict: A Critical Review," 14 *J. Conflict Res.* 389 (1970); Nisbet, "Cooperation," 3 *International Encyclopedia of the Social Sciences* (1968).

5 R. E. Leakey and R. Lewin, *Origins* (New York: Dutton, 1977), p. 223. See also Leakey and Lewin, *People of the Lake: Mankind and Its Beginnings* (New York: Anchor/Doubleday, 1978), Chpt. 12.

Other observers, however, stress competitiveness and aggression as basic human characteristics. Compare, *e.g.*, K. Lorenz, *On Aggression* (New York: Harcourt, Brace, & World, 1966) and E. Fromm, *The Anatomy of Human Destructiveness* (New York: Holt, Rinehart & Winston, 1973), and see E. Wilson, *On Human Nature* (Cambridge: Harvard Univ. Press, 1978), Chpt. 5.

6 "Introduction" to the *Report of the Secretary-General to the Twenty-Eighth U.N. General Assembly*, 28 GAOR, Supp. No. 1A, U.N. Doc. A/9001/Add. 1 (1973), p. 1, reported *N.Y. Times*, Aug. 27, 1973, p. 1. See also, *e.g.*, former Secretary of State Kissinger's statement that "never before has the world been more in need of cooperative solutions." Address "The Global Challenge and International Cooperation," delivered in Milwaukee, Wisconsin, July 14, 1975, text in 73 *Dept. St. Bull.* 149 (1975), p. 153. Also President Carter's Address to the U.N. General Assembly, March 17, 1977, text in 76 *Dept. St. Bull.* 329 (1977), and, more generally, *e.g.*, R. Heilbroner, *An Inquiry into the Human Prospect* (New York: Norton, 1974); R. Falk, *This Endangered Planet* (New York: Random House, 1971); L. Brown, *World without Borders* (New York: Random House, 1972); and M. Mesarovic and E. Pestel, *Mankind at the Turning Point: The Second Report to the Club of Rome* (New York: Dutton/Reader's Digest Press, 1974).

7 The law of international agreements is the subject of an extensive literature. See, *e.g.*, A. McNair, *The Law of Treaties* (Oxford: Clarendon Press, 1961); T. Elias, *The Modern Law of Treaties* (Dobbs Ferry, N.Y.: Oceana,

1974); I. Sinclair, *The Vienna Convention on the Law of Treaties* (Manchester: Manchester Univ. Press/Dobbs Ferry, N.Y.: Oceana, 1973); M. Whiteman, *Digest of International Law*, Vol. 5, Dept. of State Publication 7873, (1965). On the negotiation of international agreements, see, *e.g.*, F. Iklé, *How Nations Negotiate* (New York: Harper & Row, 1964).

This law is now largely codified in the 1969 Vienna Convention on the Law of Treaties, which entered into force on January 27, 1980, following ratification by 35 nations. The convention was sent to the U.S. Senate by President Nixon on November 22, 1971, S. Exec. Doc. L, 92nd Cong., 1st Sess. (1971), but has not yet been acted upon by the Senate.

The late Professor Wolfgang Friedmann early called attention to the importance of an emerging "international law of cooperation." See W. Friedmann, *The Changing Structure of International Law* (New York: Columbia Univ. Press, 1964).

8   A. Nussbaum, *A Concise History of the Law of Nations*, rev. ed. (New York: Macmillan, 1954), p. 1.

9   See Iklé, *supra* n. 3, p. 7.

10 See, *e.g.*, Briggs, "United States Ratification of the Vienna Convention," 73 *AJIL* 470 (1973).

11 Vienna Convention, Art. 2 (1) (a).

12 See, *e.g.*, W. W. Bishop, Jr., *International Law: Cases and Materials*, 3rd ed. (Boston: Little, Brown, 1971), pp. 92–93.

13 See, *e.g.*, Iklé, *supra* n. 3, p. 42.

14 Information supplied by Professor Peter H. Rohn, University of Washington Treaty Research Center. The figure of 15,000 agreements is only a rough estimate, since the number of agreements presently in force is not accurately known. The University of Washington Treaty Research Center estimates that approximately 40,000 international agreements have been concluded in the twentieth century, most of them in the last thirty-five years.

   For one useful attempt at an index, see Rohn, *World Treaty Index, supra* n. 2. Many, but not all, of these treaties are collected in the 205 volumes of the League of Nations Treaty Series and the 862 published volumes (as of 1979) of the United Nations Treaty Series (information supplied by U.N. Treaty Office).

15 See *Yearbook of International Organizations*, 17th ed. (Brussels: Union of International Assoc., 1978), table 1. These figures include only organizations based on a formal instrument of agreement between governments and having three or more member states and a permanent secretariat; if bilateral intergovernmental organizations and organizations lacking a secretariat were counted, the number of such organizations would be considerably higher.

16 Estimate supplied by Professor Peter H. Rohn, University of Washington
    Treaty Research Center. The center estimates that about 550 agreements
    per year were being concluded in the period immediately following World
    War II and that this figure had risen to 1,100 agreements per year in 1975.

17 More precisely, as of January 1, 1979, the United States was party to
    6,912 international agreements of which 6,192 were bilateral agreements
    and 720 were multilateral agreements. Of these 6,912 agreements, 966
    were entered into as formal treaties under the U.S. Constitution and 5,946
    were entered into as executive agreements under U.S. law. During the
    calendar year 1978 the United States entered into 334 new international
    agreements. Information supplied by Arthur Rovine, assistant legal ad-
    viser for treaty affairs, U.S. Department of State. See also U.S. Depart-
    ment of State, *Treaties in Force* (Jan. 1, 1979), and U.S. Department of
    State, *United States Contributions to International Organizations: 25th
    Advisory Report to the Congress for Fiscal Year 1976* (1978). U.S.
    international agreements currently in force are listed in the annual edition
    of U.S. Department of State, *Treaties in Force, supra*, and compiled in
    various collections, principally the 28 volumes (as of 1977) of U.S.
    Department of State, *U.S. Treaties*.

18 Vienna Convention, Art. 26. On the nature of the principle of *pacta sunt
    servanda*—that agreements should be carried out in good faith—see, *e.g.*,
    McNair, *supra* n. 7, p. 493; Bishop, *supra* n. 12, pp. 141–42; Kunz, "The
    Meaning and the Range of the Norm *Pacta Sunt Servanda*," 39 *AJIL* 180
    (1945); and, generally, Schachter, "Towards a Theory of International
    Obligation," 8 *Va. J. Intl. L.* 300 (1967–68).

19 See, *e.g.*, Weinstein, "The Concept of a Commitment in International
    Relations," 13 *J. Conflict Res.* 39 (1969), E. Goffman, *Strategic Inter-
    action* (Philadelphia: Univ. of Pennsylvania Press, 1969), pp. 112–13.

20 While the parties involved in cooperative transactions will often deter-
    mine between themselves through their bargaining how the risks of their
    agreements will be allocated, many developed legal systems also provide
    at least some express or implicit general rules for allocating these risks.
    Macneil, "A Primer of Contract Planning," *supra* n. 2, p. 670, notes that
    "incomplete risk planning is an inherent characteristic of the planning
    process, with the result that, to be effective, any contract legal system
    must engage in a very wide range of gap filling." Compare, for example,
    the statutory allocation of risks in commercial transactions provided by the
    Uniform Commercial Code (UCC), Art. 2 (Sales), now in force in all
    states of the United States except Louisiana. The international legal
    system, through the type of general treaty rules reflected in the Vienna
    Convention, to some extent performs a similar supportive function.

21 See, *e.g.*, L. Henkin, *How Nations Behave* (New York: Praeger, 1968);

Bilder, "The Office of the Legal Adviser: The State Department Lawyer and Foreign Affairs," 56 *AJIL* 633 (1962), pp. 648–54; Bilder, "Breach of Treaty and Response Thereto," 1967 *Proc. ASIL* 193. And see, generally, Friedmann, "The Reality of International Law: A Reappraisal," 10 *Colum. J. Transnatl. L.* 46 (1971).

22 The U.S. embassy in Tehran was seized Nov. 4, 1979. The U.S. application to the International Court was filed Nov. 29, 1979. For the text of relevant documents see *Dept. St. Bull.* (Jan. 1980), pp. 37–41, and 18 *ILM* 1464 (1979). The Court issued an order indicating provisional measures on Dec. 15, 1979, reprinted in 74 *AJIL* 266 (1980) and 19 *ILM* 139 (1980). For the Court's final judgment, see [1980] ICJ Rep. 3, reprinted 19 *ILM* 553 (1980). In the Jan. 19, 1981, agreement with Iran resolving the hostage situation, the United States agreed to withdraw the case. *N.Y. Times*, Jan. 20, 1981, p. A4.

23 See references in n. 21, *supra*; and R. Fisher, *International Crises and the Role of Law: Points of Choice* (Oxford: Oxford Univ. Press, 1978), esp. Chpt. II.

24 Henkin, *supra* n. 21, p. 48. See also R. Fisher, *supra*, p. 51: "[To] have the power to influence other states with one's promises at a time of crisis requires a reputation for principled behaviour that has been built up over time. There are various principles that one might adopt as guidelines for state behaviour, but respect for law—substantive and procedural—appears to be the most valuable counsel over the long run." And compare also former Secretary of State Kissinger's remark that "foreign governments, when they deal with the United States, make a bet in their dealings on the constancy of American policy and on the ability of the United States to carry through on whatever it is that we promise, or fail to promise, or threaten." *Washington Post*, March 31, 1975, p. A14.

25 Schelling, *supra* n. 3, p. 45. Compare Macaulay, "Non-Contractual Relations in Business: A Preliminary Study," 28 *Am. Soc. Rev.* 55 (1963), p. 63–64, commenting on nonlegal sanctions in private business transactions: "The final type of non-legal sanction is the most obvious. Both business units involved in the exchange desire to continue successfully in business and will avoid conduct which might interfere with attaining this goal. One is concerned with both the reaction of the other party in the particular exchange and with his own general business reputation. . . .

"Not only do the particular business units in a given exchange want to deal with each other again, they also want to deal with other business units in the future. And the way one behaves in a particular transaction, or a series of transactions, will color his general business reputation."

26 Chayes, *supra* n. 3, p. 968.

27 Iklé, *supra* n. 3, p. 8.

28 Bilder, "Breach of Treaty and Response Thereto," *supra* n. 20. See also A. David, *The Strategy of Treaty Termination: Lawful Breaches and Retaliations* (New Haven: Yale Univ. Press, 1975); Fisher, *supra* n. 24; Schachter, *supra* n. 18.

29 See Macaulay, *supra* n. 25, p. 61–62. See also Beale and Dugdale, "Contracts between Businessmen: Planning and the Use of Contractual Remedies," 2 *Brit. J. of Law and Society* 45 (1975).

30 The process of achieving international cooperation typically involves (1) recognition by at least one nation that its ability to attain one or more of its objectives may be affected by another nation's or other nations' behavior; (2) a tentative decision that it may be able more easily or effectively to influence the other nation or nations to behave in ways which further its objectives through offers of cooperation or reciprocal exchanges of behavior than by resorting to other options, such as "going it alone," persuasion, or coercion; (3) persuading the other nation or nations that cooperation may also be in its or their interest; (4) negotiating the terms of the cooperative arrangement; (5) formally concluding the arrangement; (6) beginning implementation of the arrangement; and (7) dealing with problems that may arise in the course of implementing the arrangement.

31 *The American Heritage Dictionary of the English Language* new college ed. 1975. For other definitions, see, *e.g.*, W. Lee, *Decision Theory and Human Behavior* (New York: Wiley, 1971), p. 117: "In everyday usage 'risk' refers to a situation or a choice that involves possible loss or danger and the loss or danger implied is apt to be substantial"; Macneil, "A Primer of Contract Planning," *supra* n. 2, p. 667: "The manmade concept of risk is a recognition that human beings are in a constant state of partial ignorance about the future, including future losses." Some decision theorists use the term *risk* in a more technical sense as applying to a situation in which the probabilities of uncertain future outcomes or events are knowns, in contrast with a situation of "uncertainty" or "ignorance" in which such probabilities are not known. See, *e.g.*, D. E. Farrar, *The Investment Decision under Uncertainty* (Englewood Cliffs: Prentice-Hall, 1962), p. 1.

32 There is an extensive literature on decisionmaking under conditions of uncertainty and risk. See, generally, *e.g.*, Lee, *supra* n. 31; Farrar, *supra* n. 31; G. L. S. Schackle, *Decision, Order, and Time in Human Affairs* (Cambridge: Cambridge Univ. Press, 1961); C. Carter, G. Meredith, and G. L. S. Schackle, *Uncertainty and Business Decisions*, 2nd ed. (Liverpool: Liverpool Univ. Press, 1953); M. J. Bowman, ed., *Expectations,*

Uncertainty and Business Behavior (New York: Social Science Research Council, Committee on Business Enterprise Research, 1958); J. Cohen, *Behavior in Uncertainty and Its Social Implications* (London: Allen and Unwin, 1964); H. Simon, "Theories of Decisionmaking in Economics and Behavioral Science," 49 *Am. Econ. Rev.* 253 (1959); Pruitt, "Pattern and Level of Risk in Gambling Decisions," 69 *Psych. Rev.* 187 (1962).

33   Marwell and Schmitt, *supra* n. 4, Chpt. 4 and pp. 15, 180–83. Lee, *supra* n. 31, p. 139, suggests that uncertainty alone, even in the absence of risk, can disrupt cooperation.

34   See, generally, *e.g.*, R. Jervis, *Perception and Misperception in International Politics* (Princeton: Princeton Univ. Press, 1976).

35   See, *e.g.*, Deutsch, *supra* n. 4, p. 53; Terhune, "The Effects of Personality on Cooperation and Conflict," in P. Swingle, *The Structure of Conflict* (New York: Academic Press, 1970); Terhune, "From National Character to Behavior: A Reformulation," 14 *J. Conflict Res.* 203 (1970).
    In an interesting set of experiments, Deutsch found that persons who were high on a scale designed to indicate authoritarian personality were generally less trusting and less likely to make cooperative choices than those who were low on the scale, and that they were also less trustworthy and tended to exploit a partner who had chosen to cooperate. Deutsch, "Trust, Trustworthiness and the F Scale," 61 *J. of Abnormal and Soc. Psych.* 138 (1960). See also K. J. Gergen, *The Psychology of Behavior Exchange* (Reading, Pa.: Addison-Wesley, 1969), p. 63.

36   The phrase is from Mario Puzo's novel *The Godfather* (New York: Putnam's, 1969).

37   See, *e.g.*, Abba Eban's statement in an interview reported in *Time*, March 6, 1978, p. 37: "I assume the Israeli government knows that autonomy carries certain risks, and that it will not stop there but will develop further. But you cannot have peace without risks."

38   For discussions of the nature and role of trust, see, especially, Deutsch, *The Resolution of Conflict*, *supra* n. 4, Chpt. 7, which is based in part upon material in Deutsch, "Cooperation and Trust: Some Theoretical Notes," in M. Jones, ed., *Nebraska Symposium on Motivation* (Lincoln: Univ. of Nebraska Press, 1962), p. 275; and Deutsch, "Trust and Suspicion," 2 *J. Conflict Res.* 267 (1958). See also, *e.g.*, Marwell and Schmitt, *supra* n. 4; Swinth, "The Establishment of the Trust Relationship," 11 *J. Conflict Res.* 335 (1967); Gergen, *supra* n. 35; Heymann, *supra* n. 3, pp. 821–23.

39   For discussion and analysis of the "rational national actor" model, see, *e.g.*, G. T. Allison, *Essence of Decision: Explaining the Cuban Missile Crisis* (Boston: Little, Brown, 1971), especially Chpt. 1; H. Morgenthau, *Politics among Nations*, 4th ed. (New York: Knopf, 1967), p. 5. Allison,

p. 254, comments: "Nations can be reified, but at a considerable cost in understanding. By personifying nations, one glides over critical characteristics of behavior where organization is the main mover." For a similar note of caution, see Chayes, *supra* n. 3, p. 907.

40 For general discussions of various other theories and models of government foreign policy decisionmaking, see, *e.g.*, Allison, *supra*; M. Halperin, *Bureaucratic Politics and Foreign Policy* (Washington, D.C.: Brookings Institution, 1974); F. E. Rourke, *Bureaucracy and Foreign Policy* (Baltimore: Johns Hopkins Univ. Press, 1972); D. H. Davis, *How the Bureaucracy Makes Foreign Policy* (Lexington: Lexington Books, 1972); R. Snyder, H. Bruck, and B. Sapin, eds., *Foreign Policy Decisionmaking: An Approach to the Study of International Politics* (Glencoe, Ill.: Free Press, 1962).

41 See, *e.g.*, Schachter, "The Invisible College of International Lawyers," 72 *Nw. U. L. Rev.* 217 (1977); Falk, "Law, Lawyers, and the Conduct of American Foreign Relations," 78 *Yale L.J.* 919 (1968–69); J. E. Haar, *The Professional Diplomat* (Princeton: Princeton Univ. Press, 1969).

CHAPTER 2: General Risk-Management Techniques

1 Schachter, "The Twilight Existence of Nonbinding International Agreements," 71 *AJIL* 296 (1977), p. 300. My discussion of nonbinding agreements draws heavily on this excellent comment.

2 *Id.*, p. 296, citing D. P. O'Connell, *International Law*, 2nd ed. (London: Stevens, 1970), 1:195, and A. McNair, *The Law of Treaties* (Oxford: Clarendon Press, 1961), p. 6.

3 Nonbinding agreements are not covered by the Vienna Convention, being generally considered as not governed by international law. See Schachter, *supra* n. 1, p. 301 and n. 19.

4 *Id.*, p. 303, n. 26, citing 73 *Dept. St. Bull.* 613 (1975).

5 *Id.*, p. 304. See also R. Fisher, *International Crises and the Role of Law: Points of Choice* (Oxford: Oxford Univ. Press, 1978), p. 41: "To be effective [a rule] need not be legally binding. It might be established by a gentleman's agreement, through tacit bargaining, through unilateral assertion followed by general acquiescence, or by some other means out of the well-stocked armoury of international diplomacy."

6 Schachter, *supra* n. 1, pp. 297–98.

7 *Id.*, pp. 303–4.

8 *Id.*, p. 301, citing MacGibbon, "Estoppel in International Law," 7 *Intl. and Comp. L.Q.* 468 (1958), and Rubin, "The International Legal Effects of Unilateral Declarations," 71 *AJIL* 1 (1977).

9 *Fisheries Case* (United Kingdom v. Norway), [1951] ICJ Rep. 116.

10 Case concerning the *Right of Passage over Indian Territory* (Portugal v. India), [1960] ICJ Rep. 6. And see, generally, A. D'Amato, *The Concept of Custom in International Law* (Ithaca: Cornell Univ. Press, 1971), Chpt. 8; R. Baxter, "Treaties and Custom," 129 *Rec. des Cours* 25 (Vol. I, 1970); Akehurst, "Custom as a Source of International Law," 47 *Brit. Y. B. Intl. L.* 1 (1974–75).

11 L. Henkin, *How Nations Behave* (New York: Praeger, 1968), p. 53.

12 See "Soviet Joins the U.S. in Pledging Observance of Lapsing Arms Pact," *N.Y. Times*, Sept. 26, 1977, p. 10; "SALT Diplomacy, Abroad and at Home" (editorial), *id.*, Sept. 27, 1977, p. 38.

Nations also frequently tacitly apply the provisions of agreements which are expected to enter into force but are still awaiting ratification or acceptance, and it has been argued that they have an obligation to do so. See, *e.g.*, the U.S. State Department's statement that the United States and Soviet Union would act as if the SALT II treaty were in effect—both observing its provisions—despite the delay in ratification announced by President Carter in early January 1980. Anderson, "Soviets, U.S., to Act as if SALT in Force," UPI, Jan. 3, 1980. See also, C. Marcy, "SALT II Still Lives," *N.Y. Times*, Jan. 29, 1980, p. A29, who reported: "According to the State Department, the principle of international law, shared by the United States and the Soviet Union, that is applicable is that 'a state should refrain from taking actions which would defeat the object and purpose of a treaty it has signed' until the treaty has been ratified and enters into force.

"Since last June, when SALT II was signed, . . . both the United States and the Soviet Union have been abiding by its terms. The Carter Administration has said it will continue to abide by the terms if the Russians do. . . .

"Obviously, unilateral, or parallel, declarations of intent to adhere to SALT II can be breached any time. Such declarations do not constitute binding commitments by either party, as would be the case with a ratified treaty." And see Whitney, "Complying with Arms Pact," *N.Y. Times*, March 24, 1980, p. A8.

13 See, *e.g.*, Turner, "The Definition of Agreement under the Sherman Act: Conscious Parallelism and Refusals to Deal," 75 *Harv. L. Rev.* 655 (1962).

14 Henkin, *supra* n. 11, p. 53.

15 *Id.*, pp. 53–54.

16 See, generally, Rubin, *supra* n. 8.

17 *Nuclear Test* cases (Australia v. France), [1974] ICJ Rep. 253, 267; (New

Zealand v. France), ICJ Rep. (1974), pp. 457, 472. See Rubin, *supra* n. 8; and Franck, "Word Made Law: The Decision of the International Court of Justice in the Nuclear Test Cases," 69 *AJIL* 612 (1975).

18 See *Congressional Review of International Agreements,* Hearings before the Subcommittee on International Security and Scientific Affairs of the House of Representatives Committee on International Relations, 94th Cong., 2nd Sess. (1976), p. 242 (memo from Monroe Leigh, legal adviser).

19 R. Baxter, "Armistices and Other Forms of Suspension of Hostilities," 149 *Rec. des Cours* 357 (Vol. I, 1976), p. 371.

20 Henkin, *supra* n. 11, p. 53n.

21 UNGA Res. 3201 (S-V1) and 3202 (S-V1), May 1, 1974.

22 OECD Council, Rec. adopted Nov. 14, 1974, OECD Doc. C(74)224 of Nov. 21, 1974, text in 14 *ILM* 242 (1975).

23 OECD, "Guidelines for Multinational Enterprises," *Declaration on International Investment and Multinational Enterprises,* text in 15 *ILM* 967 (1976), 75 *Dept. St. Bull.* 83 (1976). For a discussion of issues concerning the legal effect of such codes, see, *e.g.,* Davidow and Chiles, "The United States and the Issue of the Binding or Voluntary Nature of International Codes of Conduct Regarding Restrictive Business Practices," 72 *AJIL* 247 (1978). See also "Draft Principles of Conduct in the Field of the Environment for the Guidance of States in the Conservation and Harmonious Utilization of Natural Resources Shared by Two or More States," in *Report of the Intergovernmental Working Group of Experts on Natural Resources Shared by Two or More States,* approved by the Governing Council of the U.N. Environmental Program at its Sixth Session, UNEP GC.6/CRP.Z, May 19, 1978. The principles are reprinted in 17 *ILM* 1094 (1978), pp. 1097–99.

24 See, *e.g.,* "Statement By The Vice-Chairman of the Delegation of the United States of America in Response to the Statement by the Chairman of the Group of 77 Regarding Deep-Seabed Legislation," delivered Oct. 1, 1979 at the Third U.N. Law of the Sea Conference, concerning the legal effect of certain U.N. General Assembly resolutions relating to deep-sea bed resources: "My Government rejects outright the notion that United Nations General Assembly resolutions, including United Nations General Assembly Resolutions 2574D (XXIV) and 2749 (XXV) and irrespective of the majorities by which such resolutions are adopted, are legally binding on any State in the absence of an international agreement that gives effect to such resolutions and that is in force for that State." U.N. Doc. A/CONF. 62/93 (Oct. 1, 1979). See also, *e.g.,* E. McDowell, *Digest of United States Practice in International Law, 1975,* Dept. State

Pub. 8865 (Washington, D.C., 1976), p. 85 (letter of S. Schwebel, deputy legal adviser).

25 UNGA Res. 1962 (XVIII), Dec. 13, 1963.

26 Outer Space Treaty. Contrast also, *e.g.*, the U.N. Declaration on the Elimination of All Forms of Racial Discrimination, UNGA Res. 1904 (XVIII), 1963, with the International Convention on the Elimination of All Forms of Racial Discrimination, 1965, 660 UNTS 195.

27 UNGA Res. 217 (III), U.N. Doc. A/810 (1948), p. 71, Dec. 10, 1948.

28 See, *e.g.*, discussion in L. Sohn and T. Buergenthal, *International Protection of Human Rights* (Indianapolis: Bobbs-Merrill, 1973), pp. 514–22.

29 On the effects of U.N. General Assembly resolutions, see, generally, *e.g.*, J. Castaneda, *Legal Effect of United Nations Resolutions*, tr. A. Amoia (New York: Columbia Univ. Press, 1969); Bleicher, "The Legal Significance of Re-Citation of General Assembly Resolutions," 63 *AJIL* 444 (1969); and panel discussion by Schwebel, Osakwe, and Garibaldi, "Contemporary Views on the Sources of International Law: The Effect of U.N. Resolutions on Emerging Legal Norms," 1979 *Proc. ASIL* 300.

30 Schachter, *supra* n. 1, p. 297.

31 *Id.*, p. 299.

32 *U.S. Weekly Comp. of Presidential Docs.*, Vol. 14, No. 29 (July 24, 1978), pp. 1038–39, text in 17 *ILM* 1285 (1978). See also, *e.g.*, *Nuclear Suppliers Group: Guidelines for Nuclear Transfers*, IAEA-INFCIRC/254 (Feb. 1978), text in 17 *ILM* 220 (1978), setting out agreed but apparently not legally binding guidelines by the fifteen nuclear states concerning their policies on nuclear exports, also discussed in Barnaby, "A Gentlemen's Nuclear Agreement," 73 *New Scientist* 461 (Feb. 24, 1977); and the declaration adopted on May 30, 1974, by the governments of the Organization of Economic Cooperation and Development member countries by which they mutually pledged not to utilize restrictions on imports as a way of dealing with balance of payments difficulties caused by the oil crisis, set forth in 70 *OECD Observer* 41 (June 1974) and cited in J. Jackson, *Legal Problems of International Economic Relations* (St. Paul: West, 1977), p. 908.

33 Final Act of the Conference on Security and Cooperation in Europe, signed at Helsinki, Aug. 1, 1975, text in 14 *ILM* 1292 (1975) and 73 *Dept. St. Bull.* 323 (1975).

34 See 14 *ILM* 1292 (1975), p. 1325.

35 *Id.*

36 Schachter, *supra* n. 1; Russell, "The Helsinki Declaration: Brobdingnag or Lilliput," 70 *AJIL* 242 (1976), pp. 247–48.

37   See, *e.g.*, Goldberg, "Human Rights and the Belgrade Meeting," 30 *Hastings L. Rev.* 249 (1978); and, generally, T. Buergenthal, ed., *Human Rights, International Law, and the Helsinki Accord* (Montclair, N.J.: Allenheld, Osmun/Universe Books, 1977). Documents concerning the 1978 Belgrade Review of the Final Act are collected in 17 *ILM* 1206 (1978).

38   Henkin, "Human Rights and Domestic Jurisdiction," in Buergenthal, *supra*, pp. 21, 25.

39   On "agreements to agree," see F. Iklé, *How Nations Negotiate* (New York: Harper & Row, 1964), pp. 17–22; Macneil, "A Primer of Contract Planning," 48 *So. Calif. L. Rev.* 627 (1975), p. 662.

40   U.S.–Soviet Agreement on Cooperation in the Field of Environmental Protection, 1972, 23 UST 845, TIAS 7345, Art. 1, text also in 11 *ILM* 761 (1972).

41   See, *e.g.*, Agreement between the United Kingdom and Norway Relating to the Delimitation of the Continental Shelf between the Two Countries, London, March 10, 1965, 551 UNTS 214, Art. 4; and generally, Lagoni, "Oil and Gas Deposits across National Frontiers," 73 *AJIL* 215 (1979).

42   Judgment of the French-Spanish Arbitral Tribunal of 16 November 1957 in the Matter of the Utilization of the Waters of Lake Lanoux, text in E. Lauterpacht, ed., 24 *Intl. L. Rep.* 101 (1957), p. 128, and 12 *U.N. Rpts. of Intl. Arb. Awards* 281 (1957). The case is noted and excerpted in 53 *AJIL* 156 (1959). For discussion, see, *e.g.*, Laylin and Bianchi, "The Role of Adjudication in International River Disputes: The Lake Lanoux Case," 53 *AJIL* 30 (1959). See also the *North Sea Continental Shelf Cases*, [1969] ICJ Rep. 4, 47.

43   On option agreements, see, *e.g.*, Macneil, *supra* n. 39, p. 661.

44   See U.S.–India Agreement for Cooperation Concerning the Civil Uses of Atomic Energy, 1963, 14 UST 1484, TIAS 5446, 488 UNTS 421, Art. II. Most atomic energy bilaterals, however, are "umbrella" agreements which do not mandate supply.

45   See, generally, *e.g.*, Iklé, *supra* n. 39, pp. 8–22. Ambiguity may also, of course, be nondeliberate, reflecting unintentional misunderstandings or inherent difficulties in achieving clarity or anticipating future situations to which the rule must be applied. These difficulties are noted in Chpt. 4, Sec. 2(a), *infra*.

46   See Schachter, *supra* n. 1, pp. 297–98.

47   Compare UNGA Res. 1803 (XVII) on Permanent Sovereignty over Natural Resources, adopted Dec. 14, 1962, discussed in Schwebel, "The Story of the U.N.'s Declaration on Permanent Sovereignty Over Natural Resources," 49 *Am. Bar Assoc. J.* 463 (1963).

48 See Declaration of Principles Governing the Sea-Bed and the Ocean Floor, and the Subsoil thereof, beyond the Limits of National Jurisdiction, UNGA Res. 2749 (XXV), 1970, text in 10 *ILM* 220 (1971); and the so-called "Moratorium" Resolution, UNGA Res. 2574D (XXIV), 1969, text in 9 *ILM* 419 (1970), p. 422.

49 Comment in panel discussion appearing in J. Bhagrati, ed., *The New International Economic Order* (Cambridge: MIT Press, 1977), p. 362.

50 See, *e.g.*, Stone, "Hopes and Loopholes in the 1974 Definition of Aggression," 71 *AJIL* 224 (1977), p. 226; and, more generally, J. Stone, *Conflict through Consensus: United Nations Approaches to Aggression* (Baltimore: Johns Hopkins Univ. Press, 1977), criticizing the U.N. General Assembly's 1974 resolution defining aggression.

51 Eban, "Camp David: The Unfinished Business," 57 *Foreign Affairs* 343 (Winter 1978/79), p. 350.

52 Antarctic Treaty; Agreement between Brazil and the U.S. Concerning Shrimp, 1972, 24 UST 923, TIAS 7603, text also in 11 *ILM* 453 (1972).

53 See, *e.g.*, T. Schelling, *The Strategy of Conflict* (Cambridge: Harvard Univ. Press, 1960), pp. 45, 134–35; Swinth, "The Establishment of the Trust Relationship," 11 *J. Conflict Res.* 335 (1967), p. 343; Kelman, "A Social Psychological Approach to the Study of International Relations," in H. C. Kelman, ed., *International Behavior: A Social Psychological Analysis* (New York: Holt, Rinehart & Winston, 1965), p. 573.

54 Schelling, *supra*, p. 45.

55 G. Marwell and D. R. Schmitt, *Cooperation: An Experimental Anaylsis* (New York: Academic Press, 1975), p. 186.

56 See, *e.g.*, the series of over a dozen U.S.–Soviet agreements on a variety of relatively minor subjects reached in May 1972 (texts in 11 *ILM* 756, 761, 770, and 773); June 1973 (texts in 12 *id.* 905, 909, and 911); and June 1974 (texts in 13 *id.* 888, 892, 896, and 901). Compare also the *Document on Confidence-building Measures and Certain Aspects of Security and Disarmament*, comprising part of the *Final Act of the Conference on Security and Cooperation in Europe, supra* n. 33, which provides for measures such as prior notification of major military maneuvers, exchange of observers, and prior notification of major military movements.

57 Eban, *supra* n. 51, p. 348.

58 Research on interpersonal cooperation raises some question whether past cooperation tends to generate future cooperation. See Bixenstine, Potash, and Wilson, "Effects of Level of Cooperative Choice by the Other Player on Choices in a Prisoner's Dilemma Game," Part I, 66 *J. of Abnormal and Soc. Psych.* 308 (1963), and Part II, 67 *id.* 139 (1963).

59 K. Gergen, *The Psychology of Behavior Exchange* (Reading: Addison-Wesley, 1969), p. 66.

60 Sohn, "Step-by-Step Acceptance of the Jurisdiction of the International Court of Justice," 58 *Proc. ASIL* 131 (1964).

61 Sohn, "Disarmament and Arms Control by Territory," 17 *Bull. Atomic Scientists* 130 (April 1961); Sohn, "Zonal Disarmament and Inspection: Variations on a Theme," 18 *id.* 4 (Sept. 1962).

62 Joint U.S.–Soviet Statement and Communiqué on Strategic Offensive Arms, signed by President Ford and General Secretary Brezhnev at Vladivostok, Nov. 24, 1974, text in 71 *Dept. St. Bull.* 879 (1974). And see statement by J. Martin, Jr., U.S. representative to the Conference of the Committee on Disarmament, March 4, 1975, text in 72 *Dept. St. Bull.* 454 (1975), p. 455.

63 See, *e.g.*, U.S.–German FCN Treaty, Art. XXIV; GATT, Art. XX.

64 U.S.–German FCN Treaty, Art. XXIV (1)(d).

65 GATT, Art. XXI, discussed in J. Jackson, *World Trade and the Law of GATT* (Indianapolis: Bobbs-Merrill, 1969), pp. 748–52. On GATT generally, see also R. Hudec, *The GATT Legal System and World Trade Diplomacy* (New York: Praeger, 1975); and K. Dam, *The GATT: Law and International Economic Organization* (Chicago: Univ. of Chicago Press, 1970).

See also, *e.g.*, European Convention on Human Rights, 1950, 213 UNTS 232, Art. 15 (right of derogation from obligations in time of war or other public emergency threatening the life of the nation); International Convention for the Safety of Life at Sea, 1960, 16 UST 185, TIAS 5780, 536 UNTS 27, Art. 6 (party may suspend whole or any part of regulations in case of war or other hostilities).

66 Ocean Dumping Convention, Art. V(2).

67 International Convention on Civil and Political Rights, 1966, adopted by UNGA Res. 2200 (XXI), Dec. 16, 1966, 21 UN GAOR, Supp. No. 16, Doc. A/6316, pp. 52–58, Art. 4. For comment, see, *e.g.*, Higgins, "Derogations under Human Rights Treaties," 48 *Brit. Y.B. Intl. L.* 281 (1976–77).

68 For general discussion, see general references on treaty law cited in Chpt. 1, n. 7; J. Ruda, "Reservations to Treaties," 146 *Rec. des Cours* 95 (1975); and W. W. Bishop, Jr., "Reservations to Treaties," 103 *Rec. des Cours* 245 (1961).

69 Vienna Convention, Art. 2(d). Articles 19–23 of the convention provide detailed rules regarding reservations. See also American Law Institute, *Restatement of the Law (Second), Foreign Relations Law of the United States* (1965), secs. 124–29.

70   U.S.–Panama Canal Treaty, 1977, text in 16 *ILM* 1021 (1977), and 77 *Dept. St. Bull.* (1977), p. 483; U.S.–Panama Treaty Concerning the Permanent Neutrality of the Panama Canal, 1977, text in 16 *ILM* 1040 (1977), and 77 *Dept. St. Bull.* (1977), p. 496; with text of the Senate reservations and understandings reprinted in 17 *ILM* 827 (1978), and 78 *Dept. St. Bull.* (May 1978), pp. 52–54.

71   17 *ILM* 828–29 (1978); 78 *Dept. St. Bull.* (May 1978), p. 53.

72   See, *e.g.*, *N.Y. Times*, Nov. 1, 1979, p. 3; *id.*, Nov. 7, 1979, p. 8; and, for the possibility of Soviet rejection of the Senate reservations and amendments, *id.*, July 9, 1979, p. 4; *id.*, July 10, 1979, p. 14.

73   Oil Pollution Convention, Art. III.

74   Convention on Prohibition of Military or Any Other Hostile Uses of Environmental Modification Techniques, 1977, text in 76 *Dept. St. Bull.* 27 (1977), 16 *ILM* 88 (1977).

75   See, generally, H. Blix and J. H. Emerson, eds., *The Treaty Maker's Handbook* (Dobbs Ferry, N.Y.: Oceana, 1973), pp. 96–103.

76   International Coffee Agreement, 1962, Art. 71; *The International Coffee Agreement, 1962*, Senate Exec. Rpt. No. 1, 88th Cong., 1st Sess. (1963). See also letter from Acting Secretary of State Ball to Senator Humphrey, May 20, 1963, in 109 *Cong. Rec.* 8619 (daily ed., May 21, 1963).

77   U.S.–German FCN Treaty, Art. XXIX.

78   International Sugar Agreement, 1958, 385 UNTS 137, Art. 42.

79   Antarctic Treaty, Art. 12.

80   Universal Postal Convention, 1952, 169 UNTS 3, Art. 83. The U.N. Charter contains no provision respecting its duration.

81   Protocol of Provisional Application to the General Agreement on Tariffs and Trade, 1947, 61 Stat. (Pts. 5 and 6), TIAS 1700, 55 UNTS 308, 4 Bevans 639. See also, *e.g.*, Canada-Nicaragua Trade Agreement, 1946, 236 UNTS 229, Art. IX (provisional application pending ratification, with a right to terminate prior to exchange of ratification upon three months' notice).

82   See Vienna Convention, Art. 25. A discussion of provisional application of agreements in relation to the proposed Law of the Sea Convention prepared by the Secretariat of the Third U.N. Law of the Sea Conference is contained in U.N. Doc. A/AC.138/88 (June 12, 1973).

83   On termination and suspension of the operation of treaties generally, see Vienna Convention, Arts. 54–68. The consequences of termination and suspension are treated in Articles 70 and 72 of the convention. For typical provisions, see *Treaty Maker's Handbook, supra* n. 75, pp. 104–15. Art. 56 of the Vienna Convention provides:

1. A treaty which contains no provision regarding its termination and which does not provide for denunciation or withdrawal is not subject to denunciation or withdrawal unless:

(a) it is established that the parties intended to admit the possibility of denunciation or withdrawal; or

(b) a right of denunciation or withdrawal may be implied by the nature of the treaty.

2. A party shall give not less than twelve months' notice of its intention to denounce or withdraw from a treaty under paragraph 1.

See also A. David, *The Strategy of Treaty Termination: Lawful Breaches and Retaliations* (New Haven: Yale Univ. Press, 1975), esp. Chpts. 2 and 6; Briggs, ''Unilateral Denunciation of Treaties: The Vienna Convention and the International Court of Justice,'' 68 *AJIL* 51 (1974).

84 Nuclear Test Ban Treaty. For a legal interpretation of Article IV by the legal adviser of the U.S. Department of State, see *Hearings on the Nuclear Test Ban Treaty before the Senate Committee on Foreign Relations*, 88th Cong., 1st Sess. (1963), pp. 37–40. For a discussion of Article IV, see, *e.g.*, Chayes, ''An Inquiry into the Working of Arms Control Agreements,'' 85 *Harv. L. Rev.* 905 (1972), pp. 957–59; and, generally, Schwelb, ''The Nuclear Test Ban Treaty and International Law,'' 58 *AJIL* 642 (1964).

85 See, *e.g.*, Non-Proliferation Treaty, Art. 10(1); SALT II Treaty, Art. XIX(3).

86 See, *e.g.*, the U.S.–Tanzania Economic and Technical Cooperation Agreement, 1968, 19 UST 4614, TIAS 6448, 698 UNTS 3, para. 7.

Under Article XXXI of the GATT a party may withdraw from the GATT on six months' notice. However, under paragraph 5 of the Protocol of Provisional Application, *supra* n. 81, the period of notice is shortened to sixty days.

87 For discussions of withdrawal from international organizations, see, *e.g.*, F. Kirgis, *International Organizations in Their Legal Setting* (St. Paul: West, 1977), pp. 191–210; D. Bowett, *The Law of International Institutions*, 3rd ed. (London: Stevens, 1975), pp. 347–49; 13 M. Whiteman, *Digest of International Law*, Dept. of State Pub. 7873 (Washington, D.C., 1968), p. 229 *et seq.*; H. G. Schermers, *International Institutional Law*, 2 vols. (Leiden: A. W. Sijthoff, 1972), 1: 44–54; Feinberg, ''Unilateral Withdrawal from an International Organization,'' 39 *Brit. Y.B. Intl. L.* 189 (1963).

88 IMF Agreement, Art. 15(1); IBRD Agreement, Art. 6 (1).

89 NATO Treaty, Art. 13; FAO Constitution, Art. 19.

90   OAS Charter, Art. 112; ILO Constitution, Art. 1(5). The United States withdrew from the International Labour Organization Nov. 6, 1975, effective Nov. 6, 1977. See 77 *Dept. St. Bull*. 912 (1977). It rejoined on Feb. 18, 1980. *N.Y. Times*, Feb. 18, 1980, p. A16; *id.*, Feb. 19, 1980, p. A6.

91   See M. Whiteman, *supra* n. 87, pp. 220–28; Schwelb, "Withdrawal from the United Nations: The Indonesian Intermezzo," 61 *AJIL* 661 (1967). On experience of withdrawal from international organizations in the absence of specific provisions for withdrawal, see, generally, *e.g.*, Schermers, *supra* n.87, pp. 46–51.

92   See further discussion *infra* Chpt. 3, sec. 3.

93   Egypt-Israel Sinai Agreement.

94   Egypt-Israel Peace Treaty, Annex I and Appendix to Annex I. See, generally, Murphy, "To Bring to an End the State of War: The Egyptian-Israeli Peace Treaty," 12 *Vand. J. of Transnatl. L*. 897 (1979).

95   See, *e.g.*, Schelling, *supra* n. 53, pp. 45–46.

96   On amendment and revision, see, generally, Vienna Convention, Arts. 39–41; Dixit, "Amendment or Modification of Treaties," 10 *Indian J. Intl. L*. 37 (1970). For representative provisions, see *Treaty Maker's Handbook, supra* n. 75, pp. 223–45. On amendment to constitutive instruments of international organizations, see, *e.g.*, Bowett, *supra* n. 87, pp. 363–66; Schermers, *supra* n. 87, 2: 466–81; and R. Zacklin, *The Amendment of the Constitutive Instruments of the United Nations and Specialized Agencies* (Leiden: A. W. Sijthoff, 1968).

97   For general references to the extensive literature on dispute settlement, see citations in Chpt. 1, n. 1, *supra*.

98   See, *e.g.*, Statute of the International Court of Justice, annexed to the U.N. Charter, 59 Stat. 1055, TS 933, 3 Bevans 1153, Art. 36; S. Rosenne, *The Law and Practice of the International Court* (Leiden: A. W. Sijthoff, 1965), 1: 292–331; and, generally, references in Chpt. 1, n. 1, *supra*.

99   For representative provisions, see United Nations, *A Survey of Treaty Provisions for the Pacific Settlement of International Disputes, 1949–1962*, U.N. Sales No. 66B.V.5 (1966), and *Treaty Maker's Handbook, supra* n. 75, pp. 117–31.

100   U.S.–German FCN Treaty, Art. XXVII.

101   The Vienna Convention provides only limited dispute-settlement procedures with respect to disputes concerning the invalidity, termination, withdrawal from, or suspension of the operation of a treaty. Article 65, paragraph 3, provides that, in the event of such a dispute, the parties shall

seek a solution through the means indicated in Article 33 of the U.N. Charter. Article 66 of the convention provides:

> If, under paragraph 3 of Article 65, no solution has been reached within a period of 12 months following the date on which the objection was raised, the following procedures shall be followed:
>
> (a) any one of the parties to a dispute concerning the application or the interpretation of Article 53 or 64 may, by written application, submit it to the International Court of Justice for a decision unless the parties by common consent agree to submit the dispute to arbitration;
>
> (b) any one of the parties to a dispute concerning the application or the interpretation of any of the other articles in Part V of the present Convention may set in motion the procedure specified in the Annex to the Convention by submitting a request to that effect to the Secretary-General of the United Nations.

The annex to the convention established only a conciliation procedure. Thus, the convention provides for compulsory dispute settlement only with reference to disputes concerning Articles 53 and 64, which deal with the rule of *jus cogens*. See, generally, references in n. 83, *supra*.

102 For a different view, see Larsen, "Arbitration of the United States–French Air Traffic Dispute," 30 *J. Air Law and Commerce* 231 (1964). And see Dicker, "The Use of Arbitration in the Settlement of Bilateral Air Rights Disputes," 3 *Vand. Intl. L.J.* 124 (1970).

103 For discussion of reasons why nations are reluctant to accept compulsory third-party adjudication of treaty and other disputes, see, *e.g.*, Anand, "Role of International Adjudication," in L. Gross, ed., *The Future of the International Court of Justice* (Dobbs Ferry, N.Y.: Oceana, 1976), p. 1; Higgins, "The Desirability of Third Party Adjudication: Conventional Wisdom or Continuing Truth," in J. Fawcett and R. Higgins, eds. *International Organization: Law in Movement* (London: Oxford Univ. Press, 1974), p. 32; Shihata, "The Attitude of New States toward the International Court of Justice," 19 *Intl. Org.* 203 (1963); Owen, "Compulsory Jurisdiction of the International Court of Justice: A Study of Its Acceptance by Nations," 3 *Ga. L. Rev.* 704 (1969). For a thoughtful study of the role of third parties in dispute settlement and international processes more generally, see T. Franck, *The Structure of Impartiality: Examining the Riddle of One Law in a Fragmented World* (New York: Macmillan, 1968).

104 Vienna Convention on Diplomatic Relations, 1961, 23 UST 3227, TIAS 7502, 500 UNTS 95.

105 Vienna Convention, Arts. 65–66 and Annex; Vienna Convention on the

Succession of States in Respect of Treaties, U.N. Doc. A/CONF. 80/32 (1978), text in 72 *AJIL* 971 (1978), Arts. 41–45 and Annex. See Lavalle, "Dispute Settlement under the Vienna Convention on Succession of States in Respect of Treaties," 73 *AJIL* 407 (1979).

106 Dillard, "The World Court: Reflections of a Professor Turned Judge," 27 *Am. Univ. L. Rev.* 205 (1978), p. 228.

107 U.S. Treaty with Great Britain Relating to the Boundary Waters and Questions Arising Along the Boundary between the United States and Canada, 1909, 36 Stat. 2448 (1910), TS 548; 12 Bevans 319, Art. VII. For discussion of this experience, see, *e.g.*, Bilder, "Controlling Great Lakes Pollution: A Study in United States–Canadian Environmental Cooperation," 70 *Mich. L. Rev.* 469 (1972); and M. Cohen, "The Regime of Boundary Waters: The Canadian–United States Experience," 146 *Rec. des Cours* 219 (Vol. III, 1975).

108 Egypt-Israel Peace Treaty, Art. IV and Annex I, Art. VII.

109 Agreed Interpretations, Common Understandings, and Unilateral Statements Accompanying the SALT I Agreement, 1(b)B, and SALT II Treaty, Art. XVII.

110 See Amendment to the IMF Agreement of May 31, 1968, 20 UST 2775, TIAS 6748. For discussion, see *e.g.*, material collected in Jackson, *Legal Problems of International Economic Relations, supra* n.32, pp. 864–83.

111 Agreement on an International Energy Program, 1974, 27 UST 1685, TIAS 8278, text also in 14 *ILM* 1 (1975). See, generally, Willrich and Conant, "The International Energy Agency: An Interpretation and Assessment," 71 *AJIL* 199 (1977). Article 19 of the agreement provides for a finding by the IEA Secretariat when a reduction of oil supplies available to the group as a whole or to a participating nation "has occurred or can reasonably be expected to occur" and for the allocation of supplies in accordance with certain formulas in the case of such an emergency.

112 See, *e.g.*, UNCTAD, Report by the Secretary General, U.N. Doc. TD/B/C1/166 (1974), entitled "An Integrated Programme for Commodities"; and "U.S. Commodities Policy: A Suggested Modification of the Proposal for an International Resources Bank" (note), 17 *Va. J. Intl. L.* 279 (1977).

113 See, *e.g.*, B. Morse, "Practice, Norms, and Reform of International Humanitarian Rescue Operations," lectures delivered at the Hague Academy of International Law, August 1977, to be published in *Rec. des Cours* (1980).

Insurance concepts have also been used effectively to encourage private foreign investment by providing investors protection against such risks as expropriation and inconvertibility of earnings. See, *e.g.*, the U.S. Investment Guaranty Program established by the Foreign Assistance Act of 1969, 83 Stat. 809, 22 USC 2191–2200a, as amended by 88 Stat. 763 (1974) and administered by the U.S. Overseas Private Investment Corporation.

114   U.N. Charter, Arts. 10–17, 24–26, 33–42, and 94.

115   International Coffee Agreement, 1976, Art. 15(3). See also OAS Charter, Art. 59; EEC Treaty, Art. 189; OECD Convention, Art. 6; ICAO Convention, Art. 12.

116   For discussion of membership provisions in international organizations, see, generally, Kirgis, *supra* n. 87, pp. 77–110; Bowett, *supra* n. 87, pp. 342–44; Schermers, *supra* n. 87, 1: 33–44 and 2: 520–23.

117   NATO Treaty, Art. 10. See also, *e.g.*, EEC Treaty, Art. 237 (open only to "European" states); European Human Rights Convention, Art. 66 (open only to members of the Council of Europe). In some cases, certain states or categories of states may be subject to special disqualifications. See, *e.g.*, ICAO Convention, Arts. 92 and 93, which provide that, while most states may be freely admitted, states which fought against the Allies during the Second World War can be admitted only by a four-fifths majority vote and with the assent of any state invaded or attacked by the applicant state during that war.

118   WMO Convention, Art. 3.

119   OECD Convention, Art. 16. See also EEC Treaty, Art. 237. Most international organizations permit approval of participation by a simple or two-thirds majority of existing parties. See, *e.g.*, ILO Constitution, Art. 1(4).

120   U.N. Charter, Arts. 3 and 4. For an interpretation of Article 4 by the International Court, see Advisory Opinion on *Admission of States to the United Nations*, [1948] ICJ Rep. 57.

121   See, *e.g.*, U.N. Convention on the High Seas, 1958, 450 UNTS 82, Art. 31, which provides that the convention shall be open to "States Members of the United Nations, or of any of the specialized agencies, and by any other States invited by the General Assembly of the United Nations."

122   Article III, paragraph 1, of the Nuclear Test Ban Treaty provides that "this Treaty shall be open to all States for signature." See also, *e.g.*, Outer Space Treaty, Art. XIV(3); Convention Respecting Weights and Measures of 1875, as revised in 1921, 43 Stat. 1686, TS 673, 2 Bevans 323, 17 LNTS 45, Art. 3.

123   See also EEC Treaty, Art. 237; IMF Agreement, Art. 2(2). And see J.

Gold, *Membership and Nonmembership in the International Monetary Fund* (Washington, D.C.: International Monetary Fund, 1974).

124 See Jackson, *World Trade and the Law of GATT, supra* n. 65, pp. 100–102.

125 U.N. Charter, Art. 110.

126 Non-Proliferation Treaty, Art. 9(3).

127 Warsaw Pact, Art. 10; Antarctic Treaty, Art. XIII(5).

128 International Coffee Agreement, 1976, Art. 61. See also, *e.g.*, OAU Charter, Art. 25, which provides for entry into force upon ratification by two-thirds of the signatory states; the Vienna Convention on Diplomatic Relations, 1961, *supra* n. 104, Art. 51, which provides for entry into force on the thirtieth day after deposit of the twenty-second instrument of ratification; the Agreement Establishing the African Development Bank, 1963, 510 UNTS 46, Art. 65, which provides for entry into force upon ratification by twelve signatory governments whose aggregate subscriptions comprise not less than 65 percent of the authorized capital stock of the bank.

129 Marine Pollution Convention, Art. 15.

130 Convention on the Prevention and Punishment of the Crime of Genocide, 1948, 78 UNTS 277, Art. 15.

131 See Vienna Convention, Art. 34, which provides that "a treaty does not create either obligations or rights for a third state without its consent."

132 See, for example, the attempt to deal with this question in the recently concluded Antarctic Marine Living Resources Convention, Art. X. And see, more generally, *e.g.*, Bilder, "The Present Legal and Political Situation in Antarctica," in J. Charney, ed., *The New Nationalism and the Use of Common Spaces: Issues in Marine Pollution and the Exploitation of Antarctica*, prepared under the auspices of the American Society of International Law and scheduled for publication in 1981.

133 International Convention on the Elimination of All Forms of Racial Discrimination, adopted by UNGA Res. 2106 A(XX), Dec. 21, 1965, 20 UN GAOR, Supp. No. 14, Doc. A/6014, pp. 47–51, 660 UNTS 195. For comment, see, *e.g.*, Schwelb, "The International Convention on the Elimination of All Forms of Racial Discrimination," 15 *Intl. and Comp. L.Q.* 996 (1966). In signing the convention, the United States made the following statement: "The Constitution of the United States contains provisions for the protection of individual rights, such as the right of free speech, and nothing in the convention shall be deemed to require or to authorize legislation or other actions by the United States of America incompatible with the provisions of the Constitution of the United States of America." Text in L. B. Sohn and T. Buergenthal, *International*

Protection of Human Rights (Indianapolis: Bobbs-Merrill, 1973), pp. 861–62. For similar reservations or declarations by Austria and other countries, see *id.*, p. 861.

134　For the definition of *reservation* in Article 2(d) of the Vienna Convention, see text at *supra* n. 69.

135　See, generally, Vienna Convention, Arts. 19–23; Bowett, "Reservations to Nonrestricted Multilateral Treaties," 48 *Brit. Y. B. Intl. L.* 67 (1976–77); Mendelson, "Reservations to the Constitutions of International Organisations," 45 *Brit. Y.B. Intl. L.* 137 (1971); Schermers, *supra* n. 87, 2: 461–65; Gamble, "Reservations to Multilateral Treaties: A Macroscopic View of State Practice," 74 *AJIL* 372 (1980); and references cited in *supra* nn. 68–69.

136　International Coffee Agreement, 1976, Art. 63; Universal Copyright Convention, 1952, 6 UST 2731, TIAS 3324, 216 UNTS 132, Art. XX.

137　See Vienna Convention, Arts. 19 and 20. See also Advisory Opinion on *Reservations to the Convention on Genocide*, [1951] ICJ Rep. 15.

　　　Compare Art. 20(2) of the International Convention on the Elimination of All Forms of Racial Discrimination, 1966, 660 UNTS 195, which bars reservations which are either incompatible with the object or purpose of the convention or the effect of which would inhibit the operation of any of the bodies established by the convention, and which further provides that "a reservation shall be considered incompatible or inhibitive if at least two-thirds of the States Parties to this Convention object to it."

138　See, generally, *e.g.*, Bowett, *supra* n. 87, pp. 357–62; Schermers, *supra* n. 87, 2: 327–58, 482–534; I. Claude, *Swords into Plowshares*, 4th ed. (New York: Random House, 1971), pp. 118–62; Kirgis, *supra* n. 87, pp. 144–90; C. W. Jenks, "Unanimity, The Veto, Weighted Voting, Special and Simple Majorities, and Consensus as Modes of Decision in International Organizations," in *Cambridge Essays in International Law: Essays in Honour of Lord McNair* (Dobbs Ferry, N.Y.: Oceana, 1965), p. 48.

139　U.N. Charter, Art. 2(7).

140　For discussion of types of decisions by international organizations and the legal consequences of these decisions, see generally, *e.g.*, Schermers, *supra* n. 87, pp. 482–534. For an illustration of provisions regarding different types of decisions, see, *e.g.*, OECD Convention, Arts. 5–7.

141　See, *e.g.*, U.N. Charter, Arts. 10, 11, 13, and 14. But see, for examples of "internal" decisions which have conclusive effect, *id.*, Arts. 17, 21, and 97.

142　U.N. Charter, Art. 18. See, *e.g.*, Kerley, "Voting on Important Questions in the UN General Assembly,'' 53 *AJIL* 324 (1959). See also, *e.g.*, WMO Constitution, Art. 10(b); OAU Charter, Art. 10.

143 IAEA Statute, Art. 5(C).

144 See, *e.g.*, Zamora, "Voting in International Economic Organizations," 74 *AJIL* 566 (1980); J. Gold, *Voting and Decisions in the International Monetary Fund* (Washington, D.C.: International Monetary Fund, 1972); Gold, "Weighted Voting Power: Some Limits and Some Problems," 68 *AJIL* 687 (1974); McIntyre, "Weighted Voting in International Organizations," 8 *Intl. Org.* 484 (1954).

See also, *e.g.*, EEC Treaty, Art. 148; International Coffee Agreement, 1976, Arts. 13–15 (which require majorities of both importing members and exporting members, counted separately); IBRD Agreement, Art. 5(3); IMF Agreement, Art. 12(5)(a). For particularly complex weighting formulas, see Convention on the International Maritime Satellite Organization (INMARSAT), 1976, 15 *ILM* 1051 (1976), Art. 14; and Agreement on an International Energy Program, 1974, *supra* n. 111, Arts. 61 and 62.

145 U.N. Charter, Art. 27. See, *e.g.*, S. D. Bailey, *Voting in the Security Council* (Bloomington: Indiana Univ. Press, 1969). For other agreements which require unanimity for all decisions, or at least for certain important ones, see, *e.g.*, OECD Convention, Art. 6; EEC Treaty, Arts. 84, 99, 100, 235–38.

146 See UNGA Res. 1995, Dec. 30, 1964, 19 UN GAOR, Supp. No. 15, Doc. A/5815, p. 1. Similar conciliation procedures have been proposed for the U.N. Economic and Social Council; see *Report of the Group of Experts on the Structure of the United Nations: A New United Nations Structure for Global Economic Cooperation*, U.N. Doc. E/AC.62/9 (1975), pp. 5, 30–32.

147 See, generally, Schermers, *supra* n. 87, 2: 516–18.

148 International Whaling Convention, Art. V(3). See also Antarctic Marine Living Resources Convention, Art. IX (6); WHO Constitution, Art. 22; ICAO Convention, Arts. 37, 38, and 41; WMO Constitution, Art. 8(b).

149 See, *e.g.*, International Coffee Agreement, 1976, Art. 69(2).

150 See discussion in Bilder, *supra* n. 132. See also Antarctic Marine Living Resources Convention, Art. VII, which establishes a Commission for the Conservation of Antarctic Marine Living Resources, membership of which shall consist of those Contracting Parties which participated in the conference establishing the convention and also any subsequently acceding party "during such time as that acceding party is engaged in research or harvesting activities in relation to the marine living resources to which this Convention applies.''

CHAPTER 3: Protecting Against a Change in the Value of the Agreement

1   See, *e.g.*, Gouldner, "The Norm of Reciprocity: A Preliminary Statement," 25 *Am. Soc. Rev.* 161 (1960); K. J. Gergen, *The Psychology of Behavior Exchange* (Reading, Pa.: Addison-Wesley, 1969), p. 75 *et seq.*; Franck and Weisband, "The Role of Reciprocity and Equivalence in Systemic Superpower Interaction," 3 *N.Y.U. J. of Intl. Law and Politics* 263 (1970).

2   G. Marwell and D. R. Schmitt, *Cooperation: An Experimental Analysis* (New York: Academic Press, 1975), Chpt. 3, and pp. 178–80.

3   *Id.*, p. 180.

4   See Bilder, "Breach of Treaty and Response Thereto," 1967 *Proc. ASIL* 193; A. David, *The Strategy of Treaty Termination: Lawful Breaches and Retaliation* (New Haven: Yale Univ. Press, 1975).

5   G. Nierenberg, *Fundamentals of Negotiating* (New York: Hawthorn Books, 1973), p. 20.

6   See, *e.g.*, *Uniform Commercial Code*, secs. 2-313 (Express Warranties by Affirmation, Promise, Description, Sample), and 2-314 (Implied Warranty: Merchantibility, Usage of Trade).

7   India-Pakistan Indus Waters Treaty, 1960, 419 UNTS 125. The treaty is discussed in N. D. Gulhati, *Indus Waters Treaty: An Exercise in International Mediation* (Bombay: Allied Publishers, 1973), and R. R. Baxter, "The Indus Basin," in A. H. Garretson, R. O. Hayton, and C. J. Olmstead, eds., *The Law of International Drainage Basins* (Dobbs Ferry, N.Y.: Occana, 1967), p. 443.

8   Agreement Regarding Financial Support for the North Atlantic Ice Patrol, 1956, 7 UST 1969, TIAS 3597, 256 UNTS 171.

9   See, *e.g.*, the U.S.–Mexican Treaty Relating to the Utilization of Waters of the Rio Grande, Colorado and Tijuana, 1944, 59 Stat. 1219, TS 994, 9 Bevans 1166, 3 UNTS 313, Art. 5; and Agreement to Proceed with the Construction of Amistad Dam, 1960, 11 UST 2396, TIAS 4624, 401 UNTS 137.

10   See, generally, H. G. Schermers, *International Institutional Law*, 2 vols. (Leiden: A. W. Sijthoff, 1972), 2:392–401.

11   Convention for the Preservation of the Halibut Fishery of the Northern Pacific Ocean and Bering Sea, 1953, 5 UST 5, TIAS 2900, 222 UNTS 77, Art. III.

12   EEC Treaty, Art. 200.

13   Convention Establishing the Inter-American Tropical Tuna Commission, 1949, 1 UST 230, TIAS 2044, 80 UNTS 3, Art. I(3).

14   U.N. Charter, Art. 17(2).

15   For example, both the U.N. Development Program (UNDP) and the U.N.

International Children's Emergency Fund (UNICEF) are based on voluntary contributions; see D. Bowett, *The Law of International Institutions*, 3rd ed. (London: Stevens, 1975), p. 58; Schermers, *supra* n. 10, pp. 418–19.

16 UNGA Res. 14(I) and successor resolutions. See Bowett, *supra*, pp. 370–71; and Schermers, *supra* n. 10, pp. 395–97.

17 OAU Charter, Art. 23, which establishes a 20 percent ceiling.

18 P.L. 92-544, 86 Stat. 1109, Oct. 25, 1972.

19 Writing in 1977, Plischke noted that seventy-eight U.N. members, constituting 54 percent of the total membership, contributed at the rate of only 0.02 percent each (thus jointly paying less than 2 percent of the U.N. budget, as compared with the 25 percent paid by the United States). E. Plischke, *Microstates in World Affairs* (Washington, D.C.: American Enterprise Institute for Public Policy Research, 1977), p. 115 and, for general discussion of the assessment question, pp. 110–20.

20 Third U.N. Conference on the Law of the Sea: Revised Informal Composite Negotiating Text for the Eighth Session (March 19–April 27, 1979), U.N. Doc. A/CONF. 62/WP.10/Rev. 1 of April 28, 1979, text in 18 *ILM* 686 (1979), Arts. 140, 160(2)(j); J. Charney, "The Equitable Sharing of Revenues from Seabed Mining," in H. G. Knight, J. I. Charney, and J. L. Jacobson, *Policy Issues in Ocean Law*, American Society of International Law Studies in Transnational Legal Policy, No. 8 (St. Paul: West, 1975), p. 53.

21 See, generally, Burton, "New Stresses on the Antarctic Treaty: Toward International Legal Institutions Governing Antarctic Resources," 65 *Va. L. Rev.* 421 (1979).

22 U.S.–Austrian Agreement for Cooperation Concerning Civil Uses of Atomic Energy, 1969, 21 UST 10, TIAS 6815, Art. X.

23 See, *e.g.*, the International Wheat Agreement, 1971, 22 UST 820, TIAS 7144. On the concept of a "minimum safeguard price" for crude oil in the International Energy Program, see Willrich and Conant, "The International Energy Agency: An Interpretation and Assessment," 71 *AJIL* 199 (1977).

24 Standard U.S. Agricultural Commodities agreements with other countries under the P.L. 480 agricultural surplus disposal program typically contain a provision that the "issuance of purchase authorizations . . . shall be dependent upon the determination by the U.S. Government that such commodities are in surplus supply . . . at the time." See, *e.g.*, U.S.–India Agricultural Commodities Agreement, 1960, 11 UST 1544, TIAS 4499, 376 UNTS 279, Art. I(4).

25 See note 18, *supra*.

26 ABM Treaty, Art. III.

27 SALT II Treaty, Art. III.

28 See A. S. Becker, *Military Expenditure Limitation for Arms Control: Problems and Prospects* (Cambridge: Ballinger, 1977).

29 Compare Macneil, "A Primer of Contract Planning," 48 *So. Calif. L. Rev.* 627 (1975), p. 657.

30 U.S.–Canada Great Lakes Water Quality Agreement, 1972, TIAS 7312, text in 11 *ILM* 694 (1972). See, generally, Bilder, "Controlling Great Lakes Pollution: A Study in United States–Canadian Environmental Co-operation," 70 *Mich. L. Rev.* 469 (1972); and, on similar Colorado River problems, Brownell and Eaton, "The Colorado River Salinity Problem with Mexico," 69 *AJIL* 255 (1975).

31 Warsaw Convention for the Unification of Certain Rules Relating to International Transportation by Air, 1929, 49 Stat. 3000, TS 876, 137 LNTS 11, 2 Bevans 983, Art. 22(4).

32 See, *e.g.*, "Weighing a Basket of Currencies to Replace Dollar in Oil Pricing," *N.Y. Times*, March 17, 1978, pp. D1, D3. Similar proposals have been made for indexing prices of exports to prices of a range of imported products in connection with the proposed UNCTAD Integrated Commodity Program.

33 Compare the Washington Treaty between the United States, the British Empire, France, Italy, and Japan limiting Naval Armament, 1922, 2 Bevans 351, TS 671, 43 Stat. 1655, which limited the total tonnage of capital naval ships of the United States and British Empire to 525,000 tons each, Japan to 315,000 tons, and France and Italy to 175,000 tons each, in effect maintaining an agreed ratio between their naval power. See also the similar 1930 Treaty on Limitation and Reduction of Naval Armament, 2 Bevans 1055, TS 830, 46 Stat. 2858, 112 LNTS 65.

34 See discussion in B. S. Fisher, *The International Coffee Agreement: A Study in Coffee Diplomacy* (New York: Praeger, 1972), Chpt. 7.

35 U.S.–German FCN Treaty, Art. XIV(5).

36 *Id.*, Art. XXV(1).

37 *Id.*, Art. XXV(4).

38 See, generally, U.S. Senate, Comm. on Finance, Subcomm. on International Trade, *The Most-Favored-Nation Provision* (Executive Branch GATT Study No. 9), 93rd Cong., 1st Sess.; J. Jackson, *Legal Problems of International Economic Relations* (St. Paul: West, 1979), Chpt. 9 (on MFN provisions in GATT) and Chpt. 10 (on national treatment provisions in GATT). And see U.N. International Law Commission, *Final Draft Articles on the Most-Favored-Nation Clause in Treaties between States: Report of the U.N. International Law Commission on the Work of Its*

Thirtieth Session, U.N. Doc. A/33/192 (Aug. 30, 1978), Sec. II, pp. 4–12, text in 17 *ILM* 1518 (1978).

On commercial treaties generally, see, *e.g.*, Youngquist, "United States Commercial Treaties: Their Role in Foreign Economic Policy," 2 *Stud. in L. and Econ. Dev.* 72 (1967); Walker, "Modern Treaties of Friendship, Commerce, and Navigation," 42 *Minn. L. Rev.* 805 (1958).

39 U.S.–Netherlands Treaty of Friendship, Commerce, and Navigation, 1956, 8 UST 2043, TIAS 3942, 285 UNTS 231, Art. I(1), Art. VI(3), and Art. VI(4).

40 Compare, *e.g.*, U.S.–Canada Great Lakes Water Quality Agreement, *supra* n. 30, Art. VI.

41 See, *e.g.*, International Coffee Agreement, 1976, Art. 34, and the regulations adopted by the International Commission under the International Whaling Convention, described in *Report of the U.S. Delegation to the 27th Meeting of the International Whaling Commission* (1975), available through the U.S. Department of State.

42 See GATT, Art. XXIII.

43 Compare, *e.g.*, the U.S.–Canadian Agreement Concerning the Establishment of an International Arbitral Tribunal to Dispose of United States Claims Relating to Gut Dam, 52 *Dept. St. Bull.* 643 (1965), commented on in Lillich, "The Gut Dam Claims Agreement with Canada," 59 *AJIL* 892 (1965). The text of the Final Decision of the tribunal is reproduced in 8 *ILM* 118 (1968). See Kerley and Goodman, "The Gut Dam Claims: A Lump Sum Settlement Disposes of an Arbitral Dispute," 10 *Va. J. Intl. L.* 300 (1970).

44 For a description of "hedging" techniques, see P. A. Samuelson, *Economics*, 10th ed. (New York: McGraw-Hill, 1976), pp. 424–45.

45 On amendment and revision of treaties, see, generally, Vienna Convention, Arts. 39–41, and other references given in Chpt. 2, n. 96.

46 U.S.–United Arab Republic Air Transport Agreement, 1964, 15 UST 2202, TIAS 5706, 531 UNTS 229, Art. 12.

47 Universal Copyright Convention, 1952, 6 UST 2731, TIAS 3324, 216 UNTS 132, Art. XII. See also Antarctic Marine Living Resources Convention, Art. XXX, which provides that the depository shall call a meeting to discuss a proposed amendment if one-third of the members of the Commission on Antarctic Marine Living Resources request such a meeting.

48 IMF Agreement, Art. XVII(b).

49 GATT, Art. XXX(1). See also Convention Establishing the European Free Trade Association, 1960, 370 UNTS 3, Art. 44; Charter of the Council of Mutual Economic Assistance (COMECON), 1959, Art. 17,

text in W. E. Butler, ed., *A Source Book on Socialist Economic Organizations* (Alphen aan den Rijn: Sijthoff and Noordhoff, 1978), p. 124.

50 On amendment of the charter, see, *e.g.*, Schwelb, "The 1963/1965 Amendments to the Charter of the United Nations: An Addendum," 60 *AJIL* 371 (1966). See also the procedures contained in the Ocean Dumping Convention, Art. 15, which permits amendment to the lists of hazardous substances attached to Annex II of the convention by tacit consent of the parties after the amendment is adopted by an appropriate body of the Intergovernmental Maritime Consultative Organization and submitted to the parties for consideration. See also Marine Pollution Convention, Art. 16; and see, generally, Adede, "Amendment Procedures for Conventions with Technical Annexes: The IMCO Experience," 17 *Va. J. Intl. L.* 201 (1976–77).

51 See, *e.g.*, U.N. Charter, Art. 108; IAEA Statute, Art. 18C; ILO Constitution, Art. 36; WHO Constitution, Art. 36.

52 ICAO Convention, Art. 94(a); OAS Charter, Arts. 145 and 147. See also, *e.g.*, FAO Constitution, Art. 20(2); GATT, Art. XXX.

53 IMCO Convention, Art. 52.

54 See, *e.g.*, International Coffee Agreement, 1976, Art. 69(2) (compulsory withdrawal).

55 NATO Treaty, Art. 12; Antarctic Treaty, Art. XII.

56 International Coffee Agreement, 1962, Art. 72; Non-Proliferation Treaty, Art. VIII. On the first review conference under the Non-Proliferation Treaty, see Final Declaration of the Review Conference of the Parties to the Treaty on the Non-Proliferation of Nuclear Weapons, May 1975, reprinted in E. McDowell, ed., *Digest of United States Practice in International Law, 1975*, Dept. State Pub. 8865, (Washington, D.C., 1976), pp. 849–55.

57 See Third U.N. Conference on the Law of the Sea: Revised Informal Composite Negotiating Text, *supra* n. 16, Art. 155.

58 See, *e.g.*, GATT, Art. XXVIII(4), which authorizes the contracting parties at any time in special circumstances to authorize a contracting party to enter into negotiations for modification or withdrawal of a concession. See also International Coffee Agreement, 1976, Art. 56.

59 See Vienna Convention, Art. 62, which makes the following provisions.

Article 62

Fundamental change of circumstances

1. A fundamental change of circumstances which has occurred with regard to those existing at the time of the conclusion of a treaty, and which was not foreseen by the parties, may not be invoked as a ground for terminating or withdrawing from the treaty unless:

(a) the existence of those circumstances constituted an essential basis of the consent of the parties to be bound by the treaty; and

(b) the effect of the change is radically to transform the extent of obligations still to be performed under the treaty.

2. A fundamental change of circumstances may not be invoked as a ground for terminating or withdrawing from a treaty:

(a) if the treaty establishes a boundary; or

(b) if the fundamental change is the result of a breach by the party invoking it either of an obligation under the treaty or of any other international obligation owed to any other party to the treaty.

3. If, under the foregoing paragraphs, a party may invoke a fundamental change of circumstances as a ground for terminating or withdrawing from a treaty it may also invoke the change as a ground for suspending the operation of the treaty.

The doctrine of changed circumstances was generally recognized by the International Court in the jurisdictional phase of the Anglo-Icelandic *Fisheries Jurisdiction* case, although the Court rejected its applicability to that case. *Fisheries Jurisdiction* case (U.K. v. Iceland), [1973] ICJ Rep. 3, at pp. 17–21. On the doctrine of changed circumstances, generally, see, *e.g.*, A. David, *The Strategy of Treaty Termination, supra* n. 4, Chpt. I; G. Haraszti, "Treaties and Fundamental Changes in Circumstances," 146 *Rec. des Cours* 1 (1975); and Lissitzyn, "Treaties and Changed Circumstances (Rebus Sic Stantibus)," 61 *AJIL* 895 (1967). And compare *Uniform Commercial Code*, sec. 2-615 (Excuse by Failure of Presupposed Conditions).

60 See Chpt. 2, sec. 10, *supra* and references cited in accompanying notes.

61 On waiver provisions, see, generally, *e.g.*, F. Kirgis, *International Organizations in Their Legal Setting* (St. Paul: West, 1977), pp. 462–71; Gold, "The 'Dispensing' and 'Suspending' Powers of International Organizations," 9 *Netherlands Intl. L. Rev.* 169 (1972).

62 See, generally, Jackson, *supra* n. 38, pp. 412–18.

63 See, generally, *e.g.*, J. Jackson, *World Trade and the Law of GATT* (Indianapolis: Bobbs-Merrill, 1969), Chpt. 22.

64 See also the IMF Agreement, Art. VIII(2) and (3), which permit the Fund to approve exchange restrictions and multiple currency practices that would otherwise be illegal. See Gold, *supra* n. 61.

65 Nuclear Test Ban Treaty, Art. IV.

66 Italics added to mark the reservation. 61 Stat. 1218, reprinted in 15 *Dept. St. Bull.* 452 (1946) and also set out in *ICJ Yearbook, 1977–78*, p. 77. For references to the extensive and long debate on proposals for withdrawal of this reservation, see W. W. Bishop, Jr., *International Law: Cases and Materials*, 3rd ed. (Boston and Toronto: Little, Brown, 1971), pp. 69–74. See also the similar Declaration by the Philippines, *ICJ Yearbook, 1977–*

78, p. 71. The French Declaration of May 16, 1966, 562 UNTS 71, now withdrawn, broadly excepted disputes affecting or relating to ''national security'' or ''activities connected with national defense.''

67 GATT, Art. XXVIII.

68 See, however, the concurring opinion of Judge Lauterpacht in the *French-Norwegian Loans* case [1957] ICJ Rep. 9, suggesting that an acceptance of the compulsory jurisdiction of the International Court under Article 36, paragraph 2, of the Court's Statute, conditioned on a unilateral right to determine whether a matter is within a state's ''domestic jurisdiction'' and thus outside the Court's jurisdiction, is an illusory agreement and should be considered as ineffective.

69 GATT, Art. XXI(c).

70 U.S.–Spain Tracking Station Agreement, 1964, 15 UST 153, TIAS 5533, 511 UNTS 61, Art. 15.

71 For discussion, see, *e.g.*, J. Jackson, *Legal Problems of International Economic Relations, supra* n. 38, pp. 621–23; J. Jackson, *World Trade and the Law of GATT, supra* n. 63, Chpt. 23; U.S. Senate, Comm. on Finance, Subcomm. on International Trade, *GATT Provisions on Relief from Injurious Imports* (Executive Branch GATT Study No. 8), 93rd Cong., 2nd Sess.

72 International Sugar Agreement, 1958, 385 UNTS 137, Art. 44(3). See also the other nine paragraphs of Article 44, which provide for withdrawal under a variety of other circumstances.

73 IMF Agreement, Art. IV, 5(f).

74 See, *e.g.*, Vienna Convention, Arts. 48, 49, and 61.

Article 48

Error

1. A State may invoke an error in a treaty as invalidating its consent to be bound by the treaty if the error relates to a fact or situation which was assumed by that State to exist at the time when the treaty was concluded and formed an essential basis of its consent to be bound by the treaty.

2. Paragraph 1 shall not apply if the State in question contributed by its own conduct to the error or if the circumstances were such as to put that State on notice of a possible error.

3. An error relating only to the wording of the text of a treaty does not affect its validity; article 79 then applies.

Article 49

Fraud

If a State has been induced to conclude a treaty by the fraudulent conduct of another negotiating State, the State may invoke the fraud as invalidating its consent to be bound by the treaty.

Article 61

Supervening impossibility of performance

1. A party may invoke the impossibility of performing a treaty as a ground for terminating or withdrawing from it if the impossibility results from the permanent disappearance or destruction of an object indispensable for the execution of the treaty. If the impossibility is temporary, it may be invoked only as a ground for suspending the operation of the treaty.

2. Impossibility of performance may not be invoked by a party as a ground for terminating, withdrawing from or suspending the operation of a treaty if the impossibility is the result of a breach by that party either of an obligation under the treaty or of any other international obligation owed to any other party to the treaty.

CHAPTER 4: Protecting Against Nonperformance or Inadequate Performance by the Other State

1 The literature on arms control and disarmament is extensive. On problems of arms control agreements generally, see, *e.g.*, A. Myrdal, *The Game of Disarmament* (New York: Pantheon, 1976); Stockholm International Peace Research Institute, *Arms Control: A Survey and Appraisal of Multilateral Agreements* (New York: Crane, Russak/London: Taylor & Francis, 1978); D. Wainhouse and associates, *Arms Control Agreements: Design for Verification and Organization* (Baltimore: Johns Hopkins Press, 1968); W. C. Clemens, Jr., *The Superpowers and Arms Control* (Lexington, Mass.: D. C. Heath, 1973); A. Gotlieb, *Disarmament and International Law* (Toronto: Canadian Institute of International Affairs, 1965); Stein, "Legal Restraints in Modern Arms Control Agreements," 66 *AJIL* 255 (1972); Chayes, "An Inquiry into the Workings of Arms Control Agreements," 85 *Harv. L. Rev.* 905 (1972); Myrdal, "The International Control of Disarmament," 231 *Scientific American*, No. 4 (Oct. 1974), p. 21. On the recent SALT I and SALT II negotiations, see, *e.g.*, J. Newhouse, *Cold Dawn: The Story of SALT* (New York: Holt, Rinehart & Winston, 1973); Warnke, "SALT: An Ongoing Process," 78 *Dept. St. Bull.* 1 (April 1978); D. P. Moynihan, "Reflections: The SALT Process," *The New Yorker*, Nov. 19, 1979, p. 104; J. Newhouse, "Reflections: The SALT Debate," *The New Yorker*, Dec. 17, 1979, p. 130.

2 On armistice, truce, and peace agreements, see, generally, *e.g.*, R. Baxter, "Armistices and Other Forms of Suspension of Hostilities," 149 *Rec. des Cours* 357 (Vol. I, 1976); Bailey, "Cease-Fires, Truces, and Armistices in the Practice of the UN Security Council," 71 *AJIL* 461 (1977); Mohn, "Problems of Truce Supervision," *International Con-*

ciliation, No. 478 (1952); Levie, "The Nature and Scope of the Armistice Agreement," 50 *AJIL* 880 (1956).

3 On problems of atomic safeguards and nuclear proliferation, see, generally, *e.g.*, B. Sanders, *Safeguards against Nuclear Proliferation* (Cambridge: MIT Press, 1975); A. McKnight, *Atomic Safeguards: A Study in International Verification* (New York: UNITAR, 1971); G. Fischer, *The Non-Proliferation of Nuclear Weapons* (London: Europa, 1971); M. Willrich, ed., *International Safeguards and Nuclear Industry* (Baltimore: Johns Hopkins Univ. Press, 1973); M. Willrich, *Non-Proliferation Treaty: Framework for Nuclear Arms Control* (Charlottesville: Michie, 1969); Nye, "Non-Proliferation: A Long-Term Strategy," 56 *Foreign Affairs* 601 (April 1978); Willrich, "The Treaty on Non-Proliferation of Nuclear Weapons: Nuclear Technology Confronts World Politics," 77 *Yale L. J.* 1447 (1968); Firmage, "The Treaty on the Non-Proliferation of Nuclear Weapons," 63 *AJIL* 711 (1969); Szasz, "The Law of International Atomic Energy Safeguards," 3 *Rev. Belge Droit Intl.* 196 (1967); Willrich, "Safeguarding Atoms for Peace," 60 *AJIL* 34 (1966).

4 T. Schelling, *The Strategy of Conflict* (Cambridge: Harvard Univ. Press, 1960), p. 20. See also, *e.g.*, D. A. Baldwin, "Bargaining with Airline Hijackers," in I. W. Zartman, ed., *The 50% Solution* (Garden City, N.Y.: Anchor Press/Doubleday, 1976), p. 404.

5 On general approaches to controlling performance risks, see, *e.g.*, Heymann, "The Problem of Coordination: Bargaining and Rules," 86 *Harv. L. Rev.* 797 (1973), p. 812; G. Maiwell and D. R. Schmitt, *Cooperation: An Experimental Analysis* (New York: Academic Press, 1975), p. 16. For an example of an attempt to control performance risks in private business contracts through broad statutory rules, see the Uniform Commercial Code, adopted in almost every state of the United States.

6 Egypt-Israel Sinai Agreement and Egypt-Israel Peace Treaty. Under Articles II and III of the 1975 agreement the parties generally undertake "not to resort to the threat or use of force or military blockage against each other," and to "continue scrupulously to observe the ceasefire on land, sea and air and to refrain from all military or para-military actions against each other."

7 B. Tuchman, *A Distant Mirror: The Calamitous 14th Century* (New York: Ballantine Books, 1978), p. 190.

For a current example of the proposed use of the technique of phased release of hostages, see the report of the special Iranian parliamentary commission on the American hostages submitted to the Iranian parliament setting forth conditions for the release of the hostages, the transcript of which is printed in *N.Y. Times*, Nov. 3, 1980, p. 6. The Commission recommends, *inter alia*, that, "should some of these conditions require more time, then when all conditions are accepted by the U.S. Government, with the fulfillment of each condition a number of criminals will be released with the approval of the Islamic Government."

8   See, *e.g.*, W. Coplin, *The Functions of International Law* (Chicago: Rand McNally, 1966), p. 20; and compare Macneil, "A Primer of Contract Planning," 48 *So. Calif. L. Rev.* 627 (1975), pp. 676–77.

9   See R. Bilder, *The Role of Unilateral State Action in Preventing International Environmental Injury*, Univ. of Wisconsin–Sea Grant College Program Wis.-SG-73-219 (Sept. 1973), pp. 2–3, republished in revised version in 14 *Vanderbilt J. Transnatl. L.* (No. 1, Winter 1981).

10   Vietnam Truce Agreement.

11   See, *id.*, Arts. 2, 3, 5, and 8; see also Protocol on the Return of Captured Military Personnel and Foreign Civilians and Captured and Detained Vietnamese Civilian Personnel, text in 12 *ILM* 62 (1973).

12   See, *id.*, Arts. 2 and 7; see also Protocol on the Ceasefire in South Vietnam and the Joint Military Commissions, text in 12 *ILM* 80 (1973).

13   Secretary of State Kissinger's press conference of Jan. 21, 1973, text in 68 *Dept. St. Bull.* 155 (1973), p. 164.

14   But see H. Kissinger, *White House Years* (Boston, Toronto: Little, Brown, 1979), Chpts. xxxi–xxxiv. And see Szulc, "How Kissinger Did It," 15 *Foreign Policy* 21 (1974); Zartman, "Reality, Image and Detail: The Paris Negotiations, 1969–73" in Zartman, *supra* n. 4, p. 372.

15   See, *e.g.*, "First Phase of Cease-Fire Ends with Hopes for Peace Remote," *N.Y. Times*, March 29, 1973, p. 1; "Questions and Answers on How Truce Accord Has Affected Indochina Situation," *id.*, p. 18; texts of note by North Vietnam and U.S. sent to Peace Conference participants, *id.*, April 25, 1973, p. 10; "Sharp Response to Hanoi Disclosed by Washington," *id.*, April 24, 1973, p. 5; "Vietnam Now: Pact But No Peace," *id.*, April 27, 1973, p. 3; "Most of Truce Terms Still To Be Carried Out," *id.*, Oct. 17, 1973, p. 10. For U.S. replies to North Vietnamese charges of violation of the Vietnam cease-fire, see, *e.g.*, Dept. St. Press Release 117 dated April 24, 1973, 68 *Dept. St. Bull.* 599 (1973). See also Dr. Kissinger's testimony in July 1977 before the House International Relations Subcommittee on the alleged commitment of the United States to provide up to $4.75 billion for postwar reconstruction of North Vietnam, reported in the *N.Y. Times*, July 20, 1977, p. A5, stating that North Vietnam began to violate the agreement only a few weeks after it had been signed and that the violations continued, "so by July of 1973 we had become convinced that they had no intention of adhering to the agreement."

16 U.S.–Canada Agreement Concerning Automotive Products, 1965, TIAS 6093, 17 UST 1372, Art. VI.

17 See, *e.g.*, the description of the Department of State's Circular 175 procedure in Bilder, "The Office of the Legal Adviser: The State Department Lawyer and Foreign Affairs," 56 *AJIL* 633 (1962), pp. 651–52; and Murphy, "Treaties and International Agreements other than Treaties: Constitutional Allocation of Power and Responsibility among the President, the House of Representatives and the Senate," 23 *Kans. L. Rev.* 221 (Winter 1975), pp. 237–40.

18 See, *e.g.*, U.S.–Austria Agreement for Cooperation Concerning the Civil Uses of Atomic Energy, 1969, 21 UST 10, TIAS 6815, Art. XII(B)(1).

19 U.S.–South Africa Agreement for Cooperation Concerning the Civil Uses of Atomic Energy, 1957, 8 UST 1367, TIAS 3885, 290 UNTS 147, Art. X(B)(3).

20 Nuclear Non-Proliferation Act of 1978, P.L. 95-242, 92 Stat. 120 (1978), sec. 401. For discussion, see Bettauer, "The Nuclear Non- Proliferation Act of 1978," 10 *Law and Policy in Intl. Bus.* 1105 (1978), p. 1146. Compare also the IAEA Convention on the Physical Protection of Nuclear Material, opened for signature March 3, 1980, text in 18 *ILM* 1422 (1979).

21 See E. D. Leive, *International Regulatory Regimes* (Lexington, Mass.: D. C. Heath, 1976), 1:298.

22 See Bettauer. *supra* n. 20, p. 1145.

23 Protocol of 1978 Relating to the International Convention for the Prevention of Pollution from Ships, 1973, text in 17 *ILM* 546 (1978).

24 Chayes, *supra* n. 1, p. 949.

25 See, generally, F. Iklé, *How Nations Negotiate* (New York: Harper & Row, 1964), pp. 8–15; R. Fisher, *International Conflict for Beginners* (New York: Harper & Row, 1969), p. 119.

26 SALT II Treaty, Art. II(1).

27 *Id.*, Art. II(3).

28 See, *e.g.*, Vienna Convention, Arts. 31–33; American Law Institute, *Restatement of the Law (Second) Foreign Relations Law of the United States* (1965), secs. 146–47; and, generally, M. S. McDougal, H. D. Lasswell, and J. C. Miller, *The Interpretation of Agreements and World Public Order* (New Haven: Yale Univ. Press, 1967); McNair, *The Law of Treaties* (Oxford: Clarendon Press, 1961), pp. 432–89; Fitzmaurice, "*Vae Victis* or Woe to the Negotiators! Your Treaty or Our Interpretation of It?" 65 *AJIL* 358 (1971) (a critique of the McDougal *et al.* study); Jacobs, "Varieties of Approaches to Treaty Interpretation," 18 *Intl. and Comp. L.Q.* 318 (1969); panel discussion, "Treaty Interpretation: The

Proper Role of an Impartial Tribunal,'' 1969 *Proc. ASIL* 108; Falk, "On Treaty Interpretation and the New Haven Approach: Achievement and Prospects,'' 8 *Va. J. Intl. L.* 323 (1968).

29 See Iklé, *supra* n. 25, p. 9.

30 See *Summer Study on Verification and Response in Disarmament Agreements*, report prepared by the Institute of Defense Analysis for the Arms Control and Disarmament Agency, June 20, 1962 (Washington, D.C.: Institute of Defense Analysis, Nov. 1962 [Summary Report]), p. 2.

31 *Id.*, pp. 2–3.

32 *Id.*, p. 6.

33 *Id.*, pp. 10–11.

34 Chayes, *supra* n. 1, p. 945.

35 As quoted in 69 *U.S. News and World Report* 62 (Dec. 14, 1970), pp. 62–63.

36 As quoted in W. Safire, "Mr. Warnke's Hit List," *N.Y. Times*, April 21, 1977, p. 25. See also *N.Y. Times*, May 10, 1977, p. 3.

37 But see reports that the Soviet Union has agreed to allow seismic listening posts on its territory to aid in verification of a projected treaty banning all nuclear testing. *N.Y. Times*, Jan. 26, 1979, p. A4.

38 See, *e.g.*, *N.Y. Times*, Jan. 23, 1979, p. A12: "There is general agreement that verification of compliance by the Soviet Union is likely to prove one of the most awkward issues for the Administration in the treaty debate''; and *id.*, Feb. 25, 1978, p. 7: "The question of whether a new arms agreement could be adequately policed has emerged as a central issue in Congressional debate over the proposed [SALT II] accord, with some members of Congress expressing concern over whether the United States could guard against Soviet efforts to cheat.'' See also "Can the Russians Cheat on SALT?'' (editorial) *id.*, March 6, 1979, p. A16; and a study by U.S. Representative Les Aspin (Wis.), *SALT Verification: Prudence or Paranoia*, released March 27, 1978. On the SALT negotiations generally, see references cited in n. 1, *supra*.

39 *N.Y. Times*, Jan. 24, 1979, p. A13. See also President Carter's speech in Atlanta, Ga., Feb. 20, 1979, reported in *N.Y. Times*, Feb. 21, 1979, p. A5, in which he said: "Any SALT Treaty I sign will be adequately verifiable, using our own independent means of guaranteeing Soviet compliance with terms of the agreement. The stakes are too high to rely on trust.''

40 See, *e.g.*, the nonsecret principal findings by the U.S. Senate Select Committee on Intelligence on the ability of the United States to monitor the SALT II Treaty, made public Oct. 5, 1979, text in *N.Y. Times*, Oct. 6, 1979, p. 7, which took the position that the treaty "enhances the ability"

of the United States to monitor those components of Soviet strategic-weapons forces which are subject to the limitations of the treaty, but noted that "our reconaissance system cannot provide absolute certainty." The committee failed to draw any firm conclusion that the terms of the treaty were adequately verifiable, according to critics. See *N.Y. Times*, Oct. 5, 1979, p. A1; *id.*, Oct. 6, 1979, p. 1.

41 Report prepared by the Administration for the Senate Foreign Relations Committee, "Verification of the Proposed SALT II Agreement," released by that committee on Feb. 24, 1978, ACDA Press Release 5 of March 1, 1978, reprinted 78 *Dept. St. Bull.* 15 (April 1978). The report is worth reading in its entirety for its illustration of how nations—in this case a sophisticated nation—approach verification issues. See also *e.g.*, U.S. Dept. of State, Bureau of Public Affairs, "Verification of the SALT II Agreement," Special Report No. 56 (Aug. 1979); Secretary of Defense Brown's statement, "To have a good chance of remaining undetected, any Soviet cheating would have to be on so small a scale that it would not be militarily significant," *N.Y. Times*, July 19, 1979, p. A3; and White House statement of Oct. 5, 1979, concerning the findings of the Senate Committee on Intelligence, *supra*, reprinted 79 *Dept. St. Bull.* (Dec. 1979), p. 32, taking the position that the committee's findings "confirm that the SALT II Treaty can be monitored to a degree that justifies the Administration's conclusion that the Treaty is adequately verifiable."

42 Myrdal, "The International Control of Disarmament," *supra* n. 1, pp. 23–24.

43 *Id.*, p. 25.

44 *Id.*, p. 21. And see the detailed Administration report, "Compliance with the SALT I Agreements," released by the Department of State and the Senate Foreign Relations Committee on Feb. 28, 1978, and reprinted 78 *Dept. St. Bull.* 10 (April 1978).

See, however, the charge that the Soviet Union may have violated the spirit of a proposed treaty on underground nuclear tests, not yet ratified by either country, by detonating in July 1976 two devices that may each have exceeded the 150–kiloton limit established by the treaty, in *N.Y. Times*, Aug. 6, 1976, p. 1; *N.Y. Times*, Nov. 6, 1978, p. 3, and Feb. 1, 1979, p. A6, reporting Administration concern over Soviet efforts to conceal information on recent SS-18 missile tests; and *id.*, Feb. 16, 1980, p. 4, reporting Soviet coding of radio data in a test of a new submarine missile, in apparent violation of provisions of the pending SALT II Treaty.

45 Myrdal, "The International Control of Disarmament," *supra* n. 1, pp. 21–22. For an excellent discussion of these issues, see Chayes, *supra* n. 1, p. 945 *et seq.*

46   As quoted in Newhouse, *Cold Dawn, supra* n. 1, p. 17.

47   A. James, *The Politics of Peacekeeping* (New York: Praeger, 1969), p. 93.

48   *Id.*

49   *Id.*, pp. 93–94.

50   Iceland–U.K. Agreement Concerning British Fishing in Icelandic Waters, June 1, 1976, text in 15 *ILM* 878 (1976), para. 6 and Annex 1, para. 7.

51   See Sec. 505 of the Foreign Assistance Act of 1961, as amended, 22 U.S. Code Sec. 2314.

52   See, *e.g.*, U.S.–Austrian Atomic Energy Agreement, *supra* n. 18, Art. XII(B)(2)(i).

53   International Coffee Agreement, 1962, Art. 58.

54   Ocean Dumping Convention, Art. VI.

55   Whaling Convention, Art. VII. See also Antarctic Marine Living Resources Convention, Art. XX, which requires members of the commission to provide information on their harvesting activities.

56   Convention on Forced Labour, 1946, 39 UNTS 55, Art. XXII. For discussion of the reporting system and other implementation procedures relating to International Labour Organization conventions, see, *e.g.*, E. A. Landy, *The Effectiveness of International Supervision: Thirty Years of ILO Experience* (Dobbs Ferry, N.Y.: Oceana, 1966).

57   See, *e.g.*, Convention on the Elimination of All Forms of Racial Discrimination, 1965, 660 UNTS 195, Art. 9; Single Convention on Narcotic Drugs, 1961, 18 UST 1407, TIAS 6298, 520 UNTS 204, Arts. 13–14, 18–20; Oil Pollution Convention, Art. 12; ICAO Convention, Art. 38; European Human Rights Convention, Art. 57.

58   See *The Interdependent* (U.N. Assoc. of U.S. newsletter), Feb. 1979, p. 7.

59   Marine Pollution Convention, Annex I, Chpt. I.

60   See Lowenfeld, "International Commodity Controls: Some Lessons from the Coffee Agreement," 61 *AJIL* 785 (1967); B. Fisher, *The International Coffee Agreement: A Study in Coffee Diplomacy* (New York: Praeger, 1972), p. 90.

61   See U.S. Central Intelligence Agency, *Polar Regions Atlas* (May 1978), p. 4; U.S. Arms Control and Disarmament Agency, *Report of the United States 1975 Antarctic Inspection* (Washington, D.C., March 1975); M. Voelckel, "L'inspection en Antarctique," in G. Fisher and D. Vignes, eds., *L'inspection Internationale* (Brussels, 1976), p. 223; Simsarian, "Inspection Experience under the Antarctic Treaty and the International Atomic Energy Agency," 60 *AJIL* 502 (1966).

62 U.S.–Brazilian Agreement Concerning Shrimp, 1972, 24 UST 923, TIAS 7603, Art. V(2), text also in 11 *ILM* 453 (1972); Iceland–U.K. Agreement Concerning British Fishing in Icelandic Waters, *supra* n. 50, para. 7; Convention on the Conduct of Fishing Operations in the North Atlantic, 1967, Art. 9, ratified by the United States in 1969 but, as of 1980, not yet in force, text in 91st Cong., 1st Sess., Senate, Exec. D.

For a description of the International Inspection Scheme established under the auspices of the International Commission on Northwest Atlantic Fisheries (ICNAF), see *The Federal Ocean Program: The Annual Report of the President to the Congress on the Nation's Efforts to Comprehend, Conserve and Use the Sea* (April 1973), p. 19. And see, generally, A. W. Koers, *International Regulation of Marine Fisheries: A Study of Regional Fisheries Organizations* (West Byfleet: Fishing News Ltd., 1973), pp. 219–25; and A. W. Koers, "The Enforcement of Fishery Agreements on the High Seas: A Comparative Analysis of International State Practice," Law of the Sea Institute, Univ. of Rhode Island Occasional Paper No. 6 (June 1970).

63 See Antarctic Marine Living Resources Convention, Art. XXIV; and, more generally, Barnes, "The Emerging Antarctic Living Resources Convention," 1979 *Proc. ASIL* 272, p. 276.

64 The scheme presently operates on an annual renewable basis outside the framework of the commission and agreement. However, the United States has proposed an article in a draft protocol which would make the scheme part of the convention. See *Report of the U.S. Delegation to the 26th Meeting of the International Whaling Commission* (1974), p. 5. An earlier agreement among Japan, the Netherlands, Norway, the Soviet Union, and the United Kingdom—the International Observer Scheme for Factory Ships engaged in Pelagic Whaling in the Antarctic, signed Oct. 28, 1963, text in 3 *ILM* 107 (1964)—was never formally implemented, although certain of these countries subsequently concluded special arrangements which were implemented in 1972 and which provide for reports to be made through the International Whaling Commission. On the earlier scheme, see Surrency, "International Inspection in Pelagic Whaling," 13 *Intl. Comp. L.Q.* 666 (1964).

65 See Revised Informal Composite Negotiating Text for the Eighth Session of the Third U.N. Law of the Sea Conference, March 19–April 27, 1979, U.N. Doc. A/CONF. 62/W.P.10/Rev. 1 of April 28, 1979, Art. 73(1), text in 18 *ILM* 686 (1979), p. 722. As this is written, the conference negotiations continue and the proposed treaty text is subject to revision.

66 See, *e.g.*, U.S.–Indonesia Agreement on Cooperation Concerning Civil Uses of Atomic Energy, 1960, 11 UST 2024, TIAS 4557, 388 UNTS 287,

Art. VIII; U.S.–Austria Atomic Energy Agreement, *supra* n. 18, Art. XII. But similar provisions in the Canada-India Atomic Energy agreement were apparently ineffective in preventing India's diversion of material and development and testing in 1974 of a nuclear device. See "Canada Says India's Blast Violated Use of Atom," *N.Y. Times*, May 21, 1974, p. 1; "Canada Suspends Atom Aid to India," *id.*, May 23, 1974, p. 1; "Canada and India Fail in Talks to End Rift Over Nuclear Blast," *id.*, Aug. 3, 1974, p. 2.

67 Egypt-Israel Sinai Agreement, Annex, para. 2(B).

68 SALT I Agreement, Art. V; ABM Treaty, Art. XII.

69 See Greenwood, "Reconaissance and Arms Control," 228 *Sci. Am.* 14 (1973); and, generally, Burt, "Technology Is Essential to Arms Verification," *N.Y. Times*, Aug. 14, 1979, p. C1 (*Science Times*).

70 See, *e.g.*, *N.Y. Times*, June 19, 1979, p. A14: "The loss of American listening posts in Iran, and other factors, prompts some Senators to deny that the treaty is adequately verifiable and immune to possible Soviet cheating."

71 See references cited in n. 66, *supra*.

72 See Chayes, *supra* n. 1, pp. 954–55.

73 *N.Y. Times*, Feb. 1, 1979, p. A6.

74 See Myrdal, "International Control of Disarmament," *supra* n. 1, p. 27.

75 See, *e.g.*, the work of the Standing Group on Implementation of the Council of the International Civil Aviation Organization, which is authorized to inspect various national air navigation systems, described in T. Buergenthal, *Law-Making in the International Civil Aviation Organization* (Syracuse: Syracuse Univ. Press, 1969), p. 114.

76 *Verification and Response in Disarmament Agreements, supra* n. 30, p. 12.

77 On the U.N.'s performance of peacekeeping functions, see, generally, *e.g.*, James, *supra* n. 47, esp. Chpts. 2 and 6; I. Rikhye, M. Harbottle, and B. Egge, *The Thin Blue Line: International Peacekeeping and Its Future* (New Haven: Yale Univ. Press, 1974); J. Boyd, *United Nations Peacekeeping Operations* (New York: Praeger, 1971); D. Wainhouse and associates, *International Peace Observation: A History and Forecast* Baltimore: Johns Hopkins Press, 1966); D. Bowett, *United Nations Forces* (New York: Praeger, 1964); A. Burns and N. Heathcote, *Peacekeeping by UN Forces: From Suez to the Congo* (New York: Praeger, 1963).

78 Egypt-Israel Sinai Agreement, Annex, para. 3(A).

79 *Id.*, para. 5(C).

80 *Id.*, para. 4.

81 Egypt-Israel Peace Treaty, Annex I, Art. VI, and Appendix to Annex I, Art. VII.

82 See *N.Y. Times*, July 19, 1979, p. A10; July 20, 1979, p. A3; July 23, 1979, p. A7; July 25, 1979, pp. 1 and 8; July 26, 1979, p. 2; Aug. 2, 1979, p. A3.

83 See, *e.g.*, *N.Y. Times*, Sept. 6, 1979, p. 1.

84 Geneva Convention Relative to the Treatment of Prisoners of War, 1949, 6 UST 3316, TIAS 3364, 75 UNTS 135, Art. 126. See Forsythe, "Who Guards the Guardians? Third Parties and the Law of Armed Conflict," 70 *AJIL* 41 (1976).

85 IAEA Statute. See generally, International Atomic Energy Agency [IAEA], *The Agency's Safeguards System*, IAEA Doc. No. INFCIRC/66/ Rev. 2 (1968); IAEA, *The Structure and Content of Agreements between the Agency and States Required in Connection with the Treaty on the Non-Proliferation of Nuclear Weapons*, IAEA Doc. No. INFCIRC/153 (1971); and references cited in n. 3, *supra*.

86 U.S. Atomic energy agreements generally require the recipient nation's agreement to the application of bilateral U.S. safeguards. See, *e.g.*, U.S.–Austria Atomic Energy Agreement, *supra* n. 18, Art. XII; and, generally, W. Donnelly and B. Rather, *U.S. Agreements for Cooperation in Atomic Energy: An Analysis*, Congressional Research Service of U.S. Library of Congress (Jan. 1976). But these bilateral safeguards are suspended during any period that IAEA safeguards are being applied. See, *e.g.*, U.S.–Austria Atomic Energy Agreement, *supra*, Arts. XII and XIII.

87 See, *e.g.*, U.S.–Austria–IAEA Agreement on Application of Safeguards, 1969, 21 UST 56, TIAS 6816, 798 UNTS 77.

88 *Id.*, Part IV, sec. 23.

89 Non-Proliferation Treaty, Art. III(2), which provides: "Each non-nuclear-weapon State Party to the Treaty undertakes to accept safeguards, as set forth in an agreement to be negotiated and concluded with the IAEA in accordance with the Statute of the IAEA and the Agency's safeguard system, for the exclusive purpose of verification of the fulfillment of its obligations assumed under this Treaty with a view to preventing diversion of nuclear energy from peaceful uses to nuclear weapons or other nuclear explosive devices." See, generally, IAEA, *The Structure and Content of Agreements Required in Connection with the Treaty on Non-Proliferation, supra* n. 85. For a list of agreements concluded pursuant to this provision involving the United States, see U.S. Department of State, *Treaties in Force* (1979), p. 243.

90 E. Sullivan, "How Safe are Nuclear Safeguards?" *The Interdependent* (U.N. Assoc. of U.S. newsletter), Jan. 1979, pp. 1, 3.

91   *N.Y. Times,* April 28, 1977, p. 1. See, generally, Bettauer, *supra* n. 20; Nye, *supra* n. 3; Gleissner, "Recent U.S. Efforts to Control Nuclear Proliferation," 10 *Vand. J. Transnatl. L.* 271 (1977), pp. 278–79.

92   The Nuclear Non-Proliferation Act of 1978, P.L. 95-242, 92 Stat. 120 (1978), 22 USC secs. 3201–82 and 42 USC sec. 2074–2160a; and see, generally, Bettauer, *supra* n. 20.

93   Nuclear Non-Proliferation Act of 1978, *supra,* sec. 401, 22 USC sec. 2153(a)(1).

94   See Vienna Convention, Art. 44 (separability of treaty provisions).

95   *N.Y. Times,* Jan. 12, 1978, p. 1. See also International Atomic Energy Agency, *Communications Received from Certain Member States Regarding Guidelines for the Export of Nuclear Material, Equipment and Technology,* IAEA Doc. No. INFCIRC/254 (1978), text in 17 *ILM* 220 (1978).

96   *N.Y. Times,* Jan. 12, 1978, pp. 1 and 8.

97   See, *e.g.,* McKnight, *supra* n. 3.

98   Sullivan, *supra* n. 90. For a broader critique of the system, see also Wohlstetter, "Spreading the Bomb without Quite Breaking the Rules," 25 *Foreign Policy* 88 (Winter 1976–77).

99   Sanders, *supra* n. 3, p. 57.

100 Egypt-Israel Sinai Agreement, Art. IV. For implementation of the U.S. proposal, which occasioned some debate, see P.L. 94-110, 94th Cong., H. J. Res. 683, Oct. 13, 1975, 14 *ILM* 1482 (1975). The report of the Senate Committee on Foreign Relations, Senate Report No. 94-415, "Early Warning System in Sinai," is reprinted in 14 *id.* 1483 (1975).

101 *N.Y. Times,* July 24, 1979, p. 1; *id.,* Aug. 8, 1979, p. 1; *Time,* Aug. 20, 1979, p. 25.

102 See sec. 22 of the Foreign Assistance Act of 1974, 22 USC 2370; *N.Y. Times,* Oct. 1, 1974, p. 1, col. 4; *id.,* Oct. 17, 1974, p. 1, col. 3; *id.,* Oct. 18, 1974, p. 5, col. 1. Pursuant to a Presidential Determination under the International Security Assistance Act of 1978, the United States terminated the embargo on arms transfers to Turkey on Sept. 26, 1978. See 78 *Dept. St. Bull.* 38 (Dec. 1978).

103 See Macneil, *supra* n. 8, pp. 658–59.

104 See, *e.g.,* Convention of Establishment Between the United States and France, 1959, 11 UST 2398, TIAS 4625, 401 UNTS 75, Art. 16. But compare, *e.g.,* U.S.–German FCN Treaty, Art. XXVII(2), which provides for submission to the International Court of Justice only upon agreement of both parties.

105 See Chpt. 2, sec. 13, and references cited in Chpt. 1, n. 1 and Chpt. 2, n. 103.

106 See, *e.g.*, Antarctic Treaty, Art. 11; Antarctic Marine Living Resources Convention, Art. XXV.

107 See, *e.g.*, Genocide Convention, Art. IX (compulsory submission to International Court); U.S.–Ceylon Agreement Relating to Investment Guaranties, 1966, 17 UST 331, TIAS 5979, 586 UNTS 91, Art. 6(d) (compulsory submission to arbitration). For a complete listing of agreements conferring jurisdiction on the International Court, see *ICJ Yearbook, 1977–78*, pp. 43–94.

108 See, *e.g.*, International Coffee Agreement, 1962, Art. 61(1); ICAO Convention, Arts. 84–88; OAU Charter, Art. 27; Agreement Concerning the Status of NATO Forces, 1951, 4 UST 1792, TIAS 2846, 199 UNTS 67, Art. 16; GATT, Arts. XXII and XXIII. For reference of questions to a joint commission, see, *e.g.*, U.S.–Canadian Boundary Waters Treaty, 1909, 36 Stat. 2448, TS 548, Arts. IX and X. For discussion of the particularly interesting dispute-settlement procedures under the GATT, see, *e.g.*, J. Jackson, *World Trade and the Law of GATT* (Indianapolis: Bobbs-Merrill, 1969), Chpt. VIII; J. Jackson, *Legal Problems of International Economic Relations* (St. Paul: West, 1977), pp. 422–30; and Walker, "Dispute Settlement: The Chicken War," 58 *AJIL* 671 (1964).

109 See, *e.g.*, International Coffee Agreement, 1962, Art. 61(2)–(7).

110 See Revised Informal Composite Negotiating Text for the Eighth Session of the Third U.N. Conference on the Law of the Sea, March 19–April 27, 1979, *supra* n. 65, Part XV (Arts. 279–98) and Annexes IV–VII. And see Adede, "Settlement of Disputes Arising under the Law of the Sea Convention," 69 *AJIL* 798 (1975).

111 See M. Hudson, *International Tribunals: Past and Future* (Washington, D.C.: Carnegie Endowment, Brookings Institution, 1944), Chpt. X, who comments: "It is a striking fact that States have seldom refused to carry out or abide by the decisions of international tribunals" (p. 129). One exception was the U.K.–Albania *Corfu Channel* case, [1949] ICJ Rep. 4, 36; [1949] ICJ Rep. 244, 250, in which Albania contested the Court's jurisdiction to award damages and refused to comply with the Court's judgment imposing liability for Albania's failure to notify British ships about mines which exploded and damaged the ships in the Albanian waters of the Corfu Channel. See also the 1978 Argentina-Chile *Beagle Channel* arbitration, 17 *ILM* 632 (1978). Argentina refused to accept the judgment of the tribunal, 17 *ILM* 738 (1978), and the question was referred to Papal mediation, 18 *ILM* 1 (1979). By January 1981, Iran had not yet complied with the International Court's judgment of May 24, 1980, in the case concerning *United States Diplomatic and*

Consular Staff in Tehran, deciding that Iran should immediately release the hostages and make reparation to the United States [1980] ICJ Rep. 3. In the Jan. 19, 1981, agreement with Iran resolving the hostage situation, the United States agreed to withdraw the case.

112 See, *e.g.*, Merrills, "Interim Measures of Protection and the Substantive Jurisdiction of the International Court," 36 *Camb. L.J.* 86 (1977); Crockett, "The Effects of Interim Measures of Protection in the International Court of Justice," 7 *Calif. Western Intl. L.J.* 348 (1977); Goldsworthy, "Interim Measures of Protection in the International Court of Justice," 68 *AJIL* 258 (1974); Bilder, "The Anglo-Icelandic Fisheries Dispute," 1978 *Wis. L. Rev.* 37, p. 72 and n. 157.

113 *Fisheries Jurisdiction* cases (U.K. v. Iceland; Federal Republic of Germany v. Iceland), Orders of Aug. 17, 1972, [1972] ICJ Rep. 12 and 30, text in 11 *ILM* 1069 and 1077 (1973) (discussed in Bilder, *supra*); *Nuclear Tests* cases (Australia v. France; New Zealand v. France), Orders of June 22, 1973 [1973] ICJ Rep. 99 and 135, texts in 12 *ILM* 749 (1973); *United States Diplomatic and Consular Staff in Tehran case* (U.S. v. Iran), Order of Dec. 15, 1979, text in 74 *AJIL* 266 (1980) and 19 *ILM* 139 (1980).

114 See Kerley, "Ensuring Compliance with Judgments of the International Court of Justice," in L. Gross, ed., *The Future of the International Court of Justice* (Dobbs Ferry, N.Y.: Oceana, 1976), 1:276.

115 Treaty of Peace between Allied and Associated Powers and Germany (Treaty of Versailles), 1919, 2 Bevans 43.

116 Treaty of Friendship between Persia and the Russian Socialist Federal Republic, signed at Moscow Feb. 26, 1921, 9 LNTS 384. The treaty is discussed in Reisman, "Termination of the USSR's Treaty Right of Intervention in Iran," 74 *AJIL* 144 (1980), Arts. 4 and 6. Reisman notes that on Nov. 5, 1979, authorities in Iran announced the abrogation of the two articles in the Treaty providing for Soviet intervention, but that to date the Soviet Union had not indicated its response. *Id.*, p. 145.

117 Treaty of Guarantee between Cyprus, Greece, Turkey, and the United Kingdom, 1960, British Command Papers 1253 (Doc. XXXIV) (TS No. 5. of 1961). See, generally, T. Ehrlich, *Cyprus, 1958–1967* (New York: Oxford Univ. Press, 1974), p. 38.

118 Treaty on Relations with Cuba, 1903, 33 Stat. 2248, TS 437, 6 Bevans 1116.

119 DeConcini Condition, adopted by the U.S. Senate March 16, 1978, text in 78 *Dept. St. Bull.* (May 1978), p. 53, and 17 *ILM* 828 (1978). For text of treaty, see 77 *Dept. St. Bull.* (1977), p. 483, and 16 *ILM* 1040 (1977).

120 Leadership Amendment 20, adopted by the U.S. Senate March 10, 1978, text in 78 *Dept. St. Bull.* (May 1978), p. 52, and 17 *ILM* 827 (1978).

121   See, *e.g.*, Rubin, "The Panama Canal Treaties: Keys to the Locks," 4 *Brooklyn J. Intl. L.* 159 (1978).

122   See, *e.g.*, U.N. functions under the Egypt-Israel Sinai Agreement and Peace Treaty, described in the text at nn. 78–81, *supra*, and the references cited *supra* n. 77.

123   The example is drawn from the Anglo-Icelandic fisheries dispute and *Fisheries Jurisdiction* case, *supra* n. 113. However, while Iceland in that case had consented in a 1961 agreement with the United Kingdom to the compulsory jurisdiction of the International Court over certain disputes arising out of the agreement, it had not specifically agreed to recognize the Court's authority to issue binding orders requiring specific performance.

124   See references in n. 112, *supra*.

125   On problems of enforcement of international arbitral and judicial decisions, see, generally, *e.g.*, W. Reisman, *Nullity and Revision: The Review and Enforcement of International Judgments and Awards* (New Haven: Yale Univ. Press, 1971); E. Nantwi, *The Enforcement of International Judicial Decisions and Arbitral Awards in International Law* (Leiden: Sijthoff, 1966); W. Reisman, "Sanctions and Enforcement" in C. Black and R. Falk, eds., *The Future of the International Legal Order* (Princeton: Princeton Univ. Press, 1971), 3:273; Reisman, "Enforcement of International Judgments," 63 *AJIL* 1 (1969); Kerley, *supra* n. 114; Schachter, "The Enforcement of International Judicial and Arbitral Decisions," 54 *AJIL* 1 (1960).

126   See *supra*, n. 113.

127   See, *e.g., Lumley v. Wagner*, 1 De G.M. and G. 604 (1854 Ch. App).

128   Treaty of Versailles, *supra* n. 115, Arts. 42–44 and 159–202.

129   Non-Proliferation Treaty, Art. III(2).

130   See Schelling, *supra* n. 4, p. 135.

131   Constitution of Japan, 1946, Art. 9, text in H. Tanaka, ed., *The Japanese Legal System* (Tokyo: Univ. of Tokyo Press, 1976), p. 3.

132   *Id.*, pp. 695–96, and for a general discussion of Article 9, *id.*, Chpt. 9, and Wada, "Decisions under Article 9 of the Constitution: The Sunakawa, Eniwa, and Naganuma Decisions," 9 *Law in Japan* 117 (1976).

     Compare U.S.–Japan Peace Treaty of 1951, 3 UST 3169, TIAS 2490, 136 UNTS 45, Art. 5, text in 25 *Dept. St. Bull.* 349 (1951), which requires Japan only to accept the obligations of Article 2 of the U.N. Charter, including the obligation to refrain in its international relations from the threat or use of force against the territorial integrity or political independence of any state or in any other manner inconsistent with the purposes of the United Nations.

133   See Ehrlich, *supra* n. 117, p. 37.

134   Universal Copyright Convention, 1955, 6 UST 2731, TIAS 3324, 216 UNTS 132, Art. X; see also, *e.g.*, the 1965 U.S.–Canada Agreement Concerning Automotive Products, *supra* n. 16, Art. VI, which provides that the agreement shall enter into force definitively upon exchange of notes giving assurances that appropriate action in the respective legislatures of the two countries is completed.

135   Convention on the Law Applicable to International Sales of Goods, 1955, 510 UNTS 147, Art. 7.

136   International Covenant on Civil and Political Rights, 1966, adopted by Resolution 2200 (XXI) of the U.N. General Assembly, 21 UN GAOR, Supp. No. 16, Doc. A/6316, pp. 52–58, Art. 2(2).

137   See also, *e.g.*, L. Henkin, *The Constitution and Foreign Affairs* (Mineola, N.Y.: Foundation Press, 1972), pp. 156–67; Evans, ''Self-Executing Treaties in the United States of America,'' 30 *Brit. Y.B. Intl. L.* 178 (1953); *Restatement (Second), Foreign Relations Law of the United States, supra* n. 28, sec. 141.

138   See, *e.g.*, W. W. Bishop, Jr., *International Law: Cases and Materials*, 3rd ed. (Boston: Little, Brown, 1971), pp. 149–57; Articles 63 and 66 of the Netherlands Constitution, discussed in Van Panhuys, ''The Netherlands Constitution and International Law,'' 58 *AJIL* 88 (1964); Fatouros, ''International Law in the New Greek Constitution,'' 70 *id.* 492 (1976).

139   EEC Treaty, esp. Art. 189; and see *e.g.*, the decisions of the European Court of Justice in *Costa v. ENEL* [1964], *Comm. Mkt. L.R.* 425, CCH *Comm. Mkt. Rep.* para. 8023, and *Amsterdam Bulb B.V. v. Productschap Voor Siergewassen* [1977], *Comm. Mkt. L.R.* 218, CCH *Comm. Mkt. Rep.* para. 8391; and, see generally, Hay and Thompson, ''The Community Court and the Supremacy of Community Law: A Progress Report,'' 8 *Vand. J. Transnatl. L.* 651 (1975).

140   See Revised Informal Composite Negotiating Text, *supra* n. 65, Part XI; and, generally, for review of the various negotiating sessions, the series of articles covering developments at each session by Stevenson and Oxman and by Oxman appearing in 68 *AJIL* 1 (1974); 69 *id.* 1 (1975); 69 *id.* 763 (1975); 71 *id.* 247 (1977); 73 *id.* 1 (1979); and 74 *id.* 1 (1980).

141   See Lagoni, ''Oil and Gas Deposits across National Frontiers,'' 73 *AJIL* 215 (1979).

142   See, *e.g.*, the merger in 1958 of Egypt and Syria into the United Arab Republic, discussed in Cotran, ''Some Legal Aspects of the Formation of the United Arab Republic and the United Arab States,'' 8 *Intl. Comp. L.Q.* 346 (1959), reprinting relevant documents; and Treaty Instituting the European Coal and Steel Community, 1951, 261 UNTS 169. See

also the Treaty Instituting the European Atomic Energy Community, 1957, 298 UNTS 167, Art. 86, which vests in EURATOM ownership of all special fissionable materials in the territory of the Community, except those used for military purposes. Compare also recent proposals that plutonium reprocessing be brought under the auspices of international or regional fuel cycle arrangements; see, *e.g.*, Smith and Chayes, "Institutional Arrangements for a Multinational Reprocessing Plant" in A. Chayes and W. B. Lewis, eds., *International Arrangements for Nuclear Fuel Reprocessing Arrangements* (Cambridge: Bollinger, 1977), p. 145.

143 See, *e.g.*, Baldwin, "The Power of Positive Sanctions," 24 *World Politics* 19 (1971).

144 See, *e.g.*, Bilder, "The International Promotion of Human Rights: A Current Assessment," 58 *AJIL* 728 (1964), pp. 733–34, suggesting international prizes or other incentives for nations showing special achievements in human rights.

145 For discussion of some problems of timing of performance, see E. Goffman, *Strategic Interaction* (Philadelphia: Univ. of Pennsylvania Press, 1969), pp. 130–32.

146 See, *e.g.*, Gwertzman, "11 Years Later, Controversy and Confusion Still Surround UN's Mideast Resolution 242," *N.Y. Times*, May 6, 1978, p. 6; Rostow, "The Illegality of the Arab Attack on Israel of October 6, 1973," 69 *AJIL* 272 (1975).

147 U.N. Security Council Res. 242, adopted Nov. 22, 1967, Resolutions and Decisions of the Security Council 1967, S/INF/22/ Rev. 2, p. 8.

148 See M. Deutsch, *The Resolution of Conflict* (New Haven: Yale Univ. Press, 1973), pp. 161–62.

149 See Agreement Concerning a Military Armistice in Korea, and Temporary Supplementary Agreement, 1953, 4 UST 234, TIAS 2782, Art. III and Annex.

150 *N.Y. Times*, March 15, 1979, p. A14.

151 N. Gogol, *Dead Souls*, tr. G. Reavey (New York: Norton, 1971), p. 125. The example is drawn from S. Klatsky and M. Teitler, "On Trust," University of Wisconsin—Madison, Center for Demography and Ecology, Working Paper 73–9 (April 1973), pp. 18–19.

152 Universal Postal Convention, 1952, 169 UNTS 3, Art. 33.

153 Nuclear Non-Proliferation Act of 1978, *supra* n. 92, secs. 307 and 401.

154 Jackson, *Legal Problems of International Economic Relations, supra* n. 108, p. 429. On Article XXIII of GATT, see generally U.S. Senate, Comm. on Finance, Subcomm. on International Trade, *The GATT Provisions on Compensation and Retaliation* (Executive Branch GATT Study No. 11), 93rd Cong., 1st Sess., 1973; Jackson, *World Trade and*

the Law of GATT, supra n. 108, pp. 178–87; Hudec, "Retaliation against 'Unreasonable' Foreign Trade Practices: The New Section 301 and GATT Nullification and Impairment," 59 *Minn. L. Rev.* 466 (1975); Jackson, "The Jurisprudence of International Trade: The DISC Case in the GATT," 72 *AJIL* 747 (1978).

See also Convention Establishing the European Free Trade Association, 1960, 370 UNTS 3, Art. 31(4), which provides that if, after inquiry, the council finds by majority vote that a member has not fulfilled its obligations, the council may authorize any other member state or states to suspend corresponding obligations. Article 31(5) permits the council to authorize an interim suspension of obligations.

155 On responses to treaty breach, see generally, *e.g.*, A. David, *The Strategy of Treaty Termination: Lawful Breaches and Retaliations* (New Haven: Yale Univ. Press, 1975); Bilder, "Breach of Treaty and Response Thereto," 1967 *Proc. ASIL* 193; Briggs, "Unilateral Denunciation of Treaties: The Vienna Convention and the International Court of Justice," 68 *AJIL* 51 (1974); Reisman, "Procedures for Controlling Unilateral Treaty Terminations," 63 *AJIL* 544 (1969); B. Sinha, *Unilateral Denunciation of Treaty Because of Prior Violations of Obligations by the Other Party* (The Hague: Martinus Nijhoff, 1966); Schwelb, "Termination or Suspension of the Operation of a Treaty as a Consequence of Its Breach," 7 *Indian J. Intl. L.* 309 (1967); Esgain, "The Spectrum of Responses to Treaty Violations," 26 *Ohio State L.J.* 1 (1965).

156 The full text of Vienna Convention, Art. 60, is as follows:

Article 60

Termination or suspension of the operation of a treaty as a consequence of its breach

1. A material breach of a bilateral treaty by one of the parties entitles the other to invoke the breach as a ground for terminating the treaty or suspending its operation in whole or in part.

2. A material breach of a multilateral treaty by one of the parties entitles:

(a) the other parties by unanimous agreement to suspend the operation of the treaty in whole or in part or to terminate it either:

(i) in the relations between themselves and the defaulting State, or

(ii) as between all the parties;

(b) a party specially affected by the breach to invoke it as a ground for suspending the operation of the treaty in whole or in part in the relations between itself and the defaulting State;

(c) any party other than the defaulting State to invoke the breach as a ground for suspending the operation of the treaty in whole or in part with respect to

itself if the treaty is of such a character that a material breach of its provisions by one party radically changes the position of every party with respect to the further performance of its obligations under the treaty.

3. A material breach of a treaty, for the purposes of this article, consists in:

(a) a repudiation of the treaty not sanctioned by the present Convention; or

(b) the violation of a provision essential to the accomplishment of the objective or purpose of the treaty.

4. The foregoing paragraphs are without prejudice to any provision in the treaty applicable in the event of a breach.

5. Paragraphs 1 to 3 do not apply to provisions relating to the protection of the human person contained in treaties of a humanitarian character, in particular to provisions prohibiting any form of reprisals against persons protected by such treaties.

157 See Opinion of the Legal Adviser, Aug. 12, 1963, *Nuclear Test Ban Treaty Hearings*, Hearings before the Committee on Foreign Relations, U.S. Senate, 88th Cong., 1st Sess., on Executive M, pp. 37–40.

158 See *N.Y. Times*, July 20, 1977, p. A5.

159 See Opinion of the Legal Adviser in the *Nuclear Test Ban Treaty Hearings, supra* n. 157, p. 37. Likewise, the reporter's note to sec. 158 of *Restatement (Second), Foreign Relations Law of the United States, supra* n. 28, p. 486, indicates: "There are relatively few cases in which an international agreement has been terminated by unilateral abrogation."

160 Egypt-Israel Sinai Agreement, Annex, para. 6.

161 See Vietnam Truce Agreement, Art. 8. For disagreements regarding compliance and temporary suspension of performances by the two parties, see, *e.g.*, "Hanoi Agrees to Free Americans within Time Specified in Accord; U.S. Had Suspended Minesweeping—Pullout of Troops Also Suspended," *N.Y. Times*, March 1, 1973, p. 1; "U.S. Reviews Withdrawal from Vietnam," *id.*, March 15, 1973, p. 5.

162 Deutsch, *The Resolution of Conflict, supra* n. 148, p. 162.

163 *N.Y. Times*, Jan. 20, 1981, p. A4; For an earlier escrow proposal by U.N. Secretary General Waldheim, see *id.*, Feb. 7, 1980, p. A1.

164 See, *e.g.*, U.S.–South Africa Agreement for Cooperation Concerning the Civil Uses of Atomic Energy, 1957, *supra* n. 19, Art. X(B)(5); Bettauer, *supra* n. 20, p. 1160.

165 Nuclear Non-Proliferation Act of 1978, *supra* n. 20, sec. 401.

166 U.S.–Austria Atomic Energy Agreement, *supra* n. 18, Art. XII(B)(5).

167 See, *e.g.*, U.S.–Brazil Agreement for Cooperation Concerning Civil Uses of Atomic Energy, 1972, 23 UST 2477, TIAS 7439, Arts. VIII(H) and X(A)(3); Bettauer, *supra* n. 20, pp. 1147–50.

168 Sec. 505 of the U.S. Foreign Assistance Act of 1961, as amended, 22 USC sec. 2314.

169   See n. 102, *supra*.

170   See, *e.g.*, U.S.–Indonesia Atomic Energy Agreement: Cooperation for Civil Uses, 1960, 11 UST 2024, TIAS 4557, 388 UNTS 287, Art. IV; U.S.–Austria Atomic Energy Agreement, *supra* n. 18, Art. IX(G).

171   Compare U.S.–Austria Atomic Energy Agreement, *supra* n. 18, Art. XII(B)(3), which requires Austria to deposit in storage facilities approved by the United States any special nuclear material not currently utilized for civil purposes.

172   IAEA Statute, Art. XII(A)(7).

173   See, *e.g.*, U.S.–Japan–IAEA Agreement on Application of Safeguards by the IAEA to the U.S.–Japan Atomic Energy Cooperation Agreement, 1963, 14 UST 1265, TIAS 5429, Art. II(14); and reference in n. 87, *supra*.

174   *N.Y. Times*, Dec. 4, 1979, p. A18.

175   Macneil, *supra* n. 8, pp. 678–79.

176   International Coffee Agreement, 1962, Art. 36.

177   See, *e.g.*, L. Henkin, *How Nations Behave* (New York: Praeger, 1968), Chpt. 4; M. Whiteman, *Digest of International Law*, Dept. of State Pub. 8424 (Washington, D.C., 1968), 13:236 *et seq.*; C. Brown-John, *Multilateral Sanctions in International Law* (New York: Praeger, 1975); F. Kirgis, *International Organizations in Their Legal Setting* (St. Paul: West, 1977), pp. 475–602; H. Schermers, *International Institutional Law* (Leiden: Sijthoff, 1972), 2:581–621; Kunz, "Sanctions in International Law," 54 *AJIL* 324 (1960); Schelling, *supra* n. 4; and contrast Baldwin, *supra* n. 143.

Compare also studies of the effect of sanctions in deterring deviant behavior within national societies, such as H. Packer, *The Limits of the Criminal Sanction* (Stanford: Stanford Univ. Press, 1968); Schwartz and Orleans, "On Legal Sanctions," 34 *U. Chi. L. Rev.* 274 (1967); Chambliss, "Types of Deviance and the Effectiveness of Legal Sanctions," 1967 *Wis. L. Rev.* 703.

178   For discussions of the concept of hostage, see, *e.g.*, 11 *Encyclopaedia Britannica* 745 (1972); Schelling, *supra* n. 4, pp 135–36, 239; Deutsch, *supra* n. 148, pp. 162–63; and, noting the ambiguity of the practice, G. Schwarzenberger, *International Law as Applied by International Courts and Tribunals* (London: Stevens, 1968), 2:234. For a discussion of the use of hostages by England and France to secure observance of the Treaty of Bretigny of 1360, see Tuchman, *supra* n. 7, Chpt. 8 ("Hostage in England").

179   See, *e.g.*, the Vienna Convention on Diplomatic Relations, 1961, 23 UST 3227, TIAS 7502, 500 UNTS 95, Art. 29, which prohibits govern-

ments from holding protected persons enjoying diplomatic status; the 1973 Convention on the Prevention and Punishment of Crimes against Internationally Protected Persons, including Diplomatic Agents, text in 68 *AJIL* 384 (1974) and 13 *ILM* 41 (1974), which requires nations to outlaw the murder or kidnapping of any representative or official of a state; the Geneva Convention Relative to the Treatment of Prisoners of War, 1949, 6 UST 3316, TIAS 3364, 75 UNTS 135, Art. 3(1)(b), and the Geneva Convention Relative to the Protection of Civilian Persons in Time of War, 1949, 6 UST 3516, TIAS 3365, 75 UNTS 287, Art. 3(1)(b), which prohibit the taking of hostages in time of war; and the recently concluded but not yet in force U.N. International Convention Against the Taking of Hostages, U.N. Doc. A/C.6/34/L.23 of Dec. 4, 1979, adopted by General Assembly Res. 34/146 (XXXIV), Dec. 17, 1979, text in 18 *ILM* 1457 (1979), which extends the ban against hostage-taking to private individuals and requires prosecution or extradition of hostage takers. See *N.Y. Times*, Dec. 18, 1979, p. 1. None of these agreements appears to prohibit a consensual exchange of hostages pursuant to international agreement, although other international human rights agreements might be argued to do so.

180   Schelling, *supra* n. 4, p. 136.

181   Information supplied by Iranian Task Force, U.S. Department of State. See President Carter's Exec. Orders No. 12205, April 7, 1980, and 12211, April 17, 1980; and *N.Y. Times*, April 8, 1980, pp. A1 and A6, and *id.*, April 18, 1980, p. A1.

182   Information supplied by Iranian Task Force, U.S. Department of State.

183   R. Fisher, "My Turn: Sanctions Won't Work," *Newsweek*, Jan. 14, 1980, p. 21.

184   See, generally, discussions in Whiteman, Brown-John, Kirgis, and Schermers, *supra* n. 177.

185   See, generally, *e.g.*, Kirgis, *supra* n. 177, pp. 443–62; and compare Chayes, *supra* n. 1, pp. 955–57.

186   See, *e.g.*, ILO Constitution, Arts. 19 and 22; Valticos, "The International Labour Organization," in S. Schwebel, ed., *The Effectiveness of International Decisions* (Dobbs Ferry, N.Y.: Oceana, 1971); E. Landy, *supra* n. 55; ILO, *The Impact of International Labour Conventions and Recommendations* (Geneva: International Labour Office, 1976).

187   See, *e.g.*, D. Bowett, *The Law of International Institutions*, 3rd ed. (London: Stevens, 1975), p. 138; Schwelb, "Civil and Political Rights: The International Measures of Implementation," 62 *AJIL* 827 (1968).

188   U.N. Charter, Art. 19. See also WHO Constitution, Art. 7; ICAO Convention, Art. 62; ILO Constitution, Art. 13(4); IAEA Statute, Art. 19.

189 See Whiteman, *supra* n. 177, pp. 309–32.

190 ICAO Assembly Res. A21–6 of Oct. 4, 1974, cited in Kirgis, *supra* n. 177, p. 498.

191 IMF Agreement, Art. XV(2)(a). See, generally, Gold, "The Sanctions of the International Monetary Fund," 66 *AJIL* 737 (1972).

192 International Coffee Agreement, 1962, Art. 36; International Tin Agreement, 1975, 28 UST 4619, TIAS 8607, Art. 36.

193 See, generally, Schermers, *supra* n. 177, pp. 54–63; Sohn, "Expulsion or Forced Withdrawal from an International Organization," 77 *Harv. L. Rev.* 1381 (1964).

194 See also, *e.g.*, IAEA Statute, Art. 19(B).

195 For other provisions for expulsion, see, *e.g.*, International Coffee Agreement, 1962, Art. 69; IBRD Agreement, Art. VI(2); IMF Agreement, Art. 15(2). On experience regarding expulsion, including the League of Nations' expulsion of the Soviet Union in 1939 for aggression against Finland, and the International Monetary Fund's and International Bank's expulsion of Czechoslovakia in 1953 for failure to meet certain financial and reporting obligations, see Schermers, *supra* n. 177, pp. 57–63.

196 WMO Congress, May 1975, Res. 38 (Cg-VII), Seventh World Meteorological Congress, Abridged Report with Resolutions, 136, text in Kirgis, *supra* n. 177, pp. 526–28.

197 See Whiteman, *supra* n. 177, pp. 241–43.

198 Schermers, *supra* n. 177, p. 55.

199 Versailles Treaty, *supra* n. 115, Art. 430.

200 See, *e.g.*, the Protocol for Limiting and Regulating the Cultivation of the Poppy Plant, the Production of, International and Wholesale Trade In, and Use of Opium, 1953, 14 UST 10, TIAS 5273, 456 UNTS 3, Arts. 12 and 13, providing for a mandatory embargo which may be imposed by the Central Narcotics Board upon either a party or a nonparty to that treaty. And see, generally, Cohrrsen and Hoover, "The International Control of Dangerous Drugs," 9 *J. Intl. Law and Econ.* 81 (1974); Waddell, "International Narcotics Control," 64 *AJIL* 310 (1970).

201 U.N. Charter, Chpt. VII, and esp. Art. 39.

202 U.N. Charter, Art. 25.

203 *Id.*, Arts. 41 and 42.

204 See, generally, *e.g.*, Fitzmaurice, "The Foundations of the Authority of International Law and the Problem of Enforcement," 19 *Modern L. Rev.* 1 (1956).

205 U.N. Security Council Res. 232 of Dec. 16, 1965, 21 SCOR, Resolutions and Decisions, 1966, 1968, p. 7. On Rhodesian sanctions generally, see, *e.g.*, R. Zacklin, *The United Nations and Rhodesia: A Study*

small

in International Law (New York: Praeger, 1974); Note, "International Sanctions: United Nations Security Council Resolution-Economic Sanctions against Southern Rhodesia," 14 *Va. J. Intl. L.* 319 (1974); Kirgis, *supra* n. 177, pp. 555–99; Whiteman, *supra* n. 177, p. 392 *et seq.* U.N. sanctions were lifted on Dec. 21, 1979, following the United Kingdom's resumption of authority in Zimbabwe Rhodesia on Dec. 12, 1979, pending the holding of elections for a representative government. Security Council Res. 460 (1979), text in 19 *ILM* 258 (1980). U.S. sanctions relating to Rhodesia were lifted on Dec. 16, 1979. See Dept. of State statement of Dec. 15, 1979, 80 *Dept. St. Bull.* (Feb. 1980), p. 11.

206 U.N. Security Council Res. 418 (1977), adopted Nov. 4, 1977, 77 *Dept. St. Bull.* 859 (1977), p. 866, text in 16 *ILM* 1548 (1977). The embargo is presently limited to arms.

207 *N.Y. Times*, Jan. 14, 1980, p. A1; *id.*, Jan. 15, 1980, p. A1. The vote on the proposed resolution was held on Jan. 13, 1980. On Dec. 4, 1979, the U.N. Security Council, in Res. 457 (1979), had urged the immediate release of the hostages. On Dec. 31, 1980, the Security Council had adopted a resolution that, if the American hostages were not released within one week, all member nations should adopt "effective measures" under the Charter.

208 See *supra* n. 181.

209 See, generally, *e.g.*, I. Brownlic, *International Law and the Use of Force by States* (London: Oxford Univ. Press, 1963); but see Franck, "Who Killed Article 2(4)? or, Emerging Norms Governing the Use of Force by States," 64 *AJIL* 809 (1970).

  On economic sanctions generally, see, *e.g.*, D. Losman, *International Economic Sanctions: The Cases of Cuba, Israel and Rhodesia* (Albuquerque: Univ. of New Mexico Press, 1979); Bowett, "International Law and Economic Coercion," 16 *Va. J. Intl. L.* 245 (1976); MacDonald, "Economic Sanctions in the International System," 7 *Canadian Y.B. Intl. L.* 61 (1969).

210 *N.Y. Times*, Jan. 7, 1980, p. A7.

211 *N.Y. Times*, Jan. 13, 1980, p. 1.

212 See, generally, *e.g.*, Dinstein, "International Criminal Law," 5 *Israel Y.B. on Human Rights* 55 (1975); G. Mueller and E. Wise, eds., *International Criminal Law* (S. Hackensack, N.J.: Rothman/London: Sweet and Maxwell, 1965), esp. Chpts. 3 and 5.

213 Genocide Convention, Art. VI.

214 International Convention on the Suppression and Punishment of the Crime of Apartheid, 1973, UNGA Doc. A/RES/3068 (XXVIII) of Dec. 6, 1973, text in 13 *ILM* 50 (1974), Art. V.

215 Egypt-Israel Sinai Agreement, esp. Arts. IV and V and Annex; Egypt-

Israel Peace Agreement, esp. Art. II, Annex I, and Art. V of Appendix to Annex I.

216　See, generally, James, *supra* n. 46, esp. Chpt. 8; and other references cited in n. 76.

217　James, *supra*, p. 94.

218　Paragraph 4(b) of the Israel–U.S. Memorandum of Agreement accompanying the Egypt-Israel Sinai Agreement. The memorandum is reprinted in 14 *ILM* 1468 (1975).

219　Israel–U.S. Memorandum of Agreement accompanying the 1979 Egypt-Israel Peace Treaty, signed March 26, 1979, reprinted in 79 *Dept. St. Bull.* (May 1979), p. 61, and 18 *ILM* 537 (1979). When Egypt initially protested the U.S. extension of these assurances, the United States indicated its willingness to extend them to Egypt. See letters reprinted in 18 *ILM* 536 and 540 (1979). Similar assurances to Israel accompanying the 1975 Egypt-Israel Sinai Agreement are reprinted in *Cong. Rec.*, 94th Cong., 1st Sess., Vol. 121, No. 152 (Oct. 9, 1975), pp. S.17969–70, and in 14 *ILM* 1468–69 (1975). The extent of these commitments, and the constitutional propriety of the method of entry into them as solely executive agreements, has been subject to some debate. See, *e.g.*, the Positions of the Senate Legislative Counsel and Department of State Legal Adviser reprinted in 14 *ILM* 1585, 1593 (1975) and 15 *id.* 187, 190 (1976).

220　Israel–U.S. Memorandum of Agreement accompanying the 1979 Egypt-Israel Peace Treaty, signed March 26, 1979, reprinted in 79 *Dept. St. Bull.* (May 1979), pp. 60–61, and 18 *ILM* 533 (1979). Similar assurances to Israel accompanying the 1975 Egypt-Israel Sinai Agreement are reprinted in *Cong. Rec., supra*, pp. 1769–70, and in 14 *ILM* 1468 (1975).

221　See letter of President Carter to Congressional Committee Chairmen, April 2, 1979, reprinted in 79 *Dept. St. Bull.* (May 1979), p. 59; and the Special International Security Act of 1979, P.L. 96–35, 96th Cong., July 20, 1979, 93 Stat. 89 *et seq.*

222　See Berger, "Israeli Skeptical of Accords," *Washington Post*, May 2, 1975, p. A10.

223　*Newsweek*, Nov. 6, 1978, p. 68.

CHAPTER 5: Using Risk-Management Techniques Effectively: Limitations and Possibilities

1　The situation is noted in D. P. Moynihan, "Reflections: The SALT Process," *The New Yorker*, Nov. 19, 1979, pp. 104, 108–9, who quotes an October 5, 1979, report of the Senate Intelligence Committee as follows: ''The Soviets' unanticipated ability to emplace the much larger SS-19 in a slightly enlarged SS-11 silo circumvented the safeguards the United States thought it had obtained in SALT I against the substitution of heavy for light ICBMs.''

2 See the text of Chpt. 4 at n. 41, *supra*.

3 See also Bilder, ''Breach of Treaty and Response Thereto'' 1967 *Proc. ASIL* 193 (1967), p. 196: ''The [foreign office] official's world is one of continuing tension between his desire to maintain his own flexibility and freedom of maneuver to cope with changing circumstances and his desire for certainty and predictability on the part of foreign officials. Treaties frequently reflect an uneasy and uncertain compromise between these inconsistent objectives. Neither party intends to give up flexibility altogether, but the price each pays is in less than guaranteed expectations.''

4 Compare similar attitudes among businessmen in private contract relationships, described in Macaulay, ''Non-Contractual Relations in Business: A Preliminary Study,'' 28 *Am. Soc. Rev.* 55 (1963), p. 64: ''The greater danger perceived by some businessmen is that one would have to perform his side of the bargain to its letter and thus lose what is called 'flexibility.' Businessmen may welcome a measure of vagueness in the obligations they assume so that they may negotiate matters in the light of the actual circumstances.''

5 See President's Message to the U.S. Congress, Jan. 18, 1979, giving the Sixth Report on the Sinai Support Mission, reprinted in 79 *Dept. St. Bull.* (April 1979), p. 41.

6 Report of the U.N. Secretary General on Financing of the United Nations Peace-Keeping Forces in the Middle East, U.N. Doc. A/34/582 (Oct. 22, 1979), Annex 1, p. 2. During the calendar year 1979, U.N. appropriations for the U.N. Disengagement Observer Force (UNDOF), supervising the Syria-Israel disengagement agreement, were approximately $21 million, U.N. appropriations for the U.N. Interim Force in Lebanon (UNIFIL) were approximately $124 million, and U.N. appropriations for the U.N. Peacekeeping Force in Cyprus (UNFICYP) were approximately $24 million. Since troop-contributing governments in many cases absorbed at their own expense much of the costs incurred in providing contingents and/or logistic support for these operations, the actual costs were considerably higher. Information supplied by Office of the Under-Secretaries-General for Special Political Affairs, United Nations, letter of March 12, 1980.

7 In the *Southwest Africa* cases (Ethiopia v. South Africa, Liberia v. South Africa), [1966] ICJ Rep. 6, the applications were filed in 1960, and the

final judgment was delivered in 1966. In the case concerning the *Barcelona Traction, Light and Power Company, Limited* (Belgium v. Spain), [1970] ICJ Rep. 3, the application was filed in 1962, and the final judgment was delivered in 1970. Neither of these cases, however, was concerned primarily with treaty interpretation or application. For evidence that the Court is capable of moving with more despatch when the circumstances require, see the recent case concerning *United State Diplomatic and Consular Staff in Tehran* (U.S. v. Iran), [1980] ICJ Rep. 3, 19 *ILM* 553 (1980), a treaty case in which the Court issued its judgment within six months of the date the proceedings were instituted.

8   Compare, in the private sector, Leff, "Injury, Ignorance, and Spite: The Dynamics of Coercive Collection," 80 *Yale L.J.* 1 (1970).

9   G. Marwell and D. R. Schmitt, *Cooperation: An Experimental Analysis* (New York: Academic Press, 1975), pp. 119–27.

10   Macaulay, *supra* n. 4, p. 66.

11   Macneil, "A Primer of Contract Planning," 48 *So. Calif. L. Rev.* 627 (1975), p. 668. And compare Macaulay, *supra* n. 4, p. 64: "Detailed negotiated contracts can get in the way of creating good exchange relationships between business units. If one side insists on a detailed plan, there will be delay while letters are exchanged as the parties try to agree on what should happen if a remote and unlikely contingency occurs. In some cases they may not be able to agree at all on such matters and as a result a sale may be lost to the seller and the buyer may have to search elsewhere for an acceptable supplier. Many businessmen would react by thinking that if no one raised the series of remote and unlikely contingencies all this wasted effort could have been avoided."

12   *Newsweek*, March 19, 1979, p. 22.

13   See, *e.g.*, Marwell and Schmitt, *supra* n. 9, p. 186; Swinth, "The Establishment of the Trust Relationship," 11 *J. Conflict Res.* 335 (1967), p. 343; R. Jervis, *Perception and Misperception in International Politics* (Princeton: Princeton Univ. Press, 1976), p. 83.

14   E. E. Morison, *Turmoil and Tradition: A Study of the Life and Times of Henry L. Stimson* (Boston: Houghton Mifflin, 1960), p. 35. But Morison points out that Stimson, on his eightieth birthday, reluctantly concluded that to his dictum about trusting men to make them trustworthy must be added the qualification that "this does not always apply to a man who is determined to make you his dupe." *Id.*, p. 649.

15   See, *e.g.*, Moynihan, *supra* n. 1, pp. 146, 151.

16   *Id.*, commenting on p. 151, "If it is all unthinkable, the Soviets seem nonetheless to have been thinking about it." For the suggestion that some

American leaders think in such terms, see A. Lewis, "Thinking about the Unthinkable," (Op. Ed.) *N.Y. Times*, Feb. 14, 1980, p. A27.

17 See, generally, references cited in Chpt. 1, n. 38, *supra*.

18 Macaulay, *supra* n. 4, p. 58.

19 Speech delivered by President Carter in Atlanta, Ga., Feb. 20, 1979, reported in *N.Y. Times*, Feb. 21, 1979, p. A5.

20 See discussion in Chpt. 4, sec. 8(c)(iv), *supra*.

21 A number of commentators have suggested a broader application of social science and its techniques to problems of international law. See, *e.g.*, Falk, "New Approaches to the Study of International Law," in M. A. Kaplan, ed., *New Approaches to International Relations* (New York: St. Martins, 1968), pp. 369–70; Presidential Address by Harold Lasswell to the American Society of International Law, 66 *Proc. ASIL* 281 (1972); W. Gould and M. Barkun, *International Law and the Social Sciences* (Princeton: Princeton Univ. Press, 1970); W. Coplin, "Current Studies of the Functions of International Law: Assessment and Suggestions," 2 *Pol. Sc. Annual* 149 (1969); P. Rohn, *World Treaty Index* (Santa Barbara: ABC-Clio, 1974), 1:xi–xiii.

22 The United Nations Institute for Training and Research (UNITAR), established by UNGA Res. 1934 (XVIII) of Dec. 1, 1963, is an autonomous institution under the U.N. System, supported by voluntary contributions from member states, foundations, and other similar sources. Its purpose is to enhance, through training and research, the effectiveness of the United Nations. For a recent survey of its activities, see *Report by the Executive Director of the United Nations Institute for Training and Research* (New York: United Nations, 1979), covering the period July 1, 1978–June 30, 1979, 34 UN GAOR, Supp. No. 14, Doc. A/34/14.

   For indications of United Nations interest in measures to facilitate international agreement, see, *e.g.*, United Nations, *Laws & Practices Concerning the Conclusions of Treaties* (1953); and United Nations Institute for Training and Research (UNITAR), *Towards a Wider Acceptance of U.N. Treaties* (New York: Arno Press, 1971) (prepared by O. Schachter, M. Nawaz, and J. Fried). See also the Request for the Inclusion of an Item in the Provisional Agenda of the Thirty-Second Session of the U.N. General Assembly on *Review of the Multilateral Treaty-Making Process*, letter dated July 19, 1977, from the representatives of Australia, Egypt, Indonesia, Kenya, Mexico, the Netherlands, and Sri Lanka to the United Nations, addressed to the Secretary General, Doc. A/32/143 (July 19, 1977), which concludes: "The United Nations is the world's principal instrument of international cooperation. On any view of the matter, it seems inconsistent with the standard of efficient operation which the international community is bound to set itself that, after virtually a third of a century of intense treaty-making activity, it should not have begun to assess the adequacy of its treaty-making methods, and it is time it should start now.''

23 The Hague Academy of International Law, started in 1923 with the support of the Carnegie Endowment, maintains a Secretariat at the Peace Palace in The Hague, and, under the direction of its Curatorium, sponsors a variety of teaching and research activities relating to international law. These include a program of summer lectures at The Hague, a center for research in international law and international relations, an external program given by teams of lecturers sent to different regions throughout the world, and the holding of colloquia.

24 See T. Schelling, *The Strategy of Conflict* (Cambridge: Harvard Univ. Press, 1960), p. 20, quoted in Chpt. 4 at n. 4, *supra*. See, generally, also M. Barkun, *Law without Sanctions* (New Haven: Yale Univ. Press, 1968).

Fiction writers have suggested a number of imaginative risk-management techniques. For example, one party may attempt to protect himself against cheating by triggering the operation of a sanction against the other party which will automatically take effect if the other party fails to comply with his commitment. One novel depicts a blackmailer who protects himself from attack by his victim by letting his victim know that the damaging information is in the hands of a secret third party, who has irrevocable instructions to publish it unless periodically contacted by the blackmailer. See Trevanian, *Shibumi* (New York: Crown, 1979), p. 321. A well-known science fiction story involves a situation in which earthmen and aliens meeting in deep space want to part in peace but, for fear of future attack by the alien race on their home planets, are afraid to reveal to each other the location of their respective planets or to trust the other's promises not to attempt to trail or trace their homeward course. They resolve the problem by each destroying all of the equipment and devices on their respective spaceships which might possibly be used to trace another spaceship's homeward course, and then exchanging spaceships. See M. Leinster, "First Contact" (1945), reprinted in R. Silverberg, *Science Fiction Hall of Fame* (New York: Avon, 1971), p. 371.

25 See discussion in Chpt. 4 and references cited in nn. 212–14.

26 See, generally, references cited in Chpt. 1, n. 1, *supra*.

27 Convention on the Settlement of Investment Disputes Between States and Nationals of Other States, 1965, 17 UST 1270, TIAS 6090, 575 UNTS

159. See Broches, "The Convention on the Settlement of Investment Disputes: Some Observations on Jurisdiction," 5 *Colum. J. Transnatl. L.* 263 (1966); Note, "International Arbitration between States and Foreign Investors: The World Bank Convention," 18 *Stan. L. Rev.* 1359 (1966).

28 See discussion and citations in A. Myrdal, *The Game of Disarmament* (New York: Pantheon, 1976), pp. 304–13.

29 U.S.–German FCN Treaty, Art. XXVII(1).

Index

ABM (Anti-Ballistic Missile) Treaty: Art. III, 86; Art. XII, 268n68

African Development Bank Agreement: Art. 65, 250n128

Agreements to agree, 34–36

Agricultural commodities agreements, 254n24

Air transport agreements, consultation provisions in, 94

Air Transport Agreement (U.S.–France), 59

Air Transport Agreement (U.S.–United Arab Republic), 256n46

Algeria, as escrow agent in U.S.–Iranian hostage agreement, 165

Allison, G., on personifying national behavior, 236n39

"All States" formula, 68–69

Ambiguity: generally, 37–40; difficulty of preventing, 119; nondeliberate, 241n45

Amendment: generally, 56, 92–98; following joint agreement, 93–96; acceptance of, 95; effect of, 95–96; automatic review or revision, 96–97; on occurrence of particular circumstances, 97–98. See also Revision

American Society of International Law, 211

Amistad Dam Construction Agreement (U.S.–Mexico), 253n9

Antarctic Marine Living Resources Convention: Art. VII, 252n150; Art. IX,

252n148; Art. X, 250n132; Art. XX, 266n55; Art. XXIV, 129; Art. XXV, 271n106; Art. XXX, 256n47

Antarctic Treaty; as example of deliberate ambiguity, 40; restricted participation in, 66; effect of possible resources regime on nonparties, 71; control over decisionmaking, 76–77; profit sharing under proposed mineral regime, 85; Art. II, 271n106; Art. VII, 128–29; Art. IX, 76; Art. X, 71; Art. XII, 50, 96–97; Art. XIII, 69–70

Apartheid Convention, Art. V, 186

Arab States, position on Israeli withdrawal from occupied territories, 157

Armistice agreements, 144, 163–64, 189–90

Arms control agreements: proposals for zonal inspection, 43; withdrawal provisions in, 52–53; verification of, 120–25, 129–30; ACDA verification study, 120–22, 132; nonviolation of, 124; mentioned, 62, 106–7

Arms Control and Disarmament Agency (ACDA): verification study, 120–22, 132. See also Arms control agreements

Atomic energy agreements: as illustrating option techniques, 36; review of design and storage arrangements, 115–16; physical security measures, 116–17; recordkeeping requirements, 126; inspection by supplying nation, 129; safeguards provisions and agreements,

289

DESIGNED BY IRVING PERKINS ASSOCIATES
COMPOSED BY PIED TYPER, LINCOLN, NEBRASKA
MANUFACTURED BY CUSHING MALLOY, INC., ANN ARBOR, MICHIGAN
TEXT IS SET IN TIMES ROMAN, DISPLAY LINES IN
HELVETICA AND TIMES ROMAN

Library of Congress Cataloging in Publication Data
Bilder, Richard B., 1927–
Managing the risks of international agreement.
Includes bibliographical references and index.
1. International obligations.   2. Treaties.
3. Risk management.   I. Title.
JX4165.B47   341.3'7   80–52288
ISBN 0–299–08360–8   AACR2